Constructing Floridians

UNIVERSITY PRESS OF FLORIDA

Florida A&M University, Tallahassee
Florida Atlantic University, Boca Raton
Florida Gulf Coast University, Ft. Myers
Florida International University, Miami
Florida State University, Tallahassee
University of Central Florida, Orlando
University of Florida, Gainesville
University of North Florida, Jacksonville
University of South Florida, Tampa
University of West Florida, Pensacola

Constructing Floridians

NATIVES AND EUROPEANS IN THE
COLONIAL FLORIDAS, 1513–1783

Daniel S. Murphree

University Press of Florida

Gainesville   Tallahassee   Tampa   Boca Raton
Pensacola   Orlando   Miami   Jacksonville   Ft. Myers

Library of Congress Cataloging-in-Publication Data:
Murphree, Daniel S.
Constructing Floridians: Natives and Europeans in the colonial Floridas, 1513–1783 /
Daniel S. Murphree.
p. cm.
Includes bibliographical references and index.
ISBN 0–8130–3024–2 (alk. paper)
1. Indians of North America—First contact with Europeans—Florida. 2. Indians
of North America—Florida—Public opinion.   3. Public opinion—Florida—History.
4. Florida—History—Huguenot colony, 1562–1565. 5. Florida—History—Spanish
colony, 1565–1763. 6. Florida—History—English colony, 1763–1784. I. Title.
E78.F6M87 2006
975.9'019–dc22
2006022025

The University Press of Florida is the scholarly publishing agency for the State University
System of Florida, comprising Florida A&M University, Florida Atlantic University, Florida
Gulf Coast University, Florida International University, Florida State University, University
of Central Florida, University of Florida, University of North Florida, University of South
Florida, and University of West Florida.

University Press of Florida
15 Northwest 15th Street
Gainesville, FL 32611–2079
http://www.upf.com

Contents

Maps

Acknowledgments

Studying the development of identity in others forces one to examine his or her own views of self. In my case, as in others, identity is fashioned by time, place, and, more often than not, people. Though all the periods and locales that shaped my personal and professional identities cannot be acknowledged here, many of the institutions and individuals key to the formation of both deserve recognition for contributing to the delights within the book, if not the deficiencies of its author.

Florida State University provided an invaluable teaching opportunity in London which facilitated four months of research throughout Great Britain and Spain. The University of Texas at Tyler's History Department and College of Arts and Sciences generously allocated travel funding for Library of Congress research and numerous conference presentations.

In terms of professional development, each of the following individuals has inspired me in multiple ways: Robin Fabel, Jeff Pasley, Brock Holden, Sally Hadden, Richard Greaves, Ray Mohl, Craig Friend, and Robert Cassanello.

On a personal level, inspiration often has come in unexpected forms. Uncle John and Miss Eunice taught lessons on character that can never be duplicated. My parents, Gordon and Pat, instilled in me at a young age the love of local and the importance of global thinking. Even Amber, Homer, and Fidel provided perspective unobtainable in other ways. In the end, however, this book must be dedicated to MB. Anyone who has met her knows why.

Figure 1. Colonial Floridas.

1

Introduction

Images of Florida have influenced transnational activities and identities for over 400 years. Regardless of whether or not they were valid, written and visual depictions of the region have inspired peoples from around the world to engage in warfare, immigration, colonization, urban development, and, most recently, tourism. Inhabitants of Florida, both past and present, have acknowledged these images as well, in many ways internalizing and reacting to them more intensely than nonresidents. Floridians of various locales, from the southernmost keys to the Gulf of Mexico hinterlands, have used factual and imagined descriptions to shape their understandings of themselves and others. Distinctive Floridian identities, enhanced by an assortment of other influences, have emerged among the peninsula's ever-expanding population, fostering divisions in terms of class, religion, ethnicity, and world view. Such identities continue to develop in modern-day Florida, further diversifying a perpetually diverse populace. Remarkably, despite the region's constant evolution over the years, images upon which current identities are based differ little in substance from those constructed almost five centuries ago.

The origins of modern identity development surfaced when Indians and Europeans began forming relationships in the colonial Floridas during the sixteenth century.[1] Soon after Columbus's pivotal voyages to the New World, Calusas, Guales, Timucuans, Apalachees, and numerous other indigenous groups met and interacted with Spaniards, Frenchmen, and Britons. Almost immediately, members of all groups began to fashion perceptions of themselves in response to characteristics they deemed unusual in recently encountered "foreigners." As the decades passed, settler understandings of natives became intertwined with European conceptualizations of the local environment, failure, and independence. Colonists soon began using these factors to develop a transnational terminology to explain native differences and define a European Floridian identity. In response to both this process and other manifestations of colonialism, Indians generated their own understandings of Europeans, resisted settler encroachment both verbally and violently, and reasserted collective native Floridian identities. Interaction along these lines continued until the American Revolution, in spite of geopolitical changes and imperial competition. Foreshadowing modern trends, few factors proved more vital to these interactions than images of the Floridas and the various interpretations of those images by Floridians.

European-Indian relationships in the colonial Floridas defy simple categorization. Spanish, French, and British encounters with natives in the region rarely conformed to modes of exchange typical in other American locations. Shortly after the first contacts, colonists responded to the idea and reality of the peninsula and its hinterlands with expectations and arrangements that were significantly different from those established elsewhere. Despite repeated attempts to settle the area for more than two centuries, Europeans maintained only a marginal presence in the Floridas, especially when compared to other settings in the hemisphere that colonizers infiltrated at a much later date. The relationships between Native Americans and European Americans in the region were based on mutual limitations rather than exclusive hegemony well into the nineteenth century.

Settlers attempted to intellectually distance themselves from the Floridas Indians from the earliest contacts between the two groups. Between 1513 and 1783, Spaniards, Frenchmen, and Britons progressively racialized the native inhabitants as they struggled to control the peninsula. This process originated from extraordinarily romanticized conceptualizations of this section of the New World and subsequent exaggerated tales of its natural wonders.[2] From initial discovery until the American Revolution, Europeans consistently depicted and understood the Floridas in terms of the environment of the region. Despite contrary experiences and evidence, Spaniards, Frenchmen, and Britons continued to see the Floridas as a natural paradise full of unexploited potential. These images persisted for almost three centuries.

The reality of the Floridas contradicted this perception but did little to change consensus attitudes. European explorers and colonists repeatedly visited the region and attempted to amass economic and imperial rewards based in large degree on their steadfast illusions. Illusions rarely transformed into success, and the vast majority of new arrivals failed in their efforts. Across periods and conditions, a variety of interrelated factors obstructed significant gains and led to overall disillusionment among the colonists.

When they did not reap rewards in the Floridas equal to those of their contemporaries in other New World colonies, European immigrants searched for local justifications to explain their failures. Unable to find suitable factors that could excuse their lack of success easily and consistently, settlers focused on the natural setting, an environment that unexpectedly betrayed popular assumptions and seemed to discourage achievement. Yet that stance conflicted with viewpoints that had been dominant in Europe throughout the colonial period. Therefore, colonists blamed the human population Europeans most frequently associated with the environment, the Floridas Indians. In their attempts to vilify natives, the personification of their environmental nemesis, settlers and visitors constructed a process by which they denigrated Indians, first during times of anxiety and misfortune and eventually as a common practice. Preconceived negative images of natives intensified after 1513. New unflattering portrayals of various Indian attributes emerged and persisted with greater frequency. Over the years, Spaniards, Frenchmen, and Britons increasingly "othered" natives by implicitly racializing their differences. This process established the basis for a more explicitly defined hierarchical system of racial classification that emerged in the early nineteenth century. At the same time, racialization facilitated the creation of a unique form of pan-European identity in the region that transcended temporal, ethnic, and political boundaries.

As this process unfolded, Indians in the Floridas also attempted to reassess their identities and maintain collective independence in a suddenly disrupted and rapidly changing setting.[3] Surviving evidence indicates that Indians employed a variety of techniques to resist European domination. Through violence and savvy trading practices, Indians obstructed the earliest Spanish and French exploratory expeditions while asserting their own presence on the peninsula. Once Spanish missionaries initiated widespread efforts to convert them during the sixteenth and seventeenth centuries, natives embraced certain aspects of Christianity while exhibiting the limits of their accommodation through defiance of clergy, repudiation of teachings, and, on occasion, widespread violent rebellion.

Instead of subsiding in the eighteenth century, native resistance to marginalization increased. In response to French settlement endeavors and accompanying racialization processes along the western Gulf of Mexico coastline, native groups used an assortment of economic and military techniques of obstruction, strategies that were highlighted in the Natchez revolt of the 1720s and 1730s. Despite the disastrous results, natives developed new methods for dealing with the French and recently arrived English colonizers during the mid-eighteenth century. Migration and tribal factionalism became effective ways to express Indian resistance to imperial powers and allowed natives to reassert their strategic dominance in the region. Equally effective, indigenous peoples had succeeded in creating new pan-Indian polities by the 1780s. The most notable among these groups, the Seminoles, explicitly defied racialized categories through the nature of their development as a coherent group and persistent inhabitance of the peninsula.

The net result of European and Indian endeavors in this regard was cultural divergence. In order to erect the markers used to define their respective identities, both groups created intellectual barriers to mutual accommodation that proved unbreakable during the colonial era. In defining their own identities, European Floridians constructed fictional yet foreboding Indians. In their resistance to European colonization, Indians unintentionally augmented negative stereotypes constructed by settlers. As racialized images hardened, cross-cultural understanding degenerated. At the end of the colonial period, such images helped dictate precedents for societal development in the modern world and continued to define the Floridas and their inhabitants.

Eroding Barriers: Transnationalizing the Colonial Past of the Floridas

The early modern period of the Floridas (1517–1783) has been the subject of academic studies that incorporate a variety of methodologies and source bases. Yet investigators of European-Indian relationships in the region tend to approach their subject using rigidly defined topical, geographical, or chronological perspectives.[4] Most confine their investigations exclusively to genres such as Spanish exploration, Spanish missionization, British trade, or British warfare.[5] The majority concentrate only on particular subregions—the southern peninsula, East Florida, or West Florida.[6] Investigations that deal with the Floridas and their inhabitants focus on particular time frames—decades in general, a century at the most.[7] Studies of this type rarely probe important connections between or among zones of human habitation that are not central to the specific framework the author is using.

Though these approaches have revealed much valuable evidence, they fail to present a complete picture of European-Indian interaction throughout the colonial period. These limited foci of investigation discourage our understanding of broad themes that link different regions, periods, and population groups. While Spanish, British, and French settlement efforts differed greatly from one another and should be evaluated in terms of their unique situations, certain ideas and activities that all colonists shared must also be recognized. As historian John Elliott has noted in reference to Spanish and British efforts, "In spite of the marked differences between the two colonizing powers, the settler communities which they established had a number of characteristics and problems in common."[8] This study attempts to provide a broader perspective for interpreting the Floridas' transnational evolution and discourage further compartmentalization of the region's history.[9] It treats the region largely as a borderless international zone devoid of geopolitical hegemons during the period it covers. The varied colonists and indigenous peoples who inhabited the Floridas evaluated and acted on a daily basis with a localistic focus, though one that was constantly influenced by foreign opinions and happenings. Societal development in any subregion at any time hinged less on the activities of single nation-states or uniform ethnic/cultural standards than on the fluid mindsets and material expectations of the Floridas' population and European observers. Detecting, isolating, and contextualizing commonalities among different settlers, times, and regions will provide a fuller picture of the colonial past and the role of the early Floridas in the general social and cultural evolution of North America.[10]

Deciphering Racialization

The idea of "race" and its impact on the early development of the Floridas and its peoples have received little attention from scholars.[11] The idea as a factor in overall European-Indian relationships during the colonial period, by contrast, has received substantial attention, though scholars have reached little consensus about key issues and many questions remain unanswered.[12] The following investigation synthesizes much of the information provided in broader works and applies it specifically to the colonial Floridas. In order to resolve many of the lingering questions concerning race and its applications to European-Indian interaction during the colonial period, this study evaluates standard sources in a new light. It mines the correspondence of settlers, journals of travelers, and documents of government officials related to the Floridas for abstract references and offhand comments pertaining to racial labeling, since often the most mundane details reveal a deeper meaning than the obvious one. These sources, which have previously been explored mainly for evidence about political, economic, and military affairs, contain numerous references to intercultural interaction that have rarely been used in earlier investigations. Though these sources generally obscure or ignore the native perspective on racial viewpoints, they do reveal how European Americans attempted to frame their "othering" conceptions of the peoples they encountered in North America.[13]

Rather than join the seemingly endless "Origins Debate," this study approaches the subject from a different angle. Instead of determining when the idea of race emerged in North America, this investigation focuses on the attitudes, perceptions, and events that fostered the use of racial labels to partially justify an emerging hierarchical society. The entrenchment of legal and social discrimination only codified an intellectual process that had evolved much earlier. How and why Europeans developed their understandings of natives is just as significant as when they enacted codes institutionalizing these ideas. In this sense, racialization rather than racial classification played a much greater role in European-Indian relationships during the colonial period and thus deserves special attention.[14]

Because of its centrality to this work, the term "racialization" must be carefully defined. First and foremost, this process stemmed from Europeans' desire "to come to conclusions and make decisions out of self-interest, out of devotion to some abstract principle" and their "perceptions of the larger interests of the group" of which they claimed membership.[15] Racialization functioned on the basis of ideas generated from a variety of factors. No factor proved more influential than socially constructed images of the region. Images rather than actual incidents generally determined attitudes. Ideas rather than experiences were the initial basis for European racialization of natives in the Floridas.

These ideas would never have surfaced fully without words, however. Words, primarily in written form, allowed Europeans to express their racialized understandings of Indians and thereby expand the "othering" process.[16] Racialization could and did exist internally, and in some settlers, it never expressed itself in any other way than intellectually. But for many immigrants, racialized ideas had little value until they were expressed to other Europeans. Paraphrasing Jill Lepore's assessment of colonists' attitudes toward Indians in New England, Europeans in the Floridas could protect themselves from native differences only by writing about them.[17]

Written words describing Indians' differences allowed European settlers to assert their separateness from the region's native inhabitants. Colonists used words to erect psychological borders between themselves and Indians. These divisions allowed them to separate the worlds the two populations lived in even if the literal setting was the same. Such maneuvering paved the way to uncover additional differences while at the same time delineating "the hierarchical division between civilization and wilderness."[18] These practices also allowed Europeans to generalize their impressions of the natives they encountered. "Othering" diminished the individuality of tribes or clans and facilitated the relegation of Indians to an inferior though undefined category. Settlers could more easily exaggerate native differences if they could assign uniform characteristics to the entire population.[19]

Actual racialized depictions stemmed from ideas about the barbarity of natives. Europeans throughout the Americas frequently singled out Indians they encountered on the basis of their seemingly unbridled activities and undisciplined ways of life. Deviation from European norms indicated aberrant mores and defective character, they contended. Of all the criteria by which settlers racialized Indians, barbarity was the one that encompassed the broadest range of ideas. According to Gary Nash, Europeans consistently viewed natives as "primitive . . . bestial, cannibalistic, sexually abandoned, and, in general, moved entirely by passion rather than reason."[20] The broadness of the parameters and elasticity of the qualities that were identified as "barbaric" allowed colonists to condemn any and all aspects of Indian society and culture at will.[21]

Perceptions of native barbarity often affected European views of native spirituality. Incivility, lying, stealing, murdering, double-dealing, and unrestrained licentiousness were indications of Indian paganism to settlers generally dedicated to Christian ideals.[22] Lack of self-control along with worship of idols and resistance to biblical instruction further marked the deviance of indigenous peoples. After years of failed attempts to convert indifferent native Floridians, many European Floridians began to regard heathenism as a consequence of innate conditions. Though most settlers did not perceive Indians to be inherently evil, the fact that natives could not or would not embrace Christian theology pointed to "ineradicable qualities of savagery."[23]

Barbaric and heathen behavior soon became closely affiliated with Indian physical appearance in the minds of the colonists. Consequently, racialization transcended culture-based "othering" practices. In reference to studies on colonial French and Spanish borderlands, Thomas Holt has noted that "dated biological notions of race" fail to acknowledge how "race and culture and race and class are imbricated." Rather, in such regions, "we can discern a hybrid discourse in which biology and culture are joined."[24] Joyce Chaplin, among others, has shown how such a discourse affected settler viewpoints on Indians. Artificial differences inspired colonists to construct an "idiom" in which they criticized native bodies, eventually deeming them inferior and responsible for massive Indian depopulation. Commenting on the eighteenth century, she noted that "the colonial propensity to move toward racial distinctions is striking. The desire to strip Indian bodies of any natural affinity with America was especially foreboding: they may have been natives but they were unnatural natives."[25]

In the colonial Floridas, settlers began to view native dress, form, and skin color as "surface manifestations of inner realities." Native physical appearance signaled "behavioral, intellectual, temperamental, moral, and other" defects. References to Indians almost always highlighted elements of dress and adornment as much as physical phenotype. Hairstyles and applied dyes dominated descriptions and fascinated colonists. But the language used to describe these features tended to portray artificial adornment as permanent differences. Over the years, settler commentary essentialized such attributes and increasingly described them as manifestations of inherent deficiencies. Piercings and tattoos symbolized native distinction and intransigence to colonists progressively disappointed with the Floridas and its indigenous inhabitants. This realization enabled Europeans to racialize natives on a continual basis, regardless of actual activities or lifestyles. Perceived links between physical appearance and behavior also was the primary factor that led to the establishment of entrenched racial classifications in the nineteenth century.[26]

In view of these conditions, the term "racialization" as used in this work applies to a process, discourse, and mindset that specifically pertains to European-Indian relationships in the Floridas, though it may be suitably applied to other regions or time periods. Racialization consisted of the articulation, primarily in written form, of collective European perceptions regarding the character, behavior, spirituality, intellectual capacity, and physical appearance of native peoples of the Floridas. These views were stimulated by settler concerns over their own failure, independence, and identity in the region. This process and its manifestations evolved slowly over three centuries and existed in widely scattered settlements established by Spanish, French, and British colonists. Though it is sometimes evident in the context of legal, administrative, and military activities, racialization functioned principally as an intellectual practice confined to personal expression. Nevertheless, it generated a written vernacular that became a commonplace way for European Floridians to describe the indigenous peoples they encountered.

Despite certain similarities with modern definitions of "race" and "racism," this definition of racialization has quite different meanings from them. The available evidence indicates that though Europeans perceived and described

Indians in terms that today could be characterized as racist, they did not perceive natives to be members of a strictly defined separate class of human beings. Such official or community-driven designations did not exist until the late eighteenth century. Few settlers would have recognized their understandings of Indians as "racist," and probably Indians themselves and peoples in Europe, Africa, or Asia would not have done so either. European Americans generally did not make such references toward Indians to gain social, legal, or political privileges. Colonists in the Floridas used racialized language as a means of distancing themselves from an environment and people they could not fully understand or control. Modern observers of this situation must divorce themselves from twenty-first-century connotations of race and racism if they want to accurately evaluate the nature of European-Indian relationships in this setting.[27]

Furthermore, racialization was not inherently a demeaning or negative procedure. Again, contrary to modern understandings of racist labeling, Europeans in North America often pointed out the behavioral, religious, and physical differences of natives without damning their existence. A good example involves settler viewpoints about Indian appearance. In some instances, they perceived the natives' lack of clothing "as signaling both cultural and spiritual depravity, marking the Indians as doubly lacking."[28] Yet on other occasions, native physical appearance received praise. According to Thomas Matijasic, "If Europeans were rarely impressed by Indian dress, they generally found the physical appearance of the North Americans to be pleasing."[29] The relevance here lies not in the positive or negative connotation of the reference but in the reference itself. Europeans racialized Indians simply by pointing out on a consistent basis their overall perceptions that they were different from themselves. Exclamations of admiration and awe reinforced differences, just as exhortations of disgust and repulsion did, thereby furthering racial identification.

The impact of racialization on specific colonial actions or policies is ambiguous. On numerous occasions, racialized theorizing and discourse can be directly traced to the creation of laws, determination of strategy, and the pursuit of wars. At other times, causal relationships are less clear, and evidence that the process and its manifestations systematically altered European treatment of Indians is inconsistent. Yet over time, the existence and frequency of racialized descriptions altered settlers' conceptualizations of colonial endeavors as a whole. Racialization obscured complex and unwelcome explanations of political, economic, and military deeds or misdeeds through generalized depictions of Indians. European Floridians tended to connect overall success and failure in these endeavors in some manner to the presence and attributes of natives. Whether or not natives were relevant to the problems settlers identified, racialization meant that they routinely explained such difficulties in ways that implicated their indigenous neighbors. Consequently, natives, and their removal as obstacles, became central to colonial discourse. In the minds of many Europeans and European Americans, most New World labors ultimately hinged on roles played by Indians.

Formation of a European Floridian Identity

At its core, racialization of natives reflected the concerns and insecurities of the colonists. Colonial failures, perceived or real, prompted settlers in the Floridas to question both their personal and national capacity to dominate this portion of the New World. Unlike colonists in other American settings, who often used armed force to assert their power over natives, European Floridians typically resorted to racialized rhetoric. Lacking the resources and population superiority to physically dominate Indians at will, settlers intellectually condemned them. This occurred even after the Spanish, French, and British enjoyed relatively clear economic or military advantages over indigenous Floridians. In addition, racialization of Indians provided disgruntled colonists with a venue for expressing their various disappointments. Much like the struggling settlers of seventeenth-century Virginia, Europeans in the Floridas castigated natives, most of whom eventually "became the scapegoat for their ire."[30]

For the most part, however, racialization helped colonists define their own identity in the Floridas. Fearing that their failures would lead to domination by the environment, and therefore by Indians, Europeans racialized natives to assert their independence. "As exiles living in the wilderness far from 'civilization,'" colonists "used their negative images of Indians" to assert European superiority.[31] Racialization provided a justification and explanation for the Europeans' existence in the Floridas; it enabled Europeans to assume their cultural dominance even if they failed in their other economic, religious, and military endeavors.[32]

As a result, Spaniards, Frenchmen, and Britons achieved a collective, though seldom articulated, identity and place in this New World community based on their reactions to its difficulties.[33] Colonists rarely, if ever, noted such commonalities and tended to highlight rather than minimize their national and ethnic differences. Yet, like settlers in other areas of North America, Europeans in the Floridas found unifying (if unsolicited) connections in their multiple failures and subsequent responses to natives. As Eric Hinderaker has pointed out, images derived from racialization, danger, and misfortune sometimes "undergirded a broadly shared regional identity" among settlers.[34] European ethnic differences were minimized in this process because members of all groups encountered the same general obstacles and miseries in the region. Though in reference to a different time and location, Elizabeth Perkins accurately assessed the situation in the Floridas when she wrote that "in making decisions about strangers, preconceptions about culture norms helped to group other persons and give them a name."[35] The defining facilitator of this identity formation was an assumption and expectation of power and dominance. Europeans faced with ongoing failures, "alien" neighbors, and unclear futures sought above all else some method of control. In this regard, European settlers in the Floridas differed very little from their counterparts throughout the Western Hemisphere. All sought unquestioned supremacy of their New World and marginalization of its original inhabitants.[36]

2

Imagining an Idyllic Environment

In his Pulitzer Prize–winning book *Voyagers to the West: A Passage in the Peopling of America on the Eve of the Revolution* (1986), Bernard Bailyn devoted sixty-four pages to the Floridas and how British imperialists imagined them during the late eighteenth century. After reviewing the available historical evidence, he concluded:

> The sheer exoticism of this strange universe of cypress swamps and grassy savannas, of spectacular natural fountains and hidden lakes, of jungles of live oaks, palmettos, and towering pines crowded with screaming birds, of roaring alligators in muddy creeks, of endless sand barrens and "black, rich, soapy earth"—all of this exoticism, revealed in the reports, oral and written, received after 1763, stimulated in Britons dreamlike visions of Xanadus.

In Bailyn's opinion, though British subjects knew little else about the peninsula and its hinterlands, such depictions, along with "the forces of greed, ambition, and high entrepreneurial adventure," prompted immigrants from Great Britain and the other North American colonies to depart for the region and seek their fortunes. [1]

Though accurate, Bailyn's assessment only partially reveals the complete meaning of the Floridas to most Europeans who had never been there. From the initial explorations by Iberian adventurers until the ouster of Great Britain from the region in 1783, Spaniards, Britons, and Frenchmen viewed the Floridas through the lens of its environment. The vast majority of accounts written by European observers between the sixteenth and nineteenth centuries concentrated on the flora and fauna of the peninsula. Whether based on firsthand empirical evidence or fantastical speculation, written accounts highlighted the natural setting and its likely benefits for European empires.[2]

For the most part, Indians appear in these accounts as peripheral figures. Though depictions of native Floridians in European works will be covered at great length in subsequent chapters, it is important to note that a sizeable portion of the literature dealing with the environment of the Floridas during this time did not mention native inhabitants at all and the writings that did include references to Indians tended to address them in conjunction with evaluations of the natural setting. Particularly in the earlier works, few European authors distinguished natives from flora and fauna and preferred to treat all as a single collective entity. In these writings, Indians assumed roles as ill-defined custodians of the land and therefore, to many advocates of colonization, implicit facilitators of nature-based profits. Also of importance, these depictions appeared more frequently in accounts written by Europeans who had never been to the Floridas or had visited only briefly. As we shall see, European Floridians gradually depicted the region's natives much differently.[3]

These images of the environment are remarkable for their endurance. The "pristine" lands Spanish explorers first perceived in the sixteenth century and encountered had radically changed by the eighteenth century. Over the decades, European settlers had steadily explored the Floridas and had gradually established numerous forts, farms, plantations, and towns, in the process suffering through wars, disease, starvation, political insecurity, and economic disaster. Cognizant of these changes, a variety of chroniclers with divergent interests amassed data about the Floridas at different times and published their findings throughout Europe and the colonies. Yet the initial images endured.

Clearly, many of these accounts served as propaganda, inaccurate assessments written by individuals to promote their economic, religious, or imperial interests. But this reality provides only a partial explanation. Many people in Europe and, more important, many European settlers maintained their original impressions of the Floridas in order to rationalize a troubling situation they could not fully comprehend or explain. The Floridas were different from most North or Latin American colonies in that they failed to yield the bounties Spaniards, Frenchmen, and Britons desired. That any European group could fail to control the region and prosper from its resources was inconceivable to people accustomed to imperialist and mercantilist views of the world.[4] But the region, which was at the geographical center of the gateway to the Americas, could not easily be ignored. Therefore, rather than admit failure, officials and settlers continuously promoted the potential instead of the reality of colonial settlement in the Floridas. Lacking few other positive factors to applaud, Europeans fixated on the most visible and appealing symbol of the region—the exotic and promising natural environment.

This is not to say that Europeans did not point out negative aspects of the Floridas. Explorers and colonists often reported on the difficulties they encountered while traveling in the region or attempting to establish settlements. But most negative references surfaced in correspondence with friends, family members, or patrons living in Europe. Unlike more-positive appraisals, these complaints rarely appeared in published works. Whether through circumstance or conscious manipulation, references that downplayed the region's advantages did not get much public exposure.[5]

Iberian Impressions

Iberian impressions of the Floridas emerged during a period characterized by rapid expansion and ongoing insecurity. When Juan Ponce de León first claimed the region for Spain in 1513, the nation he represented had existed as a coherent entity for less than two decades. In a variety of regards, its unity and durability were still in question. Following the final expulsion of Muslim armies from Iberia in the 1490s, the various Christian kingdoms of the region slowly and grudgingly acquiesced to their inclusion in part of a larger national body led by the sovereigns of Castile and Aragon. The only "Spanish" identity that existed was still in its formative stages, and allegiances to the Crown proved fleeting. At the same time, spurred on by technological advances, papal prerogatives, daring adventurers, and devastating diseases, the nascent state gained imperial control of much of Latin America. Resulting mineral and agricultural riches filled the coffers of the burgeoning global power and broadened expectations about the New World among Spaniards while fears of European competition and destruction of the empire as a whole loomed large in Spanish consciousness.[6] The Floridas took shape in the Iberian mind against a backdrop of rapid transformation, great expectations, and national fear.

The first widely publicized work to mention the region originated, not surprisingly, in Spain. Written by Peter Martyr, *De Orbe Novo Decades* became available to the public in 1530.[7] Few works about North America existed up to that point, and Martyr's research is notable for the sources it used. Unlike most of his contemporaries, Martyr based his book on firsthand interviews with individuals who had actually traveled on the continent. One of these interviewees, an indigenous resident referred to as "Francisco of Chicora" by the Spanish slave traders who captured him off the coast of present-day South Carolina, provided significant detail about the geographical landscape of the Floridas. Information obtained from one of the peninsula's earliest Spanish explorers, Lucas Vázquez de Ayllón, complemented the Indian's account. Together, their observations provided much of the basis for Martyr's conclusions.[8]

Although *De Orbe Novo Decades* rarely referred to the Floridas directly, the information it contained initiated commentary on the peninsula's geographical features. Martyr believed the Floridas to be composed of one or more islands, indicating the paucity of accurate data he had. The author contended that Ponce de León first visited the region and "named it Florida, because he discovered it on the Feast of the Resurrection, which is called Pasqua Florida." This description would appear in most accounts pertaining to the region well into the eighteenth century. Martyr characterized these islands as "the daughters to Cuba or Hispaniola" and as "the guardians of what is believed to be a continent, their rocks forming a breakwater against the ocean storms." Thus, the Floridas offered protection for other possessions of the Spanish empire, an idea that would influence settlers and officials for centuries. Though these remarks were important in the construction of future European images of the region, the author's most enduring contribution to later myths was his reference to the riches of the Floridas. Seemingly as an afterthought, he wrote, "In most of these islands the Spaniards found gold in the form of grains."[9]

Subsequent Spanish accounts elaborated on the natural wealth of the Floridas. Gonzalo Fernández de Oviedo depicted Hernando de Soto's campaigns through the peninsula (1539–1543) in a lengthy work titled *La historia general y natural de las Indias*, which he wrote around 1547, though it was not published on a wide scale until much later. Based on the journals of Rodrigo Rangel, Hernando de Soto's personal assistant during the expedition, Oviedo's account undoubtedly surfaced in various other forms throughout sixteenth- and seventeenth-century Europe.[10] Rangel's information supplemented Martyr's evidence regarding the peninsula's wealth, though Rangel emphasized food resources as well. Describing the panhandle region, Oviedo wrote, "The Province of Apalache is very fertile and abundantly provided with much corn, kidney beans, pumpkins, various fruits, much venison, many varieties of birds and excellent fishing near the sea." He added that while they contained many swamps, the Floridas in general appeared to be a "pleasant country."[11]

Luis Hernández de Biedma, another member of Hernando de Soto's contingent, recorded his experiences shortly after returning to Spain in the 1540s. Like Rangel's account, Biedma's work circulated publicly only on a limited scale until Richard Hakluyt produced an English translation in 1609, though oral versions probably surfaced from time to time. In his description of Cabeza de Vaca's impressions of the Floridas, Biedma reported "that it was the richest countrie in the world." The author substantiated this claim by listing the many natural treasures he himself saw while accompanying Hernando de Soto: "There are also in Florida a great store of walnuts, and plummes, mulberries, and grapes . . . The fruites are common to all: for they grow abroad in the open fields in great abundance, without any neede of planting or dressing."[12] Not only could Europeans obtain a variety of foods from the region, but apparently they could do so with very little effort.

References to the Floridas also appeared in Portuguese publications because of that Iberian nation's interest and early participation in exploration ventures. While living in Portugal during the 1550s, the anonymous Gentleman of Elvas completed *Relaçam verdadeira*, his chronicles of Hernando de Soto's Florida experiences. He too asserted that Cabeza de Vaca praised the Floridas in discussions with Hernando de Soto, calling it "the richest land in the world."[13] In his history of Portuguese global exploration, colonial official Antonio Galvão echoed these descriptions, again focusing on the mineral wealth of the region. Referring to Ponce de León, Galvão wrote, "And because the land seemed to yeeld gold and silver and great riches, he begged it of the king Don Fernando, but he died in the discouerie of it, as many more have done."[14] Although he focused on the benefits of the Floridas, Galvão alluded to the price Europeans might pay for obtaining them.

As Spain began to colonize the region, more-detailed reports on its environment appeared in Europe. One of the first works to deal with settlement attempts appeared in 1567 under the title *Vida y hechos de Pedro Menéndez de Avilés . . . largamente se tratan las Conquistas y Poblaciones de la Provincia de la Florida*. Written by Spanish professor Bartolomé Barrientos, this study concentrated on the life of the first Spanish governor of the Floridas, Pedro Menéndez Avilés, and the fledgling coastal outpost of St. Augustine. More critical of the environment than earlier commentators, Barrientos pointed out many of the treacherous natural features of the region. Yet overall, he continued to support patterns established by earlier observers. "The coastal islands are covered with trees . . . and abound in game," he wrote, and "around them there is an abundance of shellfish, flounder and oysters." According to Barrientos, certain agricultural products of the Floridas resembled those found in Spain. He wrote that "there are also wild vineyards, cereals, and palmettos like those of Andalucia." Besides food sources, the region contained vast amounts of useful timber: "Because pine groves are numerous a quantity of tar and pitch is available. The wood necessary to build houses, ships, and boats, for which we now send to Germany, is abundant." More appealing, "this timber could be easily and cheaply transported to Spain." The author also mentioned evidence of new riches found in the Floridas. Several colonists discovered "strings of coral beads . . . turquoises, and emeralds" not far from their settlements. Such jewels only added to the bounty of the land. He concluded that "the country as a whole has a good climate, and is salubrious."[15]

But the most influential Iberian publications of the seventeenth century concentrated on the early exploration period of the Floridas rather than on ongoing colonization attempts. In 1605, Garcilaso de la Vega finished *La Florida del Ynca*, his examination of Hernando de Soto's Florida entrada. Like Barrientos, Garcilaso compared the region's produce with that found in Iberia. According to his account, Hernando de Soto found "fruits not common to Spain, such as various kinds of cherries" as well as "many species of beans and squash . . . and other varieties of vegetables." Unlike earlier observers, Garcilaso pointed out the appropriateness of the Floridas for animal husbandry. "The land is very suitable for raising all kinds of livestock," he wrote, because, "it contains good forests, pasture lands with fine streams, and swamps and lagoons with quantities of rushes for cattle."[16] With this observation, the evolving image of the land gained an additional positive attribute.

No Iberian study that referred to the Floridas had a greater impact on popular images than Antonio de Herrera's *Historia General de los hechos de los Castellanos en las Islasi tierra firme del mar Oceano*. This massive eight-volume study published between 1601 and 1615 offered Spaniards a comprehensive narrative of the empire's conquests up to the seventeenth century. Despite its length and attention to detail, however, its depictions of the Floridas differed little from those first publicized almost a century earlier. Herrera reiterated that Ponce de León named the region because of the spiritual day of its founding, though he also added that the name seemed appropriate since the land "had a very beautiful view of many and cool woodlands."[17] The main distinction between Herrera's description of the region and those discussed previously was the author's discussion of Pánfilo de Narváez's experiences on the peninsula. Information gained from the explorer's journals substantiated opinions already advanced. Herrera wrote that the "Country is cold, and has good Pasture for Cattle" and possessed "great Woods" that could be exploited. The only new information referred to the many "wild Creatures" of the Floridas, one of which surely amazed readers since it carried "its young in a Pouch, under the Belly."[18]

French Impressions

Written accounts of the Floridas had also begun to appear in France by the sixteenth century. In content and brevity, these depictions closely resembled works produced in Spain, though they also illustrated the marginalized role of the French in New World colonization. France lagged behind the Iberians in the settlement of the Americas largely because of the nation's preoccupation with continental disputes involving economic monopolies, territorial boundaries, and schisms between Catholics and Protestants. Only after Columbus had claimed most of the Caribbean borderlands for Spain did French merchants and government officials initiate significant colonization endeavors. Most failed in terms of wealth generated and lands acquired, at least in the beginning. Brief incursions into northern South America and eastern North America produced few lasting settlements, and by the seventeenth century, France enjoyed influence only in what would become Canada.[19]

Published accounts of French activities in the Floridas offered the first glimpse of the New World to many outside Spain. The earliest works concerned Fort Caroline, the only French settlement established on the peninsula's east coast. Existing for less than two years (1564–1565), the outpost generated little wealth and succumbed to Spanish soldiers, who killed most of its inhabitants and established their own fortified town named St. Augustine. France gained little from the experiment besides a humiliating defeat from an imperial adversary. Extensive French settlement in southeastern North America would not occur for another century.

Nevertheless, images of the Floridas had an enduring influence in France. The publication of an assortment of narratives indicated the interest of Frenchmen in the mysterious lands, and over the next two centuries France attempted on various occasions to gain control of the peninsula. Though France never achieved hegemony in the Floridas, the image of the region influenced generations of statesmen and potential colonists engaged in the process of attempting to understand the New World and its possibilities, dangers, and benefits.[20]

Like those of the Spanish, French accounts emphasized the natural splendor of the Floridas. In 1566, Nicolas Le Challeux, a resident of Fort Caroline, published his observations in a book titled *Discours de l'histoire de la Floride*. Of the climate, he wrote, "Sometimes when the sun is directly overhead, it is very hot; however the heat is moderated not only by the cool of the night and the dew but also by the soft rain which falls in such quantities that the ground is fertile and the crops grow strong and high." Furthermore, he added, "the country is rich in gold and in all species of animals for it has open and spacious fields." Le Challeux found the environment aesthetically pleasing. "There are quite high hills, exceedingly pleasant rivers, several kinds of trees emitting a sweet smelling sap," he recorded.[21] The French commander of Fort Caroline, René De Laudonnière, agreed with these descriptions, as did many of his French backers. In his account of the settlement published in 1586, a supporter of the colonial endeavor claimed that "without a doubt [Florida] is to be admired over any other place as to singularity and riches because it is full of unknown lands and seas, of strange people, animals, and plants."[22] Disregarding the dismal conclusion to the failed colonial experiment, Le Challeux concluded, "Considering all this, it was impossible that a man could not find there great pleasure and delight."[23]

More-detailed depictions of the Floridas appeared in Marc Lescarbot's *Histoire de la Nouvelle-France*. First published in 1609, this comprehensive study traced French involvement in North America up to the seventeenth century. Fueled by imperialist bravado, the author disputed that Ponce de León founded the Floridas, asserting that Giovanni da Verrazzano, supported by French funds, actually discovered them. Even so, Lescarbot grudgingly acknowledged that Ponce de León named the region "because it is all green and full of vegetation, even the waters being covered with grassy herbage." Referring to evidence provided by Jean Ribault, one of the first Frenchmen to visit the peninsula, Lescarbot wrote, "As for the quality of the soil, nothing finer could be seen, for it was thickly covered with tall oaks and cedars infinite in number, and above them lentiscus so sweet in smell that this alone made the spot desireable."[24] Little else in the text pertained to the Floridas except for brief comparisons of the land with other colonies in the Western Hemisphere. Lescarbot affirmed that the climate of the peninsula was much like that of Brazil, since both "provinces are without winter, and enjoy perpetual verdure." He also pointed out the advantages of French explorers in the Floridas over their counterparts in Canada. Though unsuccessful in colonization endeavors, "the Florida voyagers were the more fortunate in that they were in a country which [was] balmy, fertile, and more propitious to the health than this New France of the North."[25]

France's ouster from the Floridas and its preoccupation with settlements in Canada meant that few publications dealt with the peninsula after the early sixteenth century.[26] Even after France established what would be known as its Louisiana colony at the beginning of the eighteenth century, French writers showed little interest in areas east of the lower Mississippi River. One of the few publications to deal with the western Floridas appeared in 1768 under the title *Nouveaux Voyages aux Indies Occidentales*. This work, which was not a standard chronological history, consisted of an assortment of letters written by Jean Bernard Bossu, a French traveler in the region, to correspondents in France during the mid-1700s. Continuing past themes, Bossu's letters emphasized the bountiful natural products of the Floridas and their potential benefits for Europeans. Bossu wrote that the lands between the Mississippi River and port of Mobile were "excellent for growing indigo, tobacco, rice, corn, and sugar cane." As a result, "this country offers a delightful life to the merchants, artisans, and foreigners who inhabit it because of its healthful climate, its fertile soil, and its beautiful site."[27] Bossu saw promise in the less fertile areas as well. "Although the soil in the Mobile region is composed of thick sand, cattle thrive and the herds are growing larger," he wrote.[28] He felt that settlers could also profit from the local forests with little effort: "There are trees in the forests which produce resin and tar, and gum similar to turpentine flows from others."[29] Bossu summed up the benefits of the region by stating that "the Creator's generosity is admirable."[30]

British Impressions

Most publications that described the Floridas during the colonial era originated in England. Much more involved in the settlement of North America's eastern coastline than the Spanish or French, Britons printed a variety of accounts dealing with the region's features beginning in the late sixteenth century. Instead of tapering off over the years, the number of English publications concerned with the Floridas increased during the 1700s, especially as British colonists moved south along the Atlantic seaboard. Despite the greater number of works over a longer period of time, however, English publications continued themes established by Spanish and French authors. The actual experiences of settlers in the Floridas received little attention while the natural resources and opportunities of the land garnered much emphasis. Until the last years of Great Britain's colonization of the region during the American Revolution, such accounts influenced British subjects and their expectations of the peninsula.

Because of their eagerness for information about the New World, Englishmen at times published foreign works before they were actually printed in their home languages. Jean Ribault's accounts of Fort Caroline's future location first appeared in *The Whole and True Discoverye of Terra Florida* (1563) as an English translation. Presented as a passage in one of Richard Hakluyt's many compilations on the New World, Ribault's accounts introduced English-speakers to the alleged wealth of the Floridas. Hakluyt's translation of Ribault stated that the region possessed "golde and silver and copper . . . lead . . . turquettes and great abundance of pearles." In addition, "the countrie [was] in fertillitie apt and commodious throughout to beare & bring foorth plentifully all that men would plant . . . upon it." According to Hakluyt's translation, Ribault believed that the Floridas was "a place wonderfull fertill . . . the ground fat, so that it is likely that it would bring foorth Wheate and all other corne twise a yeere, and the commodities for livelihood, and the hope of more riches."[31]

Hakluyt published other accounts provided by individuals who had visited Fort Caroline. In 1589, he translated the journals of Frenchman René de Laudonnière, who sailed to the Floridas accompanied by dozens of Protestant families in 1564. Laudonnière wrote that "there is found among the Savages a good quantitie of Gold and Silver," though he admitted that most had been seized from shipwrecked Europeans. Laudonnière stated that "there is also in this Countrey [a] great store of grayness [grains] and herbes, whereof might be made excellent good dyes and paintings of all kind of colours."[32] Hakluyt also referred to the notes of an English visitor to Fort Caroline, John Sparke. Sparke promised that the Floridas "yeeldeth naturally grapes in great store, for in the time that the Frenchmen were there, they made 20 hogsheads of wine." This Englishman's enthusiasm for Florida surpassed that of most other observers. He proclaimed that "the commodities of this land are more then are yet knowen to any man: for besides the land it selfe, whereof there is more then any king Christian is able to inhabit, it flourisheth with medow, pasture ground, with woods of Cedar and Cypress, and other sorts, as better can not be in the world." Sparke went on to make a case for English colonization of the region. He claimed that the Floridas would surpass the prosperous West Indies settlements in terms of productivity if only they were adequately popu-lated by Europeans. Capable immigrants along with the fertile climate of the region promised "to make all things flourish therein."[33]

By the late seventeenth century, English writers had produced accounts that included comprehensive summaries of the Floridas that were largely ab-sent from earlier works. Richard Blome published *A Geographical Description of the Four Parts of the World* in 1670, which contained extensive descriptions of the Floridas. Reasoning that since "Florida being between the twenty fifth, or thirtieth and fortieth degrees of Septentrional Latitude," he asserted that "the Countrey cannot chuse but be good." Blome covered attributes of the land that previously had been scattered among earlier accounts. The Floridas "are well cloathed with trees," some of which contained bark that was an "excellent remedy for many distempers." Plentiful game lived in the region and "the Country is well stored with several sorts of Fruits, [such] as Grapes, Cherries, Plumbs, Mulberries, Chesnuts, &c." He also noted that the peninsula was "well watered with fresh Streams, which are stored with [a] variety of Fish." Early images of mineral wealth continued to linger. Despite the fact that even after many years supporting evidence had not been found for such claims, Blome insisted that the Floridas were "enriched with Mines of Gold and Silver."[34]

Though settlers who lived in the seaboard colonies of British North America had access to more knowledge about the Floridas in the early eighteenth century, most people in Great Britain still remained largely ignorant of the region. This began to change in the 1740s, when imperial warfare promised to give Great Britain increased access to the Floridas. As this possibility became a reality during the Seven Years' War of the 1750s–1760s, British writers produced several accounts that expounded on the potential benefits of settlement on the peninsula and its surrounding areas. These were different from earlier works, though. These authors not only listed the various natural attributes of the land, they also provided conclusions about how these resources could best be exploited. Yet the focus of these tracts remained the same; regardless of the presence or absence of other benefits or liabilities, the natural environment overshadowed everything else.

In 1762, Thomas Jefferys produced a book titled *A Description of the Spanish Islands and Settlements on the Coast of the West Indies* to inform Britons of the spoils that might be attained from colonial disputes. While it focused primarily on the islands of the Caribbean, Jefferys's study examined the peninsula in great detail. "The air of this region is pure and temperate, and the country in general, healthy," he wrote. In his opinion, any concerns about the soil should be forgotten. He assured his audience that the "many rivers with which Florida is watered, not only abound with fish, but render it inferior to no country, either in pleasantness or fertility. The coast indeed is sandy, but a little further from the sea, the soil is so good as to yield all sorts of grain." Jefferys pointed out that the region was suitable for raising European livestock. "Here are horses, not only for draught, but also for the saddle," he claimed, adding that cattle in the Floridas "have a long black sort of hair, or rather wool." This wool was "so fine, that with some small mixture, it is thought it would be preferable to common wool for hats, cloathing, and other necessaries." The land also abounded "with all sorts of timber," and cotton grew wild "in great plenty." Jefferys continued to promote the traditional lure of explorers to the Floridas, mineral wealth. He assured his audience that oysters in the region produced "pearls . . . many larger than ordinary."[35]

An encyclopedic depiction of the Floridas also appeared in 1762. Titled *The American Gazetteer* and compiled from a collection of earlier tracts, this work functioned as a quick reference guide for information on New World locales. As such, it provided little new information. The volume claimed that "the air of Florida is pure and temperate, and the country, in general, healthy: being but a few degrees N. of the tropic of Cancer." Much like Blome's study, this effort emphasized the cartographic coordinates of the Floridas, a pattern later commentators would follow. Repeating views of earlier writers, the compiler noted that "the country abounds with all sorts of timber and fruit trees." He specifically pointed out the presence of grapes, many of which "are larger and better than those in France."[36]

Examinations of the Floridas also began to appear frequently in certain British newspapers during the 1760s. In January 1763, the anonymous Candidus published an article in *The Scots Magazine* documenting the riches to be found in Louisiana, specifically the western Floridas. Among other things, the author commented on the many natural products available: "Indian corn, two crops a year; oats larger than ours, and the oatmeal much finer . . . vines of several kinds . . . hence wines as good and as plentiful as any country in Europe." In addition, "sheep as good as English; their wool better" lived in the region, and cotton, hemp, and flax "grow naturally wild, and may be cultivated to any extent." The most unique contributions of Candidus, however, were his opinions about why colonists should settle the lands surrounding the lower Mississippi River. The author rhetorically asked, "If these are the natural products of this country, what may we not expect from its artificial improvements?" He answered his own question: "There are products that will soon admit of improvements in so favourable a soil . . . under the cherishing wings of English liberality, labour and industry." If this course was taken, Candidus asked, "What nation in the world can parallel these? What kingdom furnishes such a list, that can boast of such staple commodities as these, and all in such plenty?"[37]

Like Candidus's article, many publications that sought to promote English settlement of the Floridas appeared after Great Britain officially gained control over the peninsula from Spain in 1763. Even though they were much more biased than earlier accounts, these efforts still generally adhered to themes established previously. The environment continued to be the primary focus, though authors gave more attention to past settlers and their inability to properly take advantage of the resources of the Floridas. Publications after 1763 came closer than earlier works to acknowledging past European failures in the area, though mainly in an attempt to promote future settlement and proper cultivation of the region.[38]

No work better reflected this new trend than William Stork's *An Account of East Florida*, published in 1765. In an introductory letter to the Marquis of Rockingham, Stork declared that he wrote the book to promote the commercial interests of the British empire and enhance the government's knowledge of its overseas colonies. In sum, he wanted to supplement the riches of Great Britain by "encouraging and promoting this young colony."[39] Stork elaborated on the need for his work. "The truth of the matter is that the country is very little known in Europe," he pointed out. Stork believed that he needed to correct erroneous perceptions as a service to the Crown. For these misunderstandings he blamed "the Spaniards, who from indolence, and a fear of the Ind seldom ventured beyond the lines of St. Augustine," and mariners, who because of the beaches they saw along the coast, portrayed the Floridas as "barren and useless." The effect was "to induce in many persons, [the idea] that the whole of Florida, ceded to Great Britain, is little better than a sandy desert." In order to correct these mistaken representations, Stork believed that he needed to prove to the reader that in terms of "climate, soil, and produce . . . the lands are of no less value than in the islands of the West-Indies."[40]

Like commentators before him, Stork compared the Floridas to different geographical regions as a means of showing their benefits. The island of Cuba, which surpassed all the North American English settlements "not only in sugar and indigo . . . but in all other productions," enjoyed only slightly better proximity to the sun than the peninsula. Consequently, "in this respect, East-Florida hath the advantage of Carolina and Georgia, as much as Cuba has the advantage of East-Florida." Many regions of Asia also compared favorably with the Floridas. The author claimed that Egypt, Persia, India, China and Japan, all of which were "famous for their riches and fertility," shared the same latitude as the peninsula.[41]

Stork used "scientific" explanations to prove the Floridas' advantageous position. He contended that the earth supporting the region was comprised of two layers of rock and clay. "The fertility of Florida is much ascribed to these two strata of clay and rock, which contributes to keep the sand moist, and prevent the rains from sinking away from the roots of the plants and trees," he wrote. These conditions and the frequency of rainfall ensured that even "the pine-barrens are covered with good grass or a perpetual verdure."[42] As a result, "tropical fruits are found in great abundance, and afford the strongest evidence that both the soil and climate are fit for sugar, cotton, indigo, and other West-India productions." Stork deviated from traditional depictions of the region by pointing out the physical comfort English settlers would enjoy in the Floridas. After inquiring of previous European settlers, he did "not find . . . that snow has ever been seen there; the winters are so mild, that the Spaniards at St. Augustine had neither chimneys in their houses, nor glass windows." Moreover, "the fogs and dark gloomy weather, so common in England, are unknown in this country." In fact, "the inhabitants of the Spanish settlements in America consider East-Florida, with respect to its healthiness, in the same light that we do the south of France."[43]

Subsequent promotions of the region singled out allegedly successful individual settlements. Another anonymous passage that appeared in the January 1766 issue of *The Scots Magazine* described the plantation established by Florida resident Denys Rolle. According to the article, "We hear that the settlement . . . is situated on a healthy elevated spot . . . and is in a very flourishing condition." Besides rice, corn, and cotton, Rolle's plantation produced "a variety of melons, cucumbers, and things of that kind, and all sorts of garden stuff." The settlement also had access to "a considerable stock of cattle, milk-cows, hogs, and all sort of poultry . . . The river abounds with fish, and the woods with deer, turkies, and many sorts of wildfowl." A variety of fruits complemented these resources, all being "the natural production of that part of the country."[44]

Descriptions of what were by the 1760s called "West Florida" and "East Florida" appeared in *The Scots Magazine* as well.[45] In the May 1766 issue, the newspaper published a letter from a British visitor to the Natchez region. He claimed that the lands on the east bank of the Mississippi River were "simply delightful, the soil the richest I ever saw, the oak, hickery, cedar, poplar, and beech, remarkably large." The traveler believed that "it would be the greatest crime in the world to suffer this part of the river to remain unsettled, as the inhabitants would reap every advantage that could be expected from the richest lands." In light of the fact that "every kind of grain that Europe produces would grow here in the greatest perfection," he deemed Natchez and its environs to be "one of the finest countries in the world."[46] A series of excerpts from a letter on East Florida were included in the June 1766 issue. They indicated that settlement of the region increased daily, no doubt precipitated by "the most authentic accounts, that the country is very fertile, fit for the raising of sugar, cotton, indigo, and other West-India productions."[47]

At the same time, British colonial officials adopted similar methods to promote settlement of the Floridas. In January 1767, *The Scots Magazine* published a proclamation issued by East Florida governor James Grant. Explicitly stating his purpose, the governor hoped to instigate "the speedy settlement of his Majesty's province of East Florida, to inform all persons of the healthiness, soil and productions thereof." Grant summarized all of the natural descriptions of Florida recorded over the past 200 years:

> The winter is so remarkably temperate . . . The lands are fertile and rich
> . . . Fruits and grains may be raised with little labour . . . There is at all
> times sufficient quantities of pasture to maintain his [the settler's] cattle
> . . . All the fruits and productions of the West Indies may be raised here
> . . . Oranges, limes, lemons, and other fruits, grow spontaneously over
> the country . . . The province abounds with mahogany and all kinds of
> timber . . . There is water-carriage every where.

Thus, the desirability of settling the region was self- evident. Further sweetening the images, Grant claimed that the environment of the Floridas also caused inhabitants to live longer. Soldiers stationed in the region "enjoyed an uninterrupted state of good health," and the "former inhabitants lived to great ages."[48]

Once Britons began to settle in the Floridas, more firsthand impressions materialized. In 1770, Captain Philip Pittman, a British soldier, published his views of the region in *The Present State of the European Settlements on the Missisippi*. Either unaware of or unsatisfied with Stork's offering, Pittman was "surprised that nobody has yet attempted to wipe off the unfavourable impressions that have taken place in the minds of many people." He wrote down his findings out of "a regard for truth, and a desire to render service to that valuable province, the welfare of which has been obstructed by ignorance and misinterpretation." Pittman believed that "from its situation and soil [the Natchez region] is the finest and most fertile part of West Florida . . . The country is well watered, hops grow wild, and all kinds of European fruits come to great perfection."[49] Colonial officials in East Florida offered their own glowing appraisals. John Gerar William De Brahm, royal surveyor for the province, published his opinions of the Floridas in 1772 under the title *Report of the General Survey in the Southern District of North America*. It contributed little new information, but De Brahm confirmed earlier reports that "the Soil consists of much fine low Land for the Culture of Rice." More impressed with the forests than anything else, he claimed that the region was "well stocked with fine Trees fit to be manufactured into Timber; those not fit for Manufactury may be tapped for drawing the Turpentine." And, as had often been mentioned before, the long-leaf forests offered "fine Pasturage for Cattle and Horses."[50] Colonial officials did their best to supplement private attempts to populate the still-illusive Floridas.

At least one widely publicized account appealed principally to Europeans already living in North America. *The New York Gazette* published a letter in September 1773 aimed at attracting settlers from the northern colonies to the Floridas. Claiming that already in the few years that Great Britain had controlled the region "some Tracts have been cultivated . . . and have yielded an increasing Produce every Year," the anonymous author hoped to show that colonists could prosper much more in the south than the north. "The Lands at and above the Natchez have been tried," according to the letter-writer, "and will produce either Wheat or Barley; and there are large Tracts suited to the raising of the greatest abundance of Hemp, Flax, Indian and Guinea Corn etc. in every Part of the Country." From this evidence, it was apparent to the author "that this Land will not only produce every Article which those of the Province proposed above the Falls of the Ohio can ever be expected to" but would eventually "be employed to Advantage in raising of Rice, Cotton and Indigo in Perfection, nay, in Time they may even produce Wine, Oyl, and Silk."[51] It appeared, at least to some, that the environment of the Floridas could produce almost anything settlers desired.

Reality

These perceptions often differed from reality, however. In a separate letter in *The New York Gazette*, the same anonymous correspondent made a state-ment that characterized European knowledge of the Floridas between 1513 and 1783: "Even at this Day, we are far from being thoroughly acquainted."[52] European understandings of the region, at least in written form, differed very little from the time of Spain's first exploration until the American Revolution. Despite the many disparate attempts to uncover the mysteries concerning the Floridas, confusion and misunderstanding remained.

Yet much of this misapprehension was intentional. Viewing the land as a distant mythical paradise enabled Spaniards, Frenchmen, and Britons to over-look failed colonization attempts and economic disappointments. Europeans concentrated on the environment because it offered endless hope for exploitation, even if colonization attempts failed in other respects. As is apparent from the literature about the Floridas, this reverence for the land's natural resources succeeded in molding overall opinion among peoples living in Europe. However, deception did not work for Europeans who actually inhabited the peninsula. Spanish, French, and British immigrants reacted to their environment in much different ways, constructing a radically different way to rationalize their failures. Images of Indians were central to this rationalization.

Figure 2. Colonial Floridas, 1513–1566.

3

The Origins of Disillusionment

In 1599, Garcilaso de la Vega published his account of Hernando de Soto's journey through what is today the southeastern United States. The work is based on the author's romantic perceptions of North America and evidence provided by expedition members, and its factual validity is questionable in many regards.[1] Nevertheless, Garcilaso's interpretation provides valuable information about the images of the Floridas that were created and perpetuated by European visitors during the sixteenth century. One passage in particular that Garcilaso attributed to Hernando de Soto captured the general opinions of colonists regarding native peoples. The explorer concluded that "all of the land of this realm is practically identical in kind and quality . . . [and] its inhabitants live, dress, eat and drink in somewhat the same manner. Even in their idols and their rites and ceremonies of paganism . . . and in their weapons, their social distinctions and their ferocity, they differ little or nothing from each other."[2]

Hernando de Soto's remarks (as represented by Garcilaso) are significant because they imply that European explorers and settlers envisioned the natives of the region and the region itself as one, as the same. In response to the difficulties prevalent in their New World, European immigrants linked the characteristics of the land with the attributes of its peoples. When expectations of riches and glory failed to materialize, romantic images of the peninsula and its promise faded and the Floridas and all they encompassed acquired new negative connotations. The disappointment of colonists manifested itself as cultural and, eventually, racialized disparagement of the indigenous peoples. Seeking explanations for their unfulfilled goals, explorers and settlers initiated a process of distancing themselves from local Indians who represented failure in the Floridas. In this manner they erected a psychological barrier that would help undermine intercultural understanding and provide an important catalyst for the formation of a European Floridian identity.

Backgrounds

The period between 1513 and 1566 in many ways marked the pinnacle of Spanish imperial power in the New World. Not only did Iberians explore and claim most coastal areas of Central and South America during these years, they also made significant incursions into interior Mexico and Peru that generated much mineral wealth for the Crown and some of its subjects. Concurrently, the longer-established island colonies of Hispaniola, Puerto Rico, Cuba, and Jamaica began to supply agricultural staples that provided both subsistence and cash crops. Aside from the growing problems associated with pirating and privateering, no European competitor could yet seriously challenge Spain's control of its New World possessions.

A similar situation existed regarding native resistance. Many indigenous peoples throughout the empire successfully resisted Iberian control for the duration of the colonial period, mostly through clinging to their cultural norms, sometimes through military efforts. But most sizeable Indian armies in Latin America and the Caribbean had been defeated or pacified by 1566. The major problems plaguing the Crown at that point involved administration of the colonies. Strategists in Madrid repeatedly grappled with bureaucratic jurisdictions and growing colonial autonomy, problems that would never be fully resolved.

These years also served as the period of most intense Spanish exploration in the Floridas. Preoccupied with "island hopping" in the Caribbean, Spaniards did not turn their attention to the Floridas until the second decade of the sixteenth century. Once it was noticed, however, the region became the site of multiple exploratory campaigns carried out by soldiers and adventurers who had recently been involved in similar endeavors to the south and west. Searching for human, mineral, and agricultural riches, conquistadors such as Juan Ponce de León, Pánfilo de Narváez, Hernando de Soto, and numerous others traversed the peninsula and its hinterlands. Although they found many hardships and few rewards, these Spaniards succeeded in mapping the region for the first time and laid the basis for different forms of colonization in later years. Equally important, they generated accounts of the Floridas and its peoples that would influence Europeans for centuries.

The Indians that Europeans first encountered in the colonial Floridas represented at least four distinct culture groups and numerous interrelated communities. In the peninsular lands south of modern-day Tampa and Fort Pierce, Calusa Indians wielded the most influence. A fisher-hunter-gatherer people probably numbering less than 10,000 at the time of contact, the Calusas used a chiefdom form of government and enforced tribute demands on the region's other sizeable native groups, the Tequesta and Ais. Timucuan-speakers, who, according to some scholars, totaled almost 200,000 people prior to European contact, inhabited the central and northwestern portions of the peninsula. Aside from language, Timucuans shared few political or ethnic allegiances, though all practiced some form of farming to supplement hunting, fishing, and gathering. About 15,000 Guale Indians lived along what is today Georgia's south Atlantic coast. Dependent on farming, hunting, gathering, and marine life for survival, the Guales resembled the Timucuans in terms of political organization, possessing no single unified system and consisting of several small independent chiefdoms that were connected through clan and kinship networks. The Apalachee Indians of northwestern Florida, who were also agriculturalists but were more politically centralized than other groups in the region, constituted the other main indigenous group Europeans encountered during this period. The Apalachee communities were home to the largest pre-contact urban site in the Floridas, which probably contained over 50,000 inhabitants in 1492.[3]

Much like the Spanish, the Indians in the Floridas experienced monumental change between the years 1513 and 1566. In addition to dealing with day-to-day issues that affected village life and intermittent conflicts with indigenous neighbors, natives encountered a new people whose ideas, material culture, and activities transformed all aspects of society. Militarily and diplomatically, Calusas, Timucuans, Guales, and Apalachees withstood European invasions, reached various forms of accommodation with colonists, and maintained control of much of their land and culture. Nevertheless, the combination of resistance efforts and the devastating diseases that accompanied explorers to native communities began the long process of decimating indigenous populations in the region, a process that ultimately undermined the coherence of all four groups.

European Exploration and Native Barbarity

Cross-cultural impressions surfaced in the earliest European writings on Indians in the Floridas. Most prevalent in the accounts of early European visitors are descriptions of Native Americans based on the concept of barbarity. In its simplest form, stripped of racial and religious connotations, the term "barbarity" (and its derivatives) referred to individual or group deviance from European standards of behavior regarding morals, manners, activities, lifestyles, and philosophies. During the early contact period, Europeans frequently used the term to describe a variety of peoples throughout the world, including, at times, other Europeans. This practice continued among immigrants in the Floridas and became common in writings that described Indians of the Americas.[4]

The idea of Indian barbarity in the Floridas emerged soon after the first major Spanish incursions into the region. In 1528, an expedition consisting of at least five ships and 500 people inadvertently landed on the western shore of the peninsula near Tampa Bay. The commander of the group, Pánfilo de Narváez, was aiming for a destination on the gulf coast east of Mexico and regretted the necessity of landing in the Floridas. Nevertheless, he sent his ships to find a better harbor to the north while most of the members in his expedition accompanied him ashore to explore the area. Unable to find the harbor, the ships departed for Cuba, leaving the landing party with few supplies. Desperate soldiers eventually killed most of the horses accompanying the group, using their organs for food. Dozens died from illness, and Timucuan and Apalachee Indians killed others. Despondent and yearning to go home, Pánfilo de Narváez and his remaining followers built rafts and attempted to sail along the coast to Mexico. None completed the journey, and most of the expedition's members, including Narváez, perished.[5]

Not all of those on the expedition died, however. Alvar Núñez Cabeza de Vaca, the most famous survivor, provided an account of the events that officials in Spain carefully preserved and revealed to the public.[6] Throughout his reports, Cabeza de Vaca alluded to the behavior and appearance of the Floridas' residents and the relationship of both to the environment. Following his account of a series of violent engagements with Apalachee Indians, he described native demeanor and tactics at length, finally concluding that "the Indians of that land are very warlike and wild and strong."[7] Cabeza de Vaca viewed the enemy's battlefield expertise as partially attributable to exceptional physical strength and alarmingly aggressive temperament. His views also reveal that Spaniards viewed these "wild" and "warlike" characteristics as atypical, or at least very different from those associated with Europeans.

Intrigued by the mysteries surrounding Pánfilo de Narváez and his experiences in the Floridas, as well as by the potential riches available there, Spanish conquistador Hernando de Soto organized an expedition, with royal backing, and sailed for the region in 1539. Like the earlier explorers, Hernando de Soto and his contingent encountered many obstacles as they proceeded through the peninsula. Hazardous travel through swamps, inconsistent food supplies, continuous threats of mutiny, and repeated violent encounters with Calusa, Timucuan and Apalachee natives hampered the men as they journeyed first north, then west. By 1541, the expedition had traversed Florida and most of the southeast but had failed to secure an empire for the Spanish Crown or wealth for the adventurers. Two years later, less than half of the members who originally left Spain for Florida escaped to Mexico. Among those missing was Hernando de Soto, who had died in June 1542.[8]

References to Indian barbarity are widespread in the accounts that document Soto's campaigns in the Floridas. Indian lifestyles and perceived instinctive behavior fascinated the explorers. Pedro Calderón, a soldier who accompanied Soto, believed that the "natives of the great kingdom of Florida are in general very brave, strong and skillful in shooting arrows" but explained their talents as partially a result of inherent predispositions:

> The children for instance, when they are three years of age and even less, in fact as soon as they are able to walk, are moved by their *natural* inclination and by the sight of what their parents do, to ask for bows and arrows. When denied these things, they themselves make them of little sticks . . . and with such implements go unendingly in search of the disgusting reptiles which they run upon in their houses . . . On account of such continuous exercises and the consequent habit the Indians have formed in shooting arrows, they are skillful and ferocious in the art.[9] (emphasis added)

In addition to reinforcing European impressions that native distinctions were the result of the peculiarities of the region, the passage promoted the idea that through instinctive practices, Indians attained unusual expertise in martial abilities, expertise that contributed to their fierceness in battle and set them apart from Europeans in the Floridas.[10]

Hernando de Soto and his men further highlighted their ideas about barbarity by commenting on the Indians' varying degrees of civilization. According to the Gentleman of Elvas, another chronicler of the expedition, Indians north of the present-day boundaries of the state were "more civilized than any people seen in all the territories of Florida, wearing clothes and shoes."[11] The Gentleman of Elvas made the assumption common among Europeans of the time that the amount and style of clothing an individual wore determined his or her degree of civilized behavior. Apparently discounting climate and geography, the soldier believed that since the natives outside of the Floridas exhibited dress styles more in line with those of Europe, they were less barbaric.[12]

As they proceeded through the Floridas, members of the expedition repeatedly commented on Indians and their defects in character. In the province of "Caluza," Hernando de Soto encountered "more than ninety villages not subject to any one, with a savage population, very warlike and much dreaded."[13] In his opinion, the lack of any visible government, laws, or leaders promoted Indian savagery. De Soto and his followers also singled out individual natives based on their expressions of barbarity. As the expedition meandered through the Floridas and the Indians learned of Soto's habit of seizing people and villages, their resistance against the requests of the Spaniards intensified. When he discovered that the cacique of a Timucuan community he identified as "Acuera" had rejected his offer of friendship, Soto "was astonished that a barbarian should manage to say such things with so much arrogance and loftiness of spirit."[14] Subsequent rejections continued to baffle Soto and his men. On another occasion, "Vitachuco [an Apalachee cacique] responded very strangely and with a boldness never heard or even imagined in an Indian" when he refused to heed Soto's commands.[15] According to Garcilaso, Vitachuco eventually attempted to murder the conquistador. Though "the Cacique rose to his feet with all imaginable savagery and fierceness and in an instant closed with the Adelantado," the native ultimately failed and he died in the ensuing struggle. In his description of the scene and its resolution, Garcilaso offered contemporary Iberian opinions on Indian barbarity and its consequences: "Vitachuco proved himself to be too strong and fierce to live. Thus one may deduce that those terrible threats—and such strange threats they were—which he had made from the first, had been born of a savageness and fierceness of spirit which, because of its rarity, had not admitted the consideration, prudence and counsel that great deeds require."[16] In the view of Hernando de Soto and his fellow Spaniards, Vitachuco's inability to master the qualities common in a civilized culture prohibited him from succeeding in his pursuits and destined him to failure.

Depictions of Indian barbarity continued to appear in the writings of Europeans who visited the Floridas. In 1549, Father Luís Cancer, a Dominican friar, attempted to convert Timucuan natives on the peninsula's west coast. A student of the famous "Indian protector" Bartolomé de Las Casas, Cancer hoped to Christianize the indigenous population prior to widespread European colonization.[17] When he first encountered Indians along the coast, the missionary carried out an experiment to evaluate the natives' true intentions:

> To see if I was free to do so, if they would let me go to the launch [a ship offshore], I was careful to tell them that I had more to give them and I was going back to get it, although in fact I already had it in my sleeve, but I had not wanted to give them all of it since I had intended to do this: I went, and came back, and found so many who wanted to embrace me that I could not get away from them. This friendship and affection was obviously based on what they thought they could get from us than on ourselves, but since this world is the route to the other, and as we all know from experience and say that love is good deeds and that gifts can break rocks, I was pleased that they should receive us so well for these material matters.[18]

Even though he began with positive intentions toward the Indians, Cancer quickly assumed that their motives for friendship were based solely on desire for material goods.

Although Spaniards were the first Europeans to explore the Floridas, other European groups soon followed. As previously mentioned, France also expressed interest in this allegedly bountiful land. René de Laudonnière's group of Protestant families, who had brought livestock and trade goods with them, established a small colony known as Fort Caroline near the mouth of the St. John's River in 1564. Even though it remained under French control for less than two years, the colony was the first substantial venue for interaction between French colonists and native inhabitants of the Floridas.[19]

Beset by problems almost immediately upon arrival, French settlers soon began comparing themselves to the Timucuan Indians they encountered. While Laudonnière expressed admiration for the natives' bravery in battle, he proclaimed that in general "they are great liars and traitors." Indian sexual practices attracted special attention: Indian priests "always carry with them a bag full of herbs and drugs to treat diseases—mainly syphilis, for they love women and girls very much, whom they call 'Daughters of the Sun.'"[20]

Laudonnière and the colonists with him shared some of the views of earlier Spanish visitors regarding the character of the Indians. On one occasion, Timucuans living along the east coast agreed to help the French repair their damaged shelters. Though pleased to have the assistance, Fort Caroline settlers questioned the motives of the natives. According to Laudonnière's account, the caciques:

proposed to all their subjects that they hasten to build another house, pointing out to them that the French were affectionate friends to them, as was obvious from the gifts and presents that they had received from them. They declared that he who did not work on it with all his ability would be regarded as worthless and as not having anything good in him (which is a reputation these barbarians fear above all other things). That was the reason that each of them began to work hard.[21]

Frenchmen also believed that native residents were expert pilferers. Laudonnière declared the Floridas Indians to be "the biggest thieves in the world because they can steal with their feet as well as their hands." And though the women appeared to be "not as thieving" as the men, females did "covet rings and chokers around their necks."[22] As had the Spaniard Father Cancer almost twenty years before, the French suspected that Indian motives for friendship stemmed from selfish interests and a preoccupation with acquiring material goods. Other European visitors to the Floridas made similar observations. In 1566, French settler Nicolas Le Challeux wrote that the Timucuans "have loose morals; they never teach or correct their children; they steal unscrupulously and claim for themselves all they can secretly carry away."[23]

The English also commented on Indian barbarity but tended to focus on their brutality and mental capacity. In 1565, English sailor John Sparke recorded his observations about Florida while accompanying the plunderer John Hawkins.[24] Sparke believed that "those people of the cape of Florida are of more savage and fierce nature, and more valiant than any of the rest." He based his opinions on tales of native cannibalism he had heard from the Spanish. According to these stories, "a frier, who taking upon him to persuade the people to subjection, was by them taken, and his skin pulled over his eares, and his flesh eaten." Other tales convinced Sparke that the Floridas Indians were "eaters of the flesh of men, aswel as the Canibals." Although he was sure that their activities were barbaric, he remained uncertain about their mental abilities. Sparke's uncertainty emanated from conflicting opinions supplied by the French and Spanish. While visiting Fort Caroline, he discovered that Indians "are called by the Spanyards *Gente triste*, that is to say Bad people, meaning thereby that they are not men of capacity: yet have the French men found them so witty in their answeres, that by the captaines owne report, a counseller with us could not give a more profound reason."[25]

In 1565, Spain effectively ousted its European competitors from the Floridas, at least for the next 200 years. The man in charge of this endeavor was

Pedro Menéndez de Avilés, an adventurer and soldier charged by the Spanish Crown with securing the peninsula for the empire. Like many Europeans before him, Menéndez de Avilés hoped to profit from his efforts in the Floridas through mining, trade, and agriculture. Also like many of his predecessors, he failed to acquire the riches he envisioned. Though he is credited with ejecting the French and establishing the settlement of St. Augustine, Menéndez de Avilés proved unable to secure the region for Spain or attract Spanish settlers and instead repeatedly engaged many of the region's Indians in battle. When he died in 1574, few of his dreams for himself or Spain had become reality in the Floridas.[26]

As these circumstances unfolded, Menéndez de Avilés formed his attitudes toward Indians and their lack of "civilization." Two years after arriving in the region, the recently appointed governor of the colony expressed his views: "The Indians were warlike, intractable, and wanted nothing to do with the Christians . . . [They] practice no austerity, but follow wherever their sensuality and bestial vice leads them."[27] He advocated severe measures to keep the Indians from rebelling against the Spanish colony, reasoning that "if in fact a man does not resist, they are such great traitors, thieves and greedy persons, that one cannot easily live with them."[28]

Menéndez de Avilés advocated strict repression of Indian dissent: "The only way to make them keep their agreements—and they are great liars and traitors—is to rout them out of their villages, burn their dwellings, cut down their plantings, seize their canoes, and destroy their fishways. Then they realize they must do the Christians' bidding, or abandon the land." Yet even these measures would not resolve all problems between the Spanish and natives. Menéndez de Avilés claimed that even the Indians living within the Spanish settlements exhibited no better behavior: "The natives at St. Augustine and at San Mateo are very treacherous and deceitful, especially since they feign friendship with the Christians for their own immediate ends. If they are not given food, clothing, iron axes, and other presents when they come to the forts, they leave in a great rage, go on the warpath, and kill any Christian they encounter."[29]

At the same time, the governor did not believe that all Indians acted in a similar manner and that some did show promise for reform. Referring to Indians living north of Saint Helena (modern Parris Island, South Carolina), he acknowledged that "the Indians give evidence of good intelligence and are not as rustic or savage as the others. Thus they can boast of established customs. In conformity with their idea of justice, they punish liars." Yet he concluded this statement by noting that "in reality all Indians are liars, and the abominate thieves."[30]

Emotional expressions by Indians further shaped European understandings of indigenous peoples of the Floridas. Spaniards and Frenchmen had difficulty understanding the value systems of the Indians and their seemingly conflicting emotional signals. The confusion of the Europeans centered on one main question: How could barbaric Indians express compassion, sympathy, and sometimes tenderness toward non-Indians? Unable to resolve this quandary, Europeans reacted with misunderstanding and distrust.

Cabeza de Vaca illustrated an example of such a scenario in his accounts of the Floridas. On one occasion, members of Cabeza de Vaca's contingent sought assistance from a group of Apalachee Indians, explaining to them that one of their boats had sunk and four Spaniards had drowned. In the minds of Cabeza de Vaca and his men, the native response was inexplicable:

> The Indians, at sight of what had befallen us, and our state of suffering and melancholy destitution, sat down among us, and from the sorrow and pity they felt, they all began to lament so earnestly that they might have been heard at a distance, and continued so doing more than half an hour. It was strange to see these men, wild and untaught, howling like brutes over our misfortunes. It caused in me as in others, an increase of feeling and a livelier sense of our calamity.[31]

Failing to understand the Indians' actions, Cabeza de Vaca and his companions reacted with confusion and a heightened degree of uncertainty regarding Indians and the standing of conquistadors among them. These situations unnerved Europeans because they indicated just how little the explorers understood about native culture and, in effect, the Floridas in general.

Forty years later, members of the Laudonnière expedition also failed to comprehend the wants and needs of the Indians. Hoping to gain more knowledge, the Frenchmen selected two Timucuan natives to take back to Europe. Initially, these Indians, "feeling more favoured than the others, considered themselves very lucky to go." Soon, however, their behavior perplexed Laudonnière's men:

> The sails forthwith were made ready and we sailed toward the big river. But the two Indians, seeing that we were apparently not going to land and were only following the middle of the channel, began to get a little nervous. Regardless of the consequences, they wanted to throw them-

selves into the water . . . However, realizing their intentions, we kept an eye on them and tried by every means to please them, which was impossible. Although they were presented with things that they prize highly, they disdained to take them and gave back everything that they had been given, thinking that such gifts put them in [our] debt and that in giving them back they would be granted their liberty.[32]

Unable to comprehend the Indians' erratic behavior and rejection of material goods, the Frenchmen grew exasperated with the Indians and eventually allowed them to go ashore.

Indian barbarity continued to be a popular topic among Europeans as they infiltrated the Floridas. Evaluated independently, these comments appear isolated and perhaps benign. Considered as a general expression of attitude, however, they indicate a growing belief among explorers and settlers that Indians and Europeans differed in multiple and significant ways. As time progressed, these differences fostered divisions between the cultures that increasingly impeded transcultural understanding.

European Exploration and the Physical Appearance of Natives

The dress and anatomy of Indians sparked lengthy comment and speculation among explorers and colonists. Though people of all cultures and regions commonly noted physical appearance in descriptions of others, the comments of Europeans about Indians were especially significant because of their frequency and the associations Europeans made between character and civilization. As would become progressively more evident, the physical distinctions Europeans made between Indians and themselves became an important vehicle for discrimination and racialization.

Not all descriptions of native appearance had negative connotations. In 1517, a Spanish ship sailing from the Yucatan took refuge from a storm in San Carlos Bay on the Floridas' southwestern coast near present-day Fort Myers. Upon going ashore and encountering local Timucuan natives, Antonio de Alaminos, the ship's pilot, recorded that "they were clad in deerskins and were very big men."[33] Ten years later, members of Pánfilo de Narváez's expedition made similar observations. These Spaniards also believed the Indians were "well built . . . [and] had large bodies" but added that "the men had one nipple pierced and a piece of cane inserted through the hole . . . and the lower lip was also pierced, with another cane there."[34] The Indians' size made an impression on the Europeans. Cabeza de Vaca and his fellow explorers noted that "all the many Indians from Florida we saw were archers, and, being very tall and naked, at a distance appear giants. Those people are wonderfully built, very gaunt and of great strength and agility."[35] This was the first time the Indians' nakedness was noted; the size of the natives was expressed with the label "giant," a term generally used at the time in association with nonhumans.

Hernando de Soto and his followers added to these descriptions during their entrada into Florida between 1539 and 1541. The Gentleman of Elvas supported earlier Spanish reactions, noting that "the Indians are well proportioned," but he disagreed with previous generalizations when he insisted that "those of the flat lands are of taller stature and better built than those of the mountains."[36] Garcilaso also established an important connection between the Indians' uncivilized behavior and their physical features. Describing the natives of the coast of northwest Florida, he wrote, "Alonso de Carmona [a member of Hernando de Soto's expedition] . . . makes particular mention of the ferocity of the Indians of the province of Apalache, saying the following, which is taken to the letter: 'These Indians of Apalache are gigantic in stature and are very valiant and spirited . . . In fact their going naked is a great help to them.'"[37] This connection between barbarity and physical features was important to the construction of later viewpoints; Europeans came to believe that nakedness and physical abnormalities contributed to wild behavior.

French depictions contributed to this image. Le Challeux emphasized the Indians' dress in his writings. He recorded that except for war decorations, "neither the men nor the women have any other clothing, except that the women girdle themselves with a small apron made of the skin of deer or other animals, tied on the left side in order to cover the most shameful part of their body." Seemingly as an afterthought, Le Challeux also wrote, "They are neither flat nosed nor thick lipped, having round, even faces, and good eye-sight."[38]

Laudonnière focused too on Indian clothing. He concluded that the males "are naked except for an animal skin covering their private parts . . . and the women have long strands of white moss wrapped around them covering their breasts and private parts."[39] In the mind of Laudonnière, natural clothing—animal or vegetation—associated Indians with the natural environment, which led him to further speculate on their appearance. Laudonnière observed that the Timucuans were "very tall, handsom, and well proportioned without any deformity . . . Their hair is very black and grows down to their hips; however, they do it up in a way that is very becoming to them." He marveled at the exotic attractiveness of one Timucuan couple in particular. The male was "one of the tallest and best built men to be found anywhere" and his wife was endowed with "Indian beauty."[40] Jean Ribault, a French explorer and contemporary of Laudonnière, held comparable opinions, writing that the Indians were "all naked and of a goodly stature, mighty, faire, and as well shapen and proportioned of bodye as any people in all the worlde."[41] In an exotic and distinctly non-European sense, Indians could be visually enticing, but it was a beauty Europeans associated with the anticipated beauty of the environment. When natives put "paint [on] their faces much and put feathers in their hair in order to appear frightening," Europeans' appreciation for native beauty dissipated.[42] An "uncivilized" appearance signified the ever-present threat that natives represented to the ideals and goals of Europeans.

Englishman John Sparke expressed amazement over the Indians' penchant for painting themselves. He marveled at the meticulous care they took in their decorating. According to Sparke, "They do not omit to paint their bodies also with curious knots, or antlike worke, as every man in his owne fancy deviseth, which painting, to make it continue the better, they use with a thorne to prickle their flesh, and dent in the same, whereby the painting may have better hold." This form of adornment represented the threat of peril to the European mind. Failing to consider that such efforts might be motivated by an assertion of identity or for cultural or spiritual reasons, Sparke assumed that Timucuans endured tattooing "to make themselves shew the more fierce."[43]

European observations about native appearance and its implications for uncivilized behavior fostered negative images of Indians. Shortly after arriving in the Floridas in 1564, Menéndez de Avilés demonstrated the impact of these images. He perceived the Timucuans to be well proportioned, "large of body . . . slender, very strong, and swift," judgments much like those his European predecessors in the Floridas had made.[44] These perceptions were starting to take on greater meaning by the time of Menéndez de Avilés's arrival. Europeans were beginning to view Indian appearance and barbarity as symbiotic. Describing shipwrecked Spaniards living along the coast of Florida, Menéndez de Avilés lamented that "they all went about naked, having become savages like the very Indians" they lived among.[45] Europeans now equated the combination of barbaric conduct and an appearance that deviated from European norms with "Indian." Benign isolated comments had combined to generate an important new stereotype that would influence European relationships with Indians for the next 300 years.

European travelers expanded these stereotypes by commenting on the skin color of the natives they met in the Floridas. Though it was mentioned far less often than barbaric activity and general physical appearance, skin color, whether artificial or natural, often surfaced in the writings of early explorers and their chroniclers. In the sixteenth century, these references did not indicate the presence of color-based racialization. However, they provided another reason for Spaniards, Frenchmen, and Englishmen to label the Indians as distinctly separate from themselves.

Father Cancer was the first to put in writing the idea that natives appeared different in color from Europeans. In 1529, he commented that when he greeted a group of Timucuans, "I was getting covered in their red dye from all the embracing that was going on, although I managed to get the worst of it on my habit to leave the skin untouched."[46] From his description, it is apparent that Cancer realized that the red coloring was artificial and impermanent. It is also clear that the dye disturbed him and was a marker of Indian deviance in his mind.

Later Spanish depictions revealed more ways Europeans "colored" the natives they encountered in the Floridas. Some accounts by members of Hernando de Soto's expedition described natives as "brown of skin," offering no commentary about the origins or meanings of the pigment to colonists.[47] On other occasions, members of the expedition pondered the significance of the natives' facial and body colors. Relating a hostile meeting between Florida Indians and Spaniards, Rodrigo Rangel noted how "they [members of the expedition] came to another plain where the Indians had taken the position, having made a very strong barricade, and within it there were many Indian braves, painted red and decorated with other colours which appeared very fine (or rather, very bad, at least it meant harm to the Christians)."[48] The Spaniard Rangel's comments resemble those of Englishman John Sparke regarding Indian face painting. Both chroniclers believed that the Indians used dyes to frighten their opponents. In addition, Rangel's passage is significant because he chose to emphasize the color "red," despite his own admission that the Indians decorated themselves with multiple colors.[49]

French adventurers in the Floridas also noticed the Indians' skin tone. Ribault believed them to be "of tawny collour."[50] Le Challeux, after much study of the natives, disagreed. He asserted that they had "a somewhat ruddy complexion."[51] Laudonnière felt that the Indians exhibited a variety of skin colors. Upon first arriving on the peninsula he claimed, "The men are olive coloured . . . Most of them are painted on the body and on the arms and thighs in beautiful patterns. The pigments cannot be removed because they are pricked into the flesh."[52] Yet on another occasion, the Indians appear anything but olive colored. Laudonnière contended that certain Indians "are painted in black all over, in beautiful designs."[53]

The uncertainty of Europeans about the origins and permanence of Indian skin color is apparent. During the early period of exploration and colonization, Spaniards, Frenchmen, and Britons could not determine any consistent shade or pigment among the natives. This uncertainty fostered feelings of alienation from the Indians. Europeans who could not master the difficulties of the terrain of the Floridas also could not resolve questions about the natives of the Floridas. In ensuing decades, the two issues melded together and became one.

The final descriptive process Europeans used to evaluate Indians involved animal imagery. Occasionally Europeans compared Indians to nonhumans, and these comparisons influenced colonists' impressions of the natives. Like references to Indians and their overall appearance, these depictions often implied little condemnation or hostility. Nevertheless, such characterizations added to racialized impressions among Europeans. Dehumanization reinforced the idea that because of their lifestyles, emotions, appearance, skin color, and nonhuman characteristics, Indians could, and perhaps should be regarded and treated as inferior.

Garcilaso introduced this imagery in his writings about Hernando de Soto. In his assessment of Spanish attitudes toward the Indians, Garcilaso recorded, "For in general these people are looked upon as simple folk without reason or understanding who in both peace and war differ very little from beasts and accordingly could not do and say things . . . worthy of memory or praise."[54] Garcilaso accurately summarized the varied European ideas regarding Indians. According to this perspective, if Indians were barbaric, emotionally unpredictable, physically abnormal, and different in skin color, they had the same qualities as nonhumans, or beasts.

Le Challeux echoed these feelings in his evaluation of Indian behavior. In 1566, he described French mistreatment of Timucuans at Fort Caroline and explained the consequences: "This caused the natives to turn from good feelings towards the French and since the desire for vengeance is planted in men's hearts by nature, and as it is also the common instinct of all animals to defend life and limb, and to remove the source of trouble, it cannot be doubted that the natives conspired and intrigued with the Spaniards to free themselves from us."[55] While he does not single out the Indians as possessing more animal-like characteristics than other groups, Le Challeux accentuated the idea that decision making by natives was based as much or more on animal instinct than anything else.

A more blatant example of "animalization" surfaces in Menéndez de Avilés' accounts of the Florida Indians. Recorded half a century after the first explorations, these writings convey just how far this idea had progressed: "When the soldier has fired, the Indian rises at a place different from the spot aimed at, as if he had been swimming underwater. So adept, and clever at this maneuver are they, that one can only be astonished. They fight by skirmishing, and jump over the brush like little deer . . . They are unencumbered by clothes, and swim like fish . . . Once on the opposite bank they shriek and mock the Christians."[56] Menéndez de Avilés directly compares natives to both deer and fish. In his eyes, their abilities are identical with those of the animals he mentions. Along with their nakedness and ridicule of Europeans (Christians), the Indians had proven through their natural capacities that they were much different from the colonists.

European Failure and Racialization

The fact that Europeans frequently referred to Indian barbarity, emotional expression, physical appearance, skin color, and beast-like characteristics is significant in itself. More illustrative of the evolution of racialization in the Floridas, however, is how these descriptions surfaced during times of European frustration. The available evidence indicates that descriptions of Indian barbarity and physical appearance became much more fervent during times of turmoil for the conquistadors and colonists. As Indians became the outlets for the anxiety and disappointment of Europeans, estrangement increased. Isolated incidents of genuine native obstruction to colonial goals could not provide sufficient excuse for the failures of Spaniards, Frenchmen, and Britons in the New World, and the Europeans constantly sought other explanations. They constructed an idea of native insufficiency, a racialized image that would serve their purposes on a consistent basis. This flexible characterization allowed Europeans to condemn the natives no matter what their actual activities were.

Juan Ponce de León, one of Spain's first explorers to visit the Floridas, laid the basis for this image of natives. Landing on the peninsula's eastern coast in April 1513, Ponce de León's expedition encountered hostile Timucuans, and very little that inspired the leader to stay in the region. Moving along the southern and western shores of the peninsula, the expedition again violently encountered Indians, this time Calusas, and at least one Spaniard died in the fighting. By June, Ponce de León had seen enough of the Floridas and had departed for Puerto Rico. Rejuvenated, he returned in 1521, hoping to establish a colony for Spain. Local natives again attacked his expedition and forced it to depart for Cuba, where Ponce de León died from a wound received while battling Florida Indians.[57]

As a consequence of his experiences, Ponce de León and his followers constructed negative impressions of both the land and its inhabitants in a way that made the indigenous peoples of the Floridas integral to Spanish explanations of misfortune in the region. According to his chronicler, Ponce de León believed that "the temperature of the region was very unsuitable and different from what he imagined, and the natives of the land [were] a very austere and very savage and belligerous [*sic*] and fierce and untamed people." Explaining his decision to leave the peninsula, Ponce de León complained, "But inasmuch as everything went wrong . . . it is believed that God was not served nor the time come for conversion of that land and province to our holy Catholic faith, since he [God] permits the devil still to keep those Indians deceived . . . and the population of hell to be augmented with their souls."[58]

Blaming Indians for failures in the Floridas became a recurring theme. Cabeza de Vaca explained Pánfilo de Narváez's decision to leave the Floridas by making parallels between the land's insufficiency and Indian obstruction. According to Cabeza de Vaca's report, his leader declared that "in view of the poverty of the land, the unfavorable accounts of the population and . . . the Indians making continual war against us . . . we determined to leave that place and go in quest of the sea."[59] Both environmental and human factors combined to frustrate European efforts, though the indigenous inhabitants received greater attention in explanations of the causes of failure. After Father Cancer was murdered in 1529 by the Timucuans he was trying to convert, the missionaries accompanying him worried about the impact his death would have on their further activities. They believed that if the expedition returned to Spain "with this news . . . they [the Spanish Crown] would conclude . . . that all these pagans deserved death, and deserved having people conquer them."[60] Indians and their perceived deviant ways threatened Spanish ventures in Florida in a number of ways.

A revealing example of European frustration and its impact on attitudes toward Indians involved Laudonnière's expedition. French settlers, who were increasingly desperate for food, began to depend on Timucuan provisions for survival. Dejected over their situation, members of the expedition became angry when the Indians demanded a large amount of merchandise in exchange for food. Laudonnière recorded his assessment of the situation:

> They brought their fish in their little boats, to which our poor soldiers were obliged to go, and very often (as I have seen) to strip off their own shirts to have one fish. If they at any time remonstrated with the savages for the excessive price they charged, those villains would answer imprudently, "If you're so fond of your merchandise, why don't you eat it, and we'll eat our fish!" They then burst out laughing and made fun of us. At this, our soldiers, losing patience, often felt like tearing them limb from limb and making them pay for their foolish arrogance.[61]

Rather than locating the source of their difficulties in the environment, the colonists blamed Indians for their grim circumstances. The natives' desire to profit from the colonists' misfortune antagonized Frenchmen already unhappy with their situation in the Floridas and led to further erosion of the Indians' standing among the Europeans.

The words of Menéndez de Avilés continued to vividly express the merging of European attitudes toward the natives of the Floridas and the land in which they lived. By 1573, the governor believed that the Indians were "so bloodthirsty," that "war [should] be made upon them, a war of fire and blood." He also advocated more severe measures. Menéndez de Avilés reasoned that it was "fitting that those Indians, because they are so wicked and perverse, and have perpetrated so many deaths and robberies should be given up and sold at auction as slaves." He asserted that "removing them from the country and taking them to the neighboring islands, Cuba, Santo Domingo, [and] Puerto Rico" would be in the best interest of the Spanish empire in general and the colonists in the Floridas in particular. Furthermore, since the Indians "persisted in their evil ways" and many of them were "infamous people, Sodomites, [and] sacrificers to the devil of many souls . . . it would greatly serve God Our Lord and your Majesty if these same were dead."[62]

The Floridas and their indigenous peoples no longer existed in the minds of Europeans as distinct entities. Decades of misfortune and intercultural misunderstandings had hardened European attitudes toward the region and its native inhabitants. The land failed to meet the expectations of Spaniards, Frenchmen, and Englishmen in terms of material wealth or glory. Indians failed to live up to European expectations of civilized human beings. Both impeded colonial designs in the New World. In response, explorers initiated a racialization process to rationalize their misfortunes in the region and define their own identity. In subsequent decades, this process would take on additional forms and further widen the intellectual gap between the indigenous and transplanted populations.

Figure 3. Colonial Floridas, 1566–1675.

4

Paradoxical Images

Spain intensified its colonization of the Floridas during the sixteenth and seventeenth centuries. Despite the nation's unfulfilled expectations, optimistic Spaniards continued to look upon the region as a potential jewel in the empire's crown. Following the expulsion of the French in the 1560s, Spanish officials envisioned the dawning of a new era in the Floridas. No longer preoccupied with ousting European adversaries from the province, Spain could devote its efforts to developing the peninsula and its hinterlands. The first, and most important, step in this process involved Christianizing the local peoples. Widespread Spanish immigration to the Floridas and exploitation of the colony's resources could begin only after the residents of the region and, by extension, the region itself embraced the Catholic faith and all it had to offer.[1]

Yet by the 1760s, when Spain lost official control of the Floridas to Great Britain, the provinces were largely un-Christianized. External conflicts and internal misadventures undermined Spanish attempts to convert the native population and establish Catholicism as the dominant religion of the land. Spanish efforts to colonize the region suffered as well. Few Europeans immigrated to the Floridas and neither the Crown nor its subjects realized monetary profits. This potential jewel of the empire never materialized.

The Spaniards' inability to Christianize the Floridas affected European attitudes toward the Indians of the region. Though other factors contributed to the failure of conversion efforts, the natives' heathenism stood out in the minds of the Spaniards as the explanation. Supply problems, church-state disputes, and foreign interventions also explained the failure, but Spanish colonists could not easily criticize these factors. Seeking more adaptable explanations and justifications for their lack of success, they focused on what they perceived as the peculiarities of the Indians and decided that their inability or unwillingness to embrace Catholicism impeded Spain's goals in the region. Colonists identified Indian paganism as the justification for their condemnation and discrimination. Their perception that native heathenism complemented native barbarity and physical abnormality facilitated this process. These conclusions enabled Spaniards to believe that Indians were responsible for their failure to Christianize the region and furthered the process by which they racialized their indigenous neighbors.

Changing Perspectives

The mission system that developed in the Floridas between 1566 and 1675 was one of the most extensive religious networks Europeans established in the New World. Stretching from St. Augustine to the western outskirts of present-day Tallahassee and from modern Miami to lands bordering Jamestown, Virginia, this assemblage of missions and neighboring Indian villages was home to hundreds of Catholic priests and perhaps over 20,000 native converts at its peak. First started by Jesuits and later dominated by Franciscans, these missions dealt with a diverse group of native peoples, most of whom were Calusas, Guales, Timucuans, and Apalachees. More than just spiritual training schools, these missions became key points of settlement for Spanish colonists in the Floridas. Priests lived side by side with soldiers on garrison duty and entrepreneurs hoping to exploit native labor and resources for trade. All became dependent on Indians for farm produce for survival and for help with manufacturing, transportation, and development of infrastructure.[2] Both Europeans and natives acculturated to each other to a certain extent and inhabited the same communities on a regular (if not always peaceful) basis. As a result, the mission network became the principle mode of Spanish colonization in the Floridas during this period and was the most prominent venue for interactions between Indians and settlers.

By the end of the seventeenth century, however, this elaborate system was visibly in decline. Spain's control of its New World possessions had steadily grown weaker as a result of inefficient trade systems, bureaucratic logjams, and increased competition for empire from France and England. The Crown and Catholic Church's subsequent reduction in support for conversion coincided with French colonization of the Louisiana region and English expansion into what would soon become the Carolinas. By 1700, Scottish traders from the English colonies had begun to undermine missionary efforts by trade with some Indians and the seizure of others for enslavement. Outnumbered Spanish settlers and soldiers provided little protection for the missions and gradually withdrew to the recently reestablished town of Pensacola or the fortress at St. Augustine for security. Though Franciscans persisted in their efforts to convert native Floridians, and they later were reinforced by the Jesuits, the combined effects of long-term Indian resentment in some areas, reduced human and material support from the Crown, and English encroachment on native populations and Spanish territory undermined their staying power. The symbolic end to this steady decline came in 1702 when a combined army of English Carolinians and assorted non-Christian Indians led by James Moore invaded St. Augustine. Through the assault failed, its defense further depleted the exposed Spanish mission network. Two years later, Moore attacked the mission outposts directly, burning most structures, killing many inhabitants, and seizing several thousand converts as slaves. Spain continued to nominally control the Floridas until 1763, but the mission system never recovered.[3] Over 100 years of mission and related settlement activity ceased and the region existed as Spanish in name only.

During the 1560s, the Indians of the Floridas viewed growing missionary endeavors with ambivalence. Some Calusas, Timucuans, Guales, and Apalachees embraced the priests and their teachings in the hope that doing so would undermine enemies, enhance traditional spiritual beliefs, accommodate colonizers, and reinforce networks of reciprocity. Others revolted violently, ridiculed missionaries, and devoted their efforts to dismantling the missions and rejecting all aspects of Spanish colonialism. Both groups of natives experienced success and failure. While some Indians became prosperous because of missionization, others watched their cultures degenerate as priests enslaved their bodies to keep the missions running. Certain chiefdoms became more powerful because of their opposition to the mission system; the reward for other opponents was the destruction of their communities and death. Generalizations about the impact of Christianization endeavors on the Indians of the Floridas are typically misleading.[4]

What is clear is that as Spanish fortunes worsened and the mission system fell apart, Indians in the Floridas suffered as well. The Calusas, Timucuans, Guales, and Apalachees all experienced radical declines in population. One scholar estimates that by 1675, less than 10,000 Apalachees, 2,500 Timucuans, and 2000 Guales survived. The number of Calusas was even smaller. When Spaniards turned over control of the Floridas to Great Britain ninety years later, the major indigenous groups of the region had ceased to exist in significant numbers and the remaining members had been assimilated into other native polities.[5] Yet even the deaths of Indians played a role in the Europeans' ongoing process of racializing native inhabitants and constructing a European Floridian identity.

Christianization and Native Paganism

In 1560, these realities lay in the future, however. In the mid-sixteenth century, Spaniards embarked on missionary endeavors with little notion of how they would end. Those colonists involved in settling the Floridas supported these efforts from the outset, some believing that paganism and its associated evils would soon be eradicated.[6] French Protestant settlers shared these views, though they had different expectations. In 1566, French colonist Nicolas Le Challeux wrote that he believed that Indians might be Christianized and "that under certain circumstances, if it is God's will, one could easily instruct them, not only in humanity and virtue, but also in holiness and religion."[7] After Spain destroyed Fort Caroline in 1565, most Spanish colonizers insisted that irrespective of the prospects for success, duty to the monarchy and the Catholic Church necessitated that efforts to convert local indigenous groups be made. In response to King Philip II's request that Pedro Menéndez de Avilés expel the French from the Floridas and secure the region for Spain, Menéndez de Avilés stated that because the Floridas were "entirely peopled by savages, without faith and law, unenlightened by the law of Our Lord Jesus Christ, his Majesty was in duty bound . . . for the conquest and settlement of that land."[8]

Jesuit Missionaries entered the region during the late sixteenth century and initially were optimistic about the prospect of converting native residents. Between July 1566 and June 1568, at least fourteen Jesuit priests sailed from Spain for the Floridas. Despite hostile encounters with Indians when they arrived, the missionaries remained enthusiastic about their undertaking.[9] In 1568, Father Juan Rogel wrote, "They [Indians] are rational animals well prepared for saving themselves. Keeping them in hand, they are a harvest so ripe that one can swing the sickle on whatever side one chooses, as they see in the minister one who is looking out for their spiritual and temporal welfare and who preaches life and doctrine to them."[10] A century later, Catholic church officials in the New World were still promoting missionary work in the Floridas. Contending that the natives "are of a docile character," Don Juan García de Palacios, the bishop of Santiago de Cuba, asserted:

> In doing this [Christianization], they [missionaries] will do a great service to God our Lord and to his Catholic Majesty . . . because of what will be achieved in the salvation of the souls and conversion of so many heathens as there are in the aforesaid provinces, in which there is no doubt but that they would gain great and eminent merit before the divine Majesty and from whose powerful hand they would receive temporal and spiritual rewards.[11]

Members of the clergy promoted the merits of missionary work in their correspondence with royal officials. Father Alonso de Posada, a lieutenant of New Spain's viceroy, believed that "the conversion of such a great multitude of Indian barbarians" in the Floridas carried out God's will. Consequently, the deity would "make easy all the means for its attainment and will provide ministers . . . for this purpose . . . since all must assist with equal obligation in such a high and sovereign ministry."[12] Priests such as Posada believed that their efforts would ensure divine rewards for both the missionaries and Spanish empire. As late as 1690, a church official declared that few activities offered more remuneration than "the conversion of more than ten thousand souls whom the Devil holds in tyranny . . . We for our part must . . . advance as much as possible a business of such seriousness and importance."[13]

Overall, however, European optimism regarding Christianization of the Floridas slowly faded. Foreign invasions, inconsistent support from Spain, and the questionable nature of some conversions diminished enthusiasm among Spaniards.[14] Increasingly, paganism and its various manifestations became more prominent in their writings about the Floridas. Facing mounting difficulties, colonists emphasized native ceremonies, barbaric practices, and physical differences when they wrote about their indigenous neighbors. In settlers' minds, the Indians' real and imagined resistance to Christianity both excused European failures and bolstered their perceptions that native residents were inferior.[15]

The pagan ceremonies in which Indians participated elicited lengthy commentary from the colonists. Early European explorers of the Floridas often remarked on the gruesome nature of these rituals. In 1539, Juan Ortiz, a member of Narváez's entrada, commented that the "Indians are worshippers of the Devil, and it is their custom to make sacrifices of the blood and bodies of their people, or of any people they can get."[16] At times, Europeans viewed native ceremonies with horror; on other occasions they reacted to them with amusement. In 1560, while accompanying Tristan de Luna's expedition in the northwestern Floridas, Father Agustín Dávila Padilla, a Dominican friar, commented on one such occasion. According to Padilla, eight Apalachee Indians entered the camp of the Spaniards, "running and without uttering a word." They removed their cacique from his horse placed him on their shoulders, and "ran with great impetuosity back the same way they had come." Throughout the process, the Indians "emitted very loud howlings, continuing them as long as their breath lasted, and when their wind gave out they barked like big dogs until they recovered it [enough] to continue the howls and prolonged shouts." These events amused the soldiers; forgetting the hardships of their journey, they, upon "observing the ceremonious superstitions of the Indians, upon seeing and hearing the mad music with which they honored their lord, could not contain their laughter." Not all the Spaniards present viewed the situation with such merriment, however. While the soldiers laughed, Father Domingo de la Anuciación, a missionary accompanying the expedition, "mourned over it, for it seemed sacrilege to him and a pact with the demon, those ceremonials which these poor people used in their blind idolatry. "[17]

Most Europeans in the Floridas shared Father Domingo's evaluation of native activities. The evil and debauchery they associated with Indian rituals overshadowed any humorous aspects. In the early 1560s, while establishing the French settlement of Fort Caroline, Laudonnière wrote that the Timucuans "have no knowledge of God, nor any religion except what is visible to them as the sun and moon. They have their priests, in whom they firmly believe, as they are great magicians, great soothsayers, and invokers of the devils."[18] Europeans especially objected to rituals involving human sacrifice. An anonymous Spanish colonist asserted that certain Calusa Indians annually killed "a Christian captive to give him to the Idol, whom they worship, to eat." He further disapproved of rituals in which the Indians wore "certain horns on the head" and "made noises like mountain animals." Unnerved by the proceedings, the Spaniard wrote that the ceremonies "never cease night or day for four months and run with such fury into such bestiality that cannot be told."[19]

Though the imperial situation in the Floridas changed after Spain expelled the French in 1565, European viewpoints concerning native ceremonies remained the same. Governor Menéndez de Avilés believed the Indians sacrificed "many to their idols, even their own children, in funerals, feasts and rejoicings, because they are great idolaters and worshipers of the Devil."[20] Requesting additional missionaries in the Floridas, he claimed that pagan ceremonies contributed to the Indians' aberrant behavior. In a letter to a Jesuit priest, Menéndez de Avilés explained his ongoing efforts to reform the natives. Though he told "them that Our Lord is in Heaven and He is Chief of all the chiefs of the earth and of all creation, and that he is angry with them for making war and killing each other like wild beasts," the Indians continued to practice their pagan ceremonies because "they are highly treacherous and unreliable."[21] A century later, Spaniards still complained about the pagan rituals of native residents. While attempting to convert Calusa Indians, Father Feliciano Lopez visited a structure used in native ceremonies. According to his description:

> One can imagine the purpose it serves. They dance around it. The walls are entirely covered with masks, one worse than the other. The cacique [has] given his word to me that we may destroy the house, but by my poor understanding, they are opposing it. May God help me and give me his divine assistance as, at this date, I am much afflicted . . . Fray Feliciano finds himself among these lambs that are stronger than lions.[22]

Despite over 150 years of efforts to Christianize them, some Indians maintained their traditional rituals. Colonists perceived their intransigence in this regard as an obstacle to European designs. They also viewed the cannibalism, "wild" activities, and amoral behavior associated with these ceremonies as further evidence of Indians' deviance.

Christianization, Barbarity, and Physical Form

Europeans regarded the general, day-to-day barbarous activities associated with Indian heathenism as additional proof of native abnormality. Over the years, the colonists most directly involved in efforts to Christianize Indians began to point out the various "barbaric" displays of the Indians more frequently. When the conversion process bogged down, as it did intermittently, their references to the Indians' vices, nakedness, and skin color became more prevalent. By the eighteenth century, Spanish allusions to Indians, especially those made by missionaries and church officials, consistently included racialized imagery.

From the early years of the sixteenth century, Spaniards' motivations for missionization stemmed from concerns about the natives' religious activities and "uncivilized" behavior. King Charles V instructed Pánfilo de Narváez "to teach the Indians in good ways . . . in order to lead them from their sins and particularly from sodomy and cannibalism." This was important so the natives could "be educated and taught good ways and habits . . . [and] live in an orderly way."[23] Concerns about the customs and order of native societies matched concerns for native souls. Europeans also focused on the "uncivilized" setting in which the natives lived. Describing a "friendly" Indian Hernando de Soto's expedition encountered, the chronicler Garcilaso lamented that the native "did not deserve to have come into the world and live in the barbarous paganism of Florida."[24] On another occasion, however, the chronicler connected native nakedness to heathen beliefs. He asserted that Indians were "a race of pagans and idolaters; they worship the sun and the moon as their principal deities," adding that "the Indian men go naked, wearing only certain little cloths . . . which modestly cover all parts of their bodies necessary to conceal."[25]

The first Spanish governor of the Floridas associated the natives' vices with their heathenism. Menéndez de Avilés believed that missionaries could help transform the Indians from "great traitors and liars" and thereby help protect the region from foreign intervention.[26] He feared that if natives were not converted, their barbarous nature and naiveté would enable French Protestants to regain a foothold in the region. Because the Indians "neither know nor fear God . . . the Lutherans would most easily dominate all the provinces of the land . . . since the natives are barbarous and devoid of the light of faith."[27] Therefore, Menéndez de Avilés reasoned, Indian paganism and barbarism threatened the security of the Spanish empire. Christianization began to look like a tool of defense in his eyes.

Beginning in the 1560s, organized missionary activity made inroads in the Floridas. Early missionaries remarked on the significant influence of pagan worship on native values. Father Rogel noted the lengths to which Guales would go to defend their customs. One cacique, discovering that the missionaries hoped to destroy his idols, "wrapped himself in a shroud [and] was determined and prepared, so that if we should burn them, he would throw himself into the fire together with his wife and children so that they might be burned along with them." Instead of seeing this as an indication of the cacique's faith in his religion, the Spaniards viewed his actions as unrestrained barbarity. Rogel shed more light on European perceptions when he commented that "there is great neglect in this village in looking to the salvation of the dark skinned people." He put into words previously conceived European ideas that connected heathenism, barbarism, and skin color. Father Rogel summarized his observations by noting that conversion efforts were necessary to help rectify the Guales' "many careless acts and the many failings they have."[28]

Other missionaries reinforced these ideas. In 1570, Jesuit priests arrived in the Floridas to initiate conversions in the region's northern tier. Eventually traveling as far north as present-day Virginia, the friars lived among Algonquian natives of Jacan near Chesapeake Bay.[29] As recorded by a chronicler of their activities, Father Luis Jerónimo de Oré, the priests contended that the Indians often rebelled and would go about "busily in despoiling the clothing, chalices, patens and sacerdotal vestments which they divided among themselves, profaning the vases and sacred objects in an abominable manner." Yet the missionaries had some success and Christianized several natives. They subsequently attached labels to non-Christian Indians based on their skin colors. According to the friars:

> We religious find it necessary to become the defenders and protectors of the Hanopiras among the Christian Indians. This term signifies a painted man because the pagans in greater part go about smeared and painted with a bright reddish color, and when this is lacking they paint themselves with soot and charcoal. In this the Indians of Florida are similar to those pagans and barbarous Indians who live in the *cordilleras* of Peru.[30]

In the late sixteenth century, European missionaries began to use the color of skin to distinguish Christians from non-Christians.

The deviant activities of natives captured the attention of other missionaries. Father Escobedo, writing in the 1580s, stressed the Indians' amoral behavior. He believed "it difficult to predict which idolatrous pagans might do" and suspected that they planned to expel the missionaries. The Timucuans he encountered on the peninsula's east coast were "evil intentioned" and "fiendish." Father Escobedo claimed that the "wickedness of the Indian" caused the natives to reject conversion efforts. At least one group of Indians he met was a "ferocious nation which wallowed in destructive vices."[31] In this environment, he could envision little headway for efforts to Christianize local residents.

By the end of the sixteenth century, missionary writings commonly depicted Indian activities as "uncivilized." Father Oré blamed the Indians' depraved customs for initiating the Guale uprising of 1597.[32] According to his description of the event, a converted Indian took offense when a missionary told him he could no longer have more than one wife. In response, "this cacique and two other Indians, like him, given to the same immoral practice, went into the interior among the pagans, without saying anything or without obtaining permission as they were wont to do on other occasions." Having already disputed the Spaniards' authority, "after a few days they returned at night with many other pagan Indians, painted and smeared with red paste, and with feathers on their heads. This among them is a sign of cruelty and slaughter." After killing the offending friar, the Guales resumed their "wicked" activities and "began to exchange women in order to give rein to their sensuality and unlawful pleasures." Among other things, this account implies that the disavowal of Christianity directly contributed to barbaric behavior. In addition, the skin color of heathen Indians remained prominent in depictions of the Guale uprising. Describing other natives involved in the rebellion, Father Oré wrote that "we encountered a great number of painted Indians, their faces smeared with red earth, and fitted out with bows and arrows. They seemed to be numberless and looked like demons."[33]

After the Guale uprising, Spanish accounts of the Indians took on a more negative tone. Juan la Cruz, a soldier manning the fort at St. Augustine, claimed that throughout the Floridas, "in all the Indians they had seen and dealt with, they had found only wickedness and cruelty."[34] Juan Menéndez Marquéz, a treasurer for the colony, continued to support missionary efforts while acknowledging the faults of the Indians. In his words, the natives were "idolaters and savages, hesitating at no crime however horrible."[35] After the rebellion, few colonists appeared to trust Indians, regardless of region or ethnic group. One traveler along Florida's northeastern coast asserted that "the Indians are great storytellers and when there is the prospect of their being given something [for it], they will invent tales."[36] Missionaries sought more protection from Spanish troops. Franciscans serving in the Floridas asked that soldiers be used to control the natives, "for they can act as wild animals and would kill our people."[37]

During the mid-seventeenth century, missionary efforts began in earnest among the Apalachee peoples of northwest Florida. Negative Spanish portrayals of these Indians resembled earlier descriptions of east coast natives. Franciscan friars living in the Apalachee missions believed that the Indians "are easily swayed to come to an agreement on an opinion, not to mention, that, as they are so fickle, what pleases them today, they detest tomorrow."[38] The physical appearance of natives continued to stimulate comment. One church official claimed that Apalachees were "fleshy, and rarely is there a small one, but they are weak and phlegmatic as regards work." Again, nakedness seemed to play a part in the Indians' barbarism: "They go naked, with only the skin [of some animal] from the waist down, and, if anything more, a coat . . . without a lining, or a blanket."[39]

Little had changed in the attitudes of the Spanish colonists toward their neighbors by the end of the seventeenth century. In 1697, Governor Laureano de Torres y Ayala asked the king for more soldiers to pacify the "heathen natives" in the southern peninsula "before their fickleness moves them to" commit barbarities among the Christianized peoples.[40] Even those Indians who seemed to adopt Catholicism were suspect because of their decadent qualities. The Council of the Indies reached the following conclusion regarding conversion attempts:

> What is apparent from . . . the statements of the religious is that as long as the religious gave provisions to the Indians and some things of those that they brought from Havana, they showed some inclination or appearance of becoming converts. And from what happened afterward [Indian uprisings] one can certify that they were moved solely by self-interest.[41]

Spaniards increasingly racialized Indians, especially when referring to violence or warfare. A high-ranking church official in St. Augustine believed that neighboring natives were "so bloodthirsty, that if some Indian from their village is killed by one from another, they do not rest until they revenge the killing either on the one who did it or on someone else from the village." In order to carry out these (what the church official characterized as) barbaric activities, natives went forth "painted all over with red ochre and with their heads full of multi-colored feathers."[42] To the Spaniards, the Indians who retained their pagan beliefs appeared to carry out the more savage acts. According to Governor Zuniga, the "inhumanities and atrocities which the pagan Indians inflict" severely disrupted daily life among the Christian natives of the Floridas.[43]

By the close of the first Spanish period in the Floridas (1565–1763), most aspects of native society had earned scorn in the writings of Spaniards. In 1728, Father Joseph de Bullones described the Floridas village of Jororo in a letter to the king. According to Bullones, the Timucuan inhabitants "were all idolaters and heathens except two or three." Missionary activity languished, according to the priest, because in his view the Indians refused to work. The villagers "wander about all year, women as well as men, searching for marine life with which they sustain themselves, killing alligators and other unclean animals, which is delectable sustenance to them." Indians living nearby also were "vile by *nature*" and hampered conversion efforts due to what he viewed as the "uselessness of the nation" (emphasis added).[44] Native intransigence increasingly indicated subhuman qualities to many Spaniards. Later Spanish observers corroborated the view that indigenous people were idle. In 1760, two Franciscans, Joseph Maria Monaco and Joseph Javier Alana, reported to the king that "the most potent reason for this rootlessness is their supreme indolence. For lacking the desire to cultivate the land, they content themselves with the fish and the small amount of wild fruit" available in the region.[45]

The heathenism, barbarity, and unusual physical appearance of Indians combined to racialize the Floridas native peoples in the minds of Spaniards. Father Monaco and Father Alana further noted that "the idolatrous errors and superstitions of this people are of the crudest sort. But what is surprising is the very tenacious attachment with which they maintain all this and the ridicule they make of beliefs contrary [to theirs]." Spaniards singled out one Indian spiritual leader in particular:

> He is considered to be the doctor for the place. His remedies are great howls and gestures that he makes over the one who is ill, adorning himself with feathers and painting himself horribly. And he is indeed a man who has in his appearance I do not know just what traces of [being] an instrument of the Devil.

Heathenism and skin color, whether perceived as inherent or applied, became intertwined. The observers noticed that "the men paint themselves variously almost every day, a custom they practice, we have learned, for the honor of the principal idol that they venerate." In light of this situation, the missionaries advocated a larger military presence in the region. In their minds, "This aid is necessary for the preservation of the Indians. These diminutive nations fight among themselves at every opportunity and they are shrinking as is indicated by the memory of the much greater number that there were just twenty years ago, so that if they continue on in their barbarous style, they will have disappeared within a few years."[46] Europeans were beginning to view heathenism and other racialized characteristics of natives as the primary factors that undermined the Floridas Indians' present and future existence.

Racialization and Failures of Christianization

References to Indian heathenism and its connection to barbarity and physical appearance appeared sporadically throughout the writings of Europeans. Much more common, however, were such references made in relation to European failures in the Floridas. Through the centuries, depictions of unsuccessful Christianization attempts increasingly included allusions to Indian heathenism and differences that Spaniards construed in racialized ways. Spaniards indirectly and at times overtly blamed their failures on Indians and their supposedly uncivilized attributes. This process continued a trend of racialization that would mark Europeans' relationships with natives of the Floridas well into the eighteenth century.

Links between Indian heathenism, racialized distinctions, and the failures of Europeans on the continent first appeared during the earliest contacts. Gonzalo Fernández de Oviedo, a chronicler of Juan Ponce de León's journey through the Floridas, remarked on the natives' resistance to Christianity. Despite "the determination of the monks and priests," the Indians failed to understand Christian teachings, he said. The missionaries had little success, "even though they preached as much as they wished," primarily because the natives were "very barbarous and idolatrous savages laden with sins and vices."[47] This experience probably influenced later Spanish opinions about enslavement of Indians in the region. In 1526, King Charles V declared that natives should not be taken as slaves except in cases "where these Indians are not prepared to allow these monks and priests to come among them and teach them good ways and habits, and preach to them Our Holy Catholic Faith."[48]

The idea of Indian deviance encouraged Europeans to assert their European identity or risk degenerating into a savage state themselves. The tales of one anonymous Spanish sailor showed the potential consequences for Europeans if they succumbed to the environment of the Floridas. The sailor, who was shipwrecked along the peninsula's eastern coast, recorded how his behavior changed after only a short time and eventually came to closely resemble that of the natives:

> I dressed myself in their fashion and in every way adapted myself to their circumstances. My appearance soon took the form of a slovenly and idle Indian. I had not clothes to cover the prow or stern. My soul was like my body—miserable and ugly and I was always ready for the pleasures of vice. The Devil was my brother and I showed my fondness for him by defending him on all occasions when I sinned for pleasure and believed the ways of evil to be most glorious.[49]

This European immigrant believed that he had degenerated from a civilized human to an evil heathen beast. The sailor wrote that he had become like an Indian, and many European readers would probably have agreed with that analysis.

Early missionaries in the Floridas blamed their failed endeavors on Indians by racializing their resistance to Christianization. After the death of Father Cancer near Tampa Bay in 1549, the Dominicans who had been accompanying him hastily returned to Spain. Claiming that the Timucuans "refused to listen," the friars proclaimed "that people so barbarous and *inhuman* as Indians had no desire to hear sermons" (emphasis added).[50] Jesuit church officials supervising missionary activity in the Floridas held similar views. In the 1560s, they sent a contingent of missionaries to the region in response to the repeated requests of Governor Menéndez de Avilés. Shortly after the missionaries arrived on the east coast, Jesuit officials decided "that it is neither useful nor is it convenient" to convert the Timucuans. They based their conclusions on the difficult living conditions of the missionaries and the fact that they were scattered among the "heathen Indians, without hope of converting them due to the barbarousness and rudeness of that nation."[51] Though they claimed membership in separate monastic orders and encountered different situations at different times, Dominican and Jesuit missionaries reached the same conclusions.

One of the earliest Jesuits to arrive in the Floridas, Father Rogel, offered extensive views on Indians and their ability to be converted. Initially, he believed that natives listened to what he said and "take it well with a strong will." However, he was cautious in his interactions with Indians who seemed interested, not wanting them to "return to the vomit of their idolatries." Father Rogel believed that the conversion process would take some time because the Indians were "simple folk and of scant understanding."[52]

Eventually he claimed to have had some success with certain Algonquians. Many converted to Christianity and seemed to adopt "civilized" lifestyles. Nonetheless, he pointed out that several natives failed to attend catechism lessons after he condemned their "idolatries and evil customs and wicked laws." In addition, conversions seemed to flourish only when the priest offered food and gifts but diminished "when the handouts ended." When that happened, "they all took off."[53]

Other Jesuits could not find any promising signs in their missionary efforts. Religious preaching among the Indians of Jacan met with little success. Father Oré described one Indian who rejected Jesuit teachings: "Despite these and other gentle words which . . . the other religious spoke to him, they could not soften him, but rather they were the occasion of spiritual hardening of the heart, for the devil reigned in his heart as he did in the heart of Judas. He forged the treachery in his breast."[54] Natives later killed the missionaries at Jacan, validating the priest's words for generations of Spaniards.

Early Franciscan missionaries in the Floridas held equally pessimistic opinions about the natives they encountered. Upon arriving on the east coast, some friars expressed dismay that the majority of the Timucuan villages continued to have substantial heathen populations, despite almost half a century of efforts to Christianize them.[55] Even Indians who seemed receptive to Catholicism frequently slipped back into their pagan ways. A Spanish observer of the situation, Hernando D'Escalante Fontaneda, wrote in 1575 that two Indians from the Floridas who were brought to Havana for conversion indicated that "baptism was not lawful for them,—they were heretics." Despite his efforts, the chronicler recorded that after the natives departed for their homeland, "it appears they have returned to their old ways, and are more wicked than they were formerly."[56] Fontaneda believed that the Indians' paganism could not be overcome and that other measures should be used to reduce their threat to the Spanish empire: "Let the Indians be taken in hand gently, inviting them to peace; then putting them under deck, husbands and wives together, sell them among the Islands, and even upon Terra-Firma for money as some old nobles of Spain buy vassals of the king. In this way, there could be management of them, and their number become diminished. This I say would be proper policy."[57] Despite laws and royal pronouncements prohibiting enslavement of the Indians, failure and disillusionment made the idea acceptable to many Spaniards disenchanted with the Floridas.

No single event was more devastating to Christianization efforts than the Guale uprising of 1597. Disgruntled Indians living in present-day northeastern Florida and southeastern Georgia revolted against the Spanish when missionaries attempted to stifle traditional marriage practices. This rebellion, which lasted almost a year, resulted in the deaths of at least five Franciscan priests and the closing of all missions in the area for almost two decades.[58] The revolt and its reverberations had a much longer impact on Spanish attitudes toward the Indians, however. Immediately after the rebellion, Governor Méndez de Canzo ordered that Guale Indians were "to serve as slaves to the soldiers who might capture them . . . inasmuch as the crime committed by the said Indians was so grave, and deserving of an equally heavy penalty and punishment."[59] Though this order was later rescinded, it demonstrates the heightened level of anxiety immediately after the uprising. The remaining missionaries in the Floridas continued to do their work, but most were "very demoralized to see how little progress they are making." Many believed that if the government's administration of the Indians did not change, "it will be pointless for the friars to waste their time there."[60]

Dejection over the Guale revolt manifested itself as further disparagement of the Indians. The idea that failure to convert Indians was attributable to native inferiority became more entrenched in the minds of Europeans. In 1600, missionaries in northern Florida reported that

there are more than eighty churches which have been built in the different missions and others [are] under construction. We are moved to do this to encourage the Indians who are incapable of good conceptions and obedience. They have always had their ministry so that they listen with little appreciation to what we preach and teach, in grave detriment to the poor newly converted Indians, notwithstanding that our teaching and converting accrues to their own good, as we aid and provide for them in their time of hunger, as when crops have failed. The Indians are so lazy, and improvident that if we did not take care of the crops after planting they would have nothing.[61]

The Indians' alleged resentment hampered conversion efforts. Many Spaniards believed that natives feared Christian teachings because they undermined the power of traditional spiritual leaders. Writing about events related to the Guale uprising, Father Rogel recorded that certain Indians "conceived a great hate against [another friar] . . . because he had revealed their secrets and profaned their religion." As a result, a local cacique sought to capture the missionary, "bring him to the temple and to sacrifice him there, giving his people to understand that however much it might disturb us, they would make us adore their idols."[62] Although Rogel had been optimistic about Christianization when he began his work in the Floridas, several decades of experience had transformed his impressions.

Not all missionaries believed their efforts were in vain, and some felt that they had successfully Christianized the Floridas. Yet even in missionary writings that promoted such beliefs, references to native heathenism and its obstruction of Spanish missionization continued to appear. In correspondence with King Philip III, Franciscan missionaries admitted that the Indians attacked the friars, "making fun of them, turning Christian more as a gesture than because they were Christian."[63] Regardless of what the outlook of missionary correspondents was, by the mid-seventeenth century, government officials had begun to question the viability of Christianization efforts. In 1657, the Council of the Indies informed the king that if missionization and administrative problems were not resolved, "the total loss of Florida is to be feared, whose conversion has cost so much wealth and concern."[64]

Missionary attitudes during the decades that followed did little to assuage the council's fears. In 1657, friars in the northeastern Floridas complained to the king about their declining standing among the Guales: "The most serious concern was the continuous bodily anguish that the said religious endured, for they found themselves reviled by the majority of Indians, deprived of the necessary provisions, and many times forsaken and alone in their convents because the Indians gave their attention solely to their dances and preparations for war to which they devoted their time, living like pagans during that period."[65] Missionaries among the Apalachees in the northwestern Floridas used physical coercion to prevent the natives from participating in non-Christian practices. These friars believed it was "necessary to punish the Indians so that they do not return to their pagan ways" or return to "the superstitions that they had in them in pre-Christian times."[66]

Other Indian revolts hardened the attitudes of Spanish colonists. In 1675, local natives rose up against Mission La Encarnación a la Santa Cruz near the confluence of the Flint and Chattahoochee rivers.[67] Those responsible included the Chacato Indians and their neighbors the Chiscas, "rebellious people, living in the woods and brought up licentiously without the subjection of culture or other conventions," in the words of Governor Hita Salazar.[68] The fear of losing native converts because of the influence of such groups and of English traders worried the Spanish. Governor Diego de Quiroga y Losada wrote that by 1688, "entire [Christian Indian] settlements fled to the woods, living in them like barbarians without attending to any of their obligations as Christians." He warned the king that many convert villages were "disappearing in this fashion and becoming depopulated."[69]

In light of these circumstances, church officials questioned the feasibility of Christianizing the Floridas. Diego Ebelino de Compostela, bishop of Santiago de Cuba, wrote that even if the Catholic Church had the resources to accomplish this goal, he "was convinced it was not possible." The bishop based his decision on the assumption that Indians in the Floridas were "numberless," were widely dispersed, and possessed "evil tendencies." In addition, the natives had "launched some uprisings and some treacherous actions implying little fidelity because while they persevere with humility as long as they recognize benefit and subjection," overall, they exhibit "damned wickedness."[70]

More Indian rebellions occurred toward the end of the seventeenth century. In 1696, Timucuans destroyed the Jororo mission in the southern portion of the peninsula, forcing the Spanish to abandon it.[71] Governor Laureano concluded that "it was a pity, because they [the missionaries] were off to a great beginning for the extention of our holy faith. But their [the Indians'] barbarism is great."[72] Missionaries continued to enter the region, though few felt confident. Describing his initial impressions of the natives upon arriving in the Floridas, Father Feliciano Lopez commented that the Indians near his mission amounted to "about one thousand, all idlers from what I have seen; I do not know how I shall accommodate myself with them."[73]

The way missionaries working in the Floridas during the late seventeenth century described the Indians they encountered resembled the descriptions of their predecessors. According to one friar, Calusas involved in an uprising at the turn of the century demanded that "if they [the missionaries] are not going to give them clothes and [food] to eat, what use was it for [Indians] to become Christians?" When the missionaries refused to provide additional gifts, the natives "began to subject the religious to some harassment, mistreating them by words and deeds and stealing from them repeatedly." Eventually the Indians declared "that they did not wish to become Christians and that the religious should leave or they would kill them."[74]

By the beginning of the eighteenth century, the Spanish commonly blamed their failure to Christianize the region on the Indians, even though other factors provided equally valid explanations. Around 1700, St. Augustine's curate rector determined that "the pagans . . . even though they [the missionaries] have urged them to accept the Catholic faith and to become Christians, do not want to."[75] The natives' inherent deficiencies were the primary cause of resistance in the minds of many colonists. Father Bullones focused on the Indians' base tendencies in his explanation of why the mission system had failed:

> The Indians . . . were in the habit of rising up and rebelling, killing the doctrineros, subjecting them to notable and harsh extortions and torments . . . and when the ones reduced were not wont to become angry, they were attacked by the heathens, with the latter always coming out winners and ours desolated. And if in one or another case this will take some time to happen, those nations are so fickle and unstable that for any whatsoever slight motive that they arrive at from their divination, they change their sites and camps to the region or territory that their omen indicates.

The combined efforts of heathen Indians and English colonists in the north undermined Spanish Christianization efforts. By 1728, Father Bullones reported that missions serving the Guales, Timucuans, and Apalachees "were depopulated and demolished," the Indians and English having "annihilated four parts out of the five that comprised the number of the reduced and converted."[76]

Later observers agreed with Bullones's viewpoints, though they tended to offer more vehement denunciations of the Indians, their heathenism, and their irreconcilable differences. In 1732, Governor Dioniso Martines de la Vega delivered his opinion about Indians to the king. He pointed out that the natives are "inclined by their *nature* to negotiate in bad faith" and therefore, "any whatsoever kindly actions that are expended on them are wasted" (emphasis added). As a consequence, he said, Indians could become Christianized only through armed force. No other factor would alter "the inveterate vice or the evil way of life of those who are adults and even of the younger ones."[77] Like many of his fellow colonists, the governor increasingly viewed native resistance as the result of inherent natural defects.

These views surfaced in a report on the Floridas Indians submitted to the governor by Father Monaco and Father Alana in 1760. The opinions they expressed reflected those of many missionaries who had labored in the Floridas over the centuries. The goal of the report was to convince the governor to use military force to control the Indians of the region:

In order to shorten [this litany] by omitting many other individual cases by which they [the Indians] have shown us their bad faith and other numerous superstitions to which we found them blindly devoted like all the American Indians, in view of the special duplicity, audacity, and obstinacy, that these [people] carry to an extreme, we consider it necessary that the conquest of their souls be supported on the same means as it has been over almost all of America, that is, that this mission be secured for some years escorted by 20 or 25 soldiers of excellent customs, with whose protection the necessary rigor can be employed in order to root out even the relics of their superstition.

They contended that military force was essential for success:

For the restraining of some Indians for their own good, who with manifest deceit make a mockery of our holy religion, maintaining the adoration of some crude [idols] almost in plain view. The time has passed on permitting some naked creatures to frustrate everything with a stubborn "We do not want it," after their having occupied the time of your Excellency and the rest of the ministers of His Majesty, and after their having caused expenses for the royal coffers. With the measures proposed, or those that your Excellency many find more appropriate, their idolatry will be abolished and the true religion will be established among this people, and in spite of the obstinate ones, who, with punishments, will come to understand what they were not able to grasp with reasonings.[78]

After decades of missionary efforts, Spanish colonizers in the Floridas believed that the only way to Christianize the land and its peoples was through military force.

Regardless of their intentions, the opinions of missionaries and settlers involved in the Christianization of the Floridas supported the racialized images of natives held by many Europeans. Emphasizing the paganism of the Indians and its associated "barbarous" behavior, these individuals contributed to the ideas about the physical abnormality and intellectual insufficiency of indigenous residents of the Floridas that the first explorers in the region had established. Although they were not as all-encompassing as the words of the explorers, references that priests and other colonists associated with missionization made proved equally influential on general attitudes toward Indians in Europe. The failure of Spaniards to Christianize the Floridas bolstered ideas that colonization of the region failed in large part due to indigenous peoples and their unchangeable differences. As a result, the racialization process in the Floridas gained further justification among Europeans in the region and additional intellectual barriers between Indians and colonists emerged in the eighteenth century.

Figure 4. Colonial Floridas, 1675–1763.

5

Reevaluating the Western Floridas

During the eighteenth century, Spain lost its monopoly on colonization of the Floridas. France again settled parts of the region in the 1690s and maintained a continuous presence there until the Seven Years' War of 1756–1763.[1] French explorers, missionaries, soldiers, traders, and settlers infiltrated the western coastal regions and northwestern hinterlands of the peninsula. Although nominally attached to "Louisiana," according to mapmakers in France, this area, which stretched from Pensacola in the east to New Orleans in the west and from the Gulf of Mexico coastline as far north as the thirty-fourth parallel, actually shared many of the social, demographic, and environmental characteristics of the peninsula. For these reasons, as well as because of economic and geopolitical factors, most Europeans and many Indians considered the land to be an extension of the Floridas by the dawn of the nineteenth century.[2]

This region also resembled other parts of the Floridas in terms of European contact with the native population. Patterns of interaction established by Spaniards along the east coast, southern peninsula, and panhandle region reappeared among the French in the western Floridas. Though numerous scholars have contended that immigrants from France generally exhibited more tolerance and were more willing to compromise in their relationships with natives of the New World than other colonizers did,[3] evidence pertaining to this area indicates that processes of racialization developed in the French settlements much as they had among those of the Spanish in other parts of the Floridas.

Like those from Spain, colonists from France came to the western Floridas with expectations of material wealth and general prosperity. Strategists in Paris hoped the area would become a valuable new addition to the empire, one that would enhance the power and prestige of the nation while hindering colonial opponents. Both administrators and immigrants became disillusioned with the situation that developed during the first half of the eighteenth century. Much like the Spanish in the east, French colonists experienced failure and disappointment in a variety of endeavors. The region produced little profit for individuals, business ventures, or the national treasury; the number of colonists never met expectations, and boundary disputes promoted endless imperial warfare. In order to rationalize and explain their situation, settlers looked for impediments on which to blame their misfortune. Lacking other factors that they could easily and consistently hold responsible, French colonists targeted the Indians. As living representatives of the setting that stymied French advancement, regional natives were ideal scapegoats. Additionally, disillusionment enhanced previously established negative attitudes of many French émigrés toward natives and helped justify discrimination and maltreatment. The result was that French Floridians gradually racialized local Indians in a process that intensified over time.

The French experience in the Floridas, however, was different from that of the Spanish in terms of the eventual consequences. French racialization of the Indians of the western Floridas ultimately culminated in a military campaign aimed at the extermination of one of the most prominent Indian groups in the region, the Natchez. The events surrounding this campaign exacerbated colonists' racialized understandings of all native groups in the area and influenced subsequent French policy in the Gulf South. Of equal significance, this policy and its aftermath helped worsen European relationships with Native Americans and further eroded any semblance of cultural accommodation in the Floridas.[4]

As in other regional locales, the process of racialization evolved slowly in the western Floridas and assumed a variety of forms. Long before any general conflict arose between French settlers and the Natchez, French explorers began to evaluate Indians by their differences in appearance and lifestyle. Over the years, as disillusionment grew, these references to native character, barbarity, paganism, nudity, clothing, physical features, and, finally, skin color coalesced into a single negative meaning: Indians differed significantly from Europeans and these differences impeded colonial ambitions in North America.

Different Backgrounds

The French fared much better in the Western hemisphere in the late seventeenth and early eighteenth centuries than they had previously. While France was still beset by ongoing wars with European rivals, a new generation of imperialistic government leaders and a growing and ambitious merchant class promoted greater efforts to secure New World possessions. In the Caribbean, France obtained control of several important islands through conquest and diplomacy. Among them were Martinique, Guadeloupe, Dominica, and Haiti, all of which provided profitable cash crops. In addition, Haiti was a strategic fortification in the midst of heavily traveled trade routes. To the north, French colonization of New France (Canada) began slowly but by mid-century had created fledging settlements that were almost self-sufficient in terms of foodstuffs and had developed a lucrative fur trade with local Indians. Though not many settlers emigrated there, enough interest had been generated in the region to sponsor exploration and the creation of outposts throughout the Great Lakes backcountry and south along the Mississippi River.[5]

Partially as a result, a greater French presence in the western Floridas took shape as the seventeenth century drew to a close. Exploratory expeditions conducted by Fathers Jacques Marquette and Louis Jolliet, René Robert Cavelier, Sieur de La Salle, and a host of others showed that the mouth of the Mississippi River opened into the Gulf of Mexico. This realization, along with the wealth that could be earned in the fur trade with local natives and the seizure of Spanish holdings to the west, galvanized interest among many in France. Spain's resettlement of Pensacola in 1698 by military force precipitated the landing of French troops on the gulf coast of the western Floridas led by Pierre le Moyne de Iberrille and a concentrated effort by officials in Paris to secure the region from imperial competitors. A trickle of immigrants from France led to the establishment of outposts at Biloxi (1699), Mobile (1702), and New Orleans (1718) along the coast as well as Fort Rosalie (1716), about 250 miles north of the Gulf of Mexico on the Mississippi River. A frontier exchange economy developed in the region based on the deerskin trade and limited plantation agriculture.[6] As these events took place, French colonizers began to evaluate the natives of the western Floridas much as their predecessors had evaluated indigenous people of the eastern Floridas a century and a half before.

Indians living in the gulf hinterlands in the early eighteenth century differed in significant ways from those living on the peninsula during the sixteenth and seventeenth centuries. The Creeks, a heterogeneous confederation numbering about 10,000 people, enjoyed a centralized position in the region. Living along the Coosa, Tallapoosa, and Chattahoochee rivers, Creeks slowly began moving south to infiltrate the lands left vacant by Apalachees and Timucuans while incorporating a diverse array of native communities. The Choctaws, who inhabited much of modern Mississippi's southern tier, also had a decentralized political system. Their population was slightly larger than that of the Creeks, about 12,000, and ethnic and language commonalities facilitated group cohesion. Less prominent in the colonial Floridas were the Chickasaws, cultural ancestors of the Choctaws, who lived north of the Yazoo River and counted between 3,000 and 4,000 natives as members. The *petites nations* that inhabited the lands bordering the lower Mississippi consisted of much smaller, though distinct, populations, the remnants of groups that had once been prominent during the pre-contact era.[7] The Natchez, who lived on the western fringes of the Floridas, stood out as the native peoples that most closely resembled the Calusas, Timucuans, or Apalachees. This community, which was one of the last remaining components of the Mississippian culture and was comprised of only a few thousand people, enjoyed influence in the upper reaches of the western Floridas until the early eighteenth century.[8]

Collectively, these groups maintained a much stronger position relative to European colonizers than their predecessors to the east had. Natives in the western Floridas used the presence of competing empires (Spain on the peninsula, England in the Carolinas, and France in Louisiana) to bolster their strategic positions and limit colonial power. European reliance on native-supplied deerskins, slaves, and military support created an environment where compromise became the norm. Creek, Choctaw, and Chickasaw influence increased during the period, and until the 1720s the *petites nations* and Natchez enjoyed a relative stability and autonomy that belied their numbers. Natives shaped the nature of intercultural relations as much as, and sometimes more than, the colonizers. But native power only increased European racialization processes. Initially unable to dominate the region economically, spiritually, or militarily, Europeans again resorted to characterizations of Indians that denounced them for their differences from Europeans.

French Colonizers and Native Barbarity

References to Indian barbarity appeared frequently in the writings of French visitors during this period and earlier. In the 1650s, César de Rochefort, an adventurer who traveled extensively throughout the Caribbean and the Gulf of Mexico, offered his impressions of the natives he encountered when he visited the peninsula's shores. Perhaps influenced by the accounts of Laudonnière and Ribault written over a century earlier, Rochefort claimed that the Indians were "very obstinate in their opinions, easily angered, and much addicted to revenge."[9] The first French visitors to the western Floridas in the late seventeenth century echoed his impressions. Father de Montigny, a Catholic missionary visiting the Taensa Indians along the lower Mississippi River, commented on the natives' many "abuses," especially those associated with the burial of the dead.[10] The work ethic and material culture of the Indians elicited comment as well. Upon encountering natives on the east bank of the Mississippi River near New Orleans, Pierre le Moyne de Iberville wrote, "They [the Indians] are highly indolent . . . they are the most destitute Indians that I have ever encountered, having neither conveniences nor works of art."[11]

By 1700, France had established rudimentary settlements in the Louisiana-Florida borderlands and more European immigrants had begun to arrive. André Pénicaut, a carpenter, accompanied one of the earliest exploratory missions. As he traveled through the region this inquisitive colonist kept a journal in which he recorded numerous descriptions of the *petites nations* members he encountered. Much like Iberville, Pénicaut expressed concerns about the character of the natives. In 1700, he wrote that "they live solely from hunting because . . . there is plenty of game in the region. That is why they are not industrious and are very little devoted to the cultivation of the soil."[12] Such observations convinced some French officials that the *petites nations* could be easily controlled. Villantray de la Sauvole, a French officer in the western Floridas, stated, "I dare to flatter myself that the savages will do blindly everything that we want," mostly because "they are very lazy."[13]

Few of the early French immigrants in the western Floridas commented on the local natives more than the Catholic priest Paul Du Ru. Like Father de Montigny, Father Du Ru was troubled by the burial ceremonies of the *petites nations* he witnessed after arriving in 1700. More disconcerting than these "evil customs," however, were the "less terrible but more ridiculous . . . medicine men of these tribes." Believing the efforts of these men to be useless, Father Du Ru abhorred their practice of gathering around a dying man and breathing "through his mouth, ears, etc. as strongly as they can."[14] Other ceremonies also provoked disapproving remarks from the priest. On one occasion he witnessed a mourning ritual in which native females imbibed large amounts of water and endlessly howled "in a most horrible manner." Finding it difficult to describe the scene, the priest wrote, "One cannot imagine anything more utterly crude than this ceremony, for the poor women next make horrible efforts to spew up this water which they have drunk."[15] Father Du Ru seemed to hold native females in higher regard than their male counterparts. He said that the Indian men in the western Floridas were "unusually difficult to reform, being *naturally* more indolent and idle. It is the women who do nearly all the work" (emphasis added).[16] The indolence of natives became a recurring them in French writings, as did the idea that it resulted from inherent deficiencies. Du Ru wrote that after "studying the character of these people," he discovered that "their whole desire is to get from everyone what they want, though without violence and without treachery."[17] In his opinion, the Indians' general lack of exertion hampered the Europeans' ability to understand native peoples. Father Du Ru found it difficult to believe that *petites nations* Indians "will go without things that we regard as absolutely necessary, merely because it would require a little effort to get them."[18]

Subsequent descriptions of the Indians' barbaric activities triggered a wide range of reactions among the French. In 1700, Father James Gravier claimed that *petites nations* Indians on the east bank of the Mississippi River practiced "polygamy, steal and are very vicious, the girls and the women more than the men and boys, among whom there is much to reform before anything can be expected of them."[19] Other French observers viewed the Indians' activities in a different light. Charles Levasseur, who journeyed through the western Floridas the same year, characterized natives around the recently established French outpost of Mobile as having "a strong, merry temperament; they dance and play almost always."[20] Pénicaut also perceived Indian barbarity as harmless at times. In 1706, he explained his efforts to teach the French language to *petites nations* natives. When the Indians attempted to speak the language, "they made me die of laughing, with their savage pronunciation." Later he confessed that in his mind, "the only savage thing about them is their language."[21] As Pénicaut's language reveals, however, regardless of the perspective with which Frenchman viewed Indians, in the end, above all other characteristics, natives were still "savage."

The absence of French females in the western Floridas in many ways intensified European perceptions of the Indians as uncivilized. Male settlers routinely cohabitated with native females, and government officials disliked this arrangement. King Louis XIV believed that "Frenchmen . . . who live in extreme debauchery with the Indian women . . . [are] prejudicial to religion, to the good of the service and to the increase of the colony."[22] Political authorities living in the region agreed. Bernard Diron d'Artaguiette, one of the province's commissaries, simply asserted that "the Indian women are easy."[23] Other officials believed that French intermarriage with the natives would eventually destroy the colony. General Commissioner Jean-Baptiste Duclos contended that Frenchmen who married Indian females "have themselves become almost Indians, residing among them and living in their manner."[24] All authorities held the same general implicit viewpoint: Indian females made French males uncivilized, a situation that could not be tolerated.

Descriptions of native barbarity continued unabated during the second decade of the eighteenth century, when the French presence in North America reached its height. In 1713, General Commissioner Duclos feared that new settlers in the colony would encounter "an infinite number of Indians the greater part of whom are treacherous, cruel and capable of assassinating them after having received them in a friendly manner."[25] Several colonial officials concurred, though their condemnation was less overt. Jean Baptiste le Moyne de Bienville, at different times a military leader and governor of the province, reported to his colleagues that "the Indians are governed more by self-interest than by reason."[26] The viewpoints of colonial officials resembled those of newly arriving Frenchmen. Jean-François Bertet de la Clue, a sailor who visited Mobile in 1720, recorded that "these people are not much given to cultivating the land," since "their strongest passion is hunting."[27] Both Bienville and La Clue supported the growing sentiment among settlers in the Floridas that local natives acted more on primal instincts than logic, generally to the detriment of French interests.

As immigrants interacted more frequently with the region's Indians, comments about the natives' barbarity and its effect on the colony began to appear. In 1721, Father Pierre François Xavier de Charlevoix commenced missionary work among Indians living in the gulf coast hinterlands of the western Floridas. While he claimed that the natives needed little help from Europeans regarding morality, he commented that "the Muscogulges or Creeks are a proud, haughty and arrogant race of men," a fact he found disconcerting, since they also were "perpetually exercising their arms."[28] These characteristics, along with perceptions that natives relied on passion instead of reason as the basis for their decisions, disturbed provincial officials. In 1724, Jean Baptiste Bénard de La Harpe cautioned against the departure of certain French officials from the region, arguing that their absence "could bring disorder not only though the desertions of the troops and the inhabitants, but also through the inconstancy of the Indian nations, who are only faithful to the French because of the esteem and love which they bear for M. de Bienville."[29]

Opinions about the Indians' lack of reason bolstered ideas that they were incapable of living in the same manner as Europeans. This sentiment was implied in La Harpe's journal when he wrote that "few old men are seen among the Indians, either because they kill each other before arriving at old age or because they destroy their good health through exhausting work."[30] Later, La Harpe more blatantly questioned the intellectual abilities of Indians. He wrote that no definitive proof of the origins of Indians in North America existed because native oral accounts were suspect and Indians "were ignorant of Scripture, making use only of painted characters and of knots of different colors."[31] In La Harpe's view, the Indians of the western Floridas did not have sufficient mental discipline to record their history or maintain their existence.

Few French inhabitants of the region enjoyed greater familiarity with the local Indians or offered more criticism of their lifestyles than Bienville. In reports to his superiors in France, he acknowledged the bravery of the Chickasaws but said that they "breathe nothing but war."[32] Bienville saw the *petites nations* in a different light, however. According to his letters, the "Chaouachas" were "by *nature* slothful and indolent . . . wondering and nomadic" and the "Ouachas" were "of the same character . . . wandering here and there in the woods and along the lakes, without law and even without subordination to their so-called chiefs" (emphasis added).[33] Lawlessness and laziness were common themes in the governor's descriptions. *Petites nations* on the west bank of the Mississippi River were "by *nature* sluggish and slothful, very little devoted to the cultivation of the land," and the Arkansas Indians were "very cowardly, and very lazy and rely entirely upon the work of their women for the requirements of life" (emphasis added).[34] Considering Bienville's prominence in the western Floridas, his attitudes probably either influenced French settlers or reflected their own viewpoints.

Later writings emphasized the Indians' failure to contribute to the colonists' goals. Étienne de Périer, governor of the region from 1726 to 1732, stated that French settlers should abstain from enslaving the natives, not for moral reasons but because "they are not suited for anything else than for fishing and hunting, since it is impossible to get any service from them for the trades or the cultivation of the earth."[35] The French deemed Indians unsuitable for forced labor and also felt that they could provide little reliable military assistance. Edmé Salmon, a commissary responsible for the western Floridas, reported to Paris that the Choctaws could never be counted on to support French military operations because "it is morally impossible among spirited people without laws" to coordinate strategy in the European manner.[36] In the minds of many French settlers, their Indian neighbors offered little of value to the colony or its European inhabitants.

Incapable of adequately assisting the colony's development, local Indians degenerated in the minds of French Americans. By the 1730s, Bienville was claiming that the natives' character was "unstable and superstitious."[37] Despite his earlier comments about the admirable characteristics of the large tribes in the region, the governor had come to view those natives with contempt. The Choctaws were difficult to deal with due to the tribe's "*natural* inconstancy, small authority of its chiefs and especially the jealousy that almost always divides them" (emphasis added).[38] Significantly, after several years of living and working with Indians, Bienville attributed their deficiencies in part to inherent "natural" flaws.

Decades of French condemnation of Indian barbarity produced dismissive accounts of the native peoples. In 1775, Antoine Le Page du Pratz, a French resident of the colony, published a brief history of the Louisiana-Florida region in which he speculated on the significance of the local tribes. Commenting on the hardships within native communities, the author claimed that "the Indian women are far better off when slaves to the French, than if married at home."[39] Le Page du Pratz reluctantly dealt with native culture and society in his work; only after being prodded by "some persons of distinction" did he broach the subject. In his mind, "the arts and manufactures of the natives are so insignificant, when compared with ours, that I should not have thought of treating them."[40] These sentiments generally reflected those held by most French colonists in the western Floridas, sentiments that provided the initial stage in the process of racialization.

French Colonizers and Native Paganism

French settlers in the western Floridas, much like their Spanish counterparts in the east, condemned native paganism. French missionary work in the region, which was never as extensive as the efforts of Spaniards to Christianize indigenous peoples, took place along the east bank of the Mississippi River throughout the early eighteenth century. As they engaged in these conversion attempts, representatives of the Church developed attitudes toward the Indians based on their differences from Europeans. Government officials and private citizens also commented on the natives' spiritual beliefs and potential to become Christians. As in the eastern Floridas, when conversion efforts stalled or failed, Frenchmen tended to blame the Indians and their unwillingness or inability to embrace the faith. Over the years, these attitudes hardened and merged with viewpoints on native barbarity to further the process of racialization.

Initial French comments on native spirituality revealed opinions about native simplicity. In 1666, Rochefort noted that the Indians "are extremely apt to give credit to their dreams, and they have some old dotards among them, who openly make it their business to interpret them, and foretell what things shall happen after them."[41] Early attempts to convert the native residents of the western Floridas proved disappointing. Father Zenobius Membré, who accompanied La Salle's expedition down the Mississippi River in 1682, wrote that despite his efforts, the "Indians, though of the most advanced and best instructed, were not yet capable" of living as Christians.[42] After investigating the natives' spiritual beliefs, the missionary concluded that most had little familiarity with the tenets of Roman Catholicism. Although he proclaimed that the *petites nations* appeared friendly, he decided that "they have no true idea of religion by a regular worship" and maintained "a particular veneration . . . for the sun, which they recognize as him who made and preserves all."[43]

Other French observers acknowledged native spiritual beliefs by commenting on the various structures in which the Indians worshipped. Around 1699, "Thaumur de la Source" visited Taensa villages and noted that "they have a pretty large temple, with three columns well made, serpents and other like superstitions."[44] Similarly, Pénicaut recorded his interaction with the Taensas, at one point describing an incident involving the destruction of one of their temples:

A frightful thunderstorm suddenly arose: lightning struck their temple, burned all their idols, and reduced their temple to ashes. Immediately the savages ran out in front of their temple making horrible shrieks, tearing out their hair, and raising their arms aloft. Facing their temple they seized dirt and smeared it on their bodies and their faces. Fathers and mothers brought their children and strangled them and cast them into the fire. M. d'Hyberville was so horrified at such brutality that he commanded us to put a stop to that frightful performance.[45]

Episodes such as this, along with the observers' written depictions of serpents and "superstitions" associated with the temples, augmented negative attitudes among the French toward native spiritual beliefs.

During the early years of the eighteenth century, French immigrants began to make connections between native barbarity and paganism. While he was optimistic that the western Floridas Indians could be converted, Father Du Ru admitted that "the barbarians . . . seem to have only a very vague idea [of spirituality] . . . Their whole cult and religion is limited to the performance of their duties to the dead."[46] The priest questioned Indian devotion to pagan beliefs. He believed that they were "superstitious, but not particularly attached to their superstitions, believing, or at least pretending to believe and to admire whatever is told them about religion."[47] Nonetheless, Du Ru began to doubt the missionaries' ability to convert Indians in the western Floridas. After witnessing a ceremony in which a native community destroyed its pagan symbols and appeared to embrace Christian teachings, he wrote: "I am, at the same time, pleased and unhappy at the sight of these spectacles. I am delighted to see the symbol of our faith become an object of veneration to the Savages, but at the same time, I cannot stifle a groan on seeing that it is really futile, for, even within sight of this salutary cross, many of these poor blind people will perish miserably through lack of knowing its virtue."[48] Writings about similar disappointments linked Indian paganism and the overall differences between natives and Europeans.

As French settlement of the region increased, accounts of Indian paganism stressed the aberrant behavior of the natives. After viewing ceremonies held by the "Mobiliens, Tomez, and the Nanaiabas," Pénicaut wrote, "I believe it is the devil they are invoking, since they issue forth from this hut with the fury of men possessed and then make magic such as perambulating the straw-filled skin of an otter dead for more than two years." He concluded this description by adding that "the ones that do these kinds of tricks—whether magical or otherwise—are esteemed very highly by the other savages."[49] Missionaries substantiated tales of ceremonies that were unconventional to European eyes. Father Poisson, a Jesuit priest working in the area, claimed that native "dances, as you may imagine, are fantastical. The regularity with which they observe the cadences is as surprising as their contortions and exertions." He too began to have doubts about the ability of the French to Christianize the Indians. In correspondence, the priest wrote, "Pray that I may retain my strength to consecrate it to the conversion of the Indians. Judging from a human point of view there is not much good to expect from them, at least in the beginning."[50]

Many Frenchmen in the western Floridas shared Father Poisson's pessimism. In a request for a greater presence of missionaries among the natives in 1725, Father Raphael claimed that building more establishments for Indian education was "the only means we have in the present circumstances for working for the salvation of these poor people."[51] The prevailing sentiment among French colonists in the western Floridas was that conversion efforts were unsuccessful. As late as 1774, Le Page du Pratz maintained that "these people [Indians] have not religion expressed in any external worship. The strongest evidence that we discover of their having religion at all, are their temples, and the eternal fire therein kept up by some of them."[52] The image of Indian paganism remained dominant among the French. This image eventually contributed to a racialized understanding of the indigenous peoples of the Floridas that united disparate negative impressions of natives.

French Colonizers and Native Physical Appearance

Perceptions of Native American physical appearance further augmented the process of racialization. From initial contacts, explorers and colonists commented on the unusual attire (or lack thereof), size, features, tattoos, and skin color of the Indians. Such markers transformed essentially culture-based differences between the two groups into social and physical distinctions. Grouping barbarism and paganism with appearance allowed settlers to create a race-based definition of natives that made no distinctions about differences among indigenous peoples. Though some Indians might not have exhibited uncivilized or heathen behavior, to French eyes they were all were essentially different in form from Europeans.

Native nudity and clothing generally elicited comments from French observers in the Floridas when they first met the indigenous inhabitants. Rochefort resembled earlier explorers of the region in noting that most Indians wore "neither Caps nor any thing instead of Shoes, but they cover the body with the skins of Bears or Tygers."[53] Explorers in the western Floridas frequently disagreed about the amount of clothing natives wore, probably because of the varied clothing practices of individual native groups. A member of La Salle's contingent reported in 1682 that on the Mississippi River he "met four women completely naked as they all are in that country."[54] Along the gulf coast, Pénicaut noticed a slightly different situation. Among the Pascagoulas, "all the savages—the men and the boys—went as naked as one's hand; but the women and the girls wore a single hank of moss which passed between their legs and covered their nakedness."[55]

Though few Frenchmen indicated profound displeasure with Indian nudity, the fact that so many referred to it indicates the significance of appearance to their perceptions of the Indians of the western Floridas. Father Montigny, while disapproving of native nakedness, felt confident that he could change the custom. In his mind, "it will not be very difficult when I know the language a little to reform this abuse, which among them makes no impression, they being accustomed to it from childhood."[56] In his travels throughout Louisiana and the western Floridas, Iberville repeatedly noted the *petites nations* natives' lack of clothing. On one occasion he mentioned meeting "ten men clothed only in loincloths" and on another commented, "All the men are naked, without being self-conscious. The women wear only a sash of bark . . . they are sufficiently concealed by this garment, the strands being in continuous motion."[57] La Clue, on the other hand, pointed out the influence of Europeans on native dressing habits. In 1720, he recorded that natives living near Mobile were "all nude and wear only a belt around their bodies from which a piece of cloth hangs before and behind and covers a part of their nudity. This they call trousers."[58] Others used animal imagery to convey their impressions. Father Du Ru wrote, "The men wear skins and red linen cloth. The women have on the dresses of bark . . . with a fringe of the same material, about their waist, that falls down like the nets which one puts on our horses in summer to protect them from flies."[59] Father Charlevoix offered the briefest description: "As to their dress, a few leaves of trees, or a piece of bark was sufficient for them."[60]

Along with clothing, the physical size and features of the Indians garnered much attention in French accounts of the western Floridas. French immigrants expressed amazement about the skull-altering practices of many tribes along the lower Mississippi River.[61] A chronicler of La Salle's expedition on the waterway remarked that among the "Corroa" Indians, "All the people in this nation have flat heads. As soon as they are born, the mothers take great care to flatten them between two boards, which they put in front and in back."[62] Frenchmen with experiences among natives in other parts of North America considered this practice unique. Father Membré believed that the western Floridas natives "are very different from our Canada Indians in their houses, dress, manners, inclinations, and customs, and even in the form of the head, for theirs is flat."[63]

Iberville had little appreciation for the appearance of indigenous peoples, especially the females. In his journal he wrote, "I have not seen any of them [native females] who were pretty." The explorer based his opinion on the natives' modifications of their bodies, especially their teeth. He discovered that "the women beautify themselves by blackening their teeth with dyes made from ground herbes. They remain black temporarily and eventually become white again."[64] Iberville's remarks on native males merged physical and cultural perceptions. After meeting a Taensa headman, the explorer explained, "The chief is a man 5 feet 3 or 4 inches, rather thin . . . To me he seemed the most tyrannical Indian I have beheld, as beggarly as the others . . . all tall men, well made, quite idle."[65]

French immigrants noted other aspects of the natives' physique as well. Pénicaut described the Indians he encountered in the western Floridas as "heavy and thickset."[66] The natives' lack of body hair particularly awed the carpenter. Using animal imagery, he recorded:

These savages have no hair on them whatever except the hair on their heads. The men as well as the women and girls remove the hair from their faces as well as from other parts of the body; they remove hair with shell ash and hot water as one would remove the hair from a suckling pig.[67]

Father Charlevoix remarked at length on the Choctaws and Creeks he encountered in the western Floridas. Referring to the females, he noted, "they are I believe the smallest race of women yet known, seldom above five feet high, and I believe the greater number never arrive to that stature; their hands and feet are not larger than those of Europeans of nine or ten years of age." On the other hand, "the men are of gigantic stature, a full size larger than Europeans; many of them above six feet." Father Charlevoix concluded his descriptions by claiming that some bands of the "Uches, and Savannucas" looked slightly different in that they were "rather taller and slenderer, and their complexion brighter."[68]

Le Page du Pratz's history of the western Floridas magnified the impact of Indian appearance on attitudes of the French toward their indigenous neighbors in the region. The author believed that "all the natives of America in general are extremely well made; very few of them are to be seen under five feet and a half, and very many of them above that." In general, "they are long waisted; their head is upright and somewhat flat in the upper part, and their features are regular; they have black eyes, and thick black hair without curls." Though "the men are almost all large," to Le Page du Pratz, "the women are more plump and fleshy." These descriptions are significant because of Le Page du Pratz's explanation of why Indians had these physical attributes: "I have always been inclined to think, that the care they take of their children in their infancy contributes greatly to their fine shapes, tho' the climate has also its share in that, for the French born in Louisiana are all large, well shaped, and of good flesh and blood."[69] While he seemed to imply that French and native bodies in the region developed similarly, Le Page du Pratz's contention that environmental factors determined physical development reinforced beliefs about differences between Europeans and Indians. To French Americans, the western Floridas themselves, the obstacle to French success, helped blur differences between the two groups and thus threatened settler identity. Unable to punish the environment, Europeans chose to racialize its offspring.

Indian tattooing was another factor that distanced natives from Europeans. As early as 1699, Iberville commented in his journal that *petites nations* Indians "tattoo their faces and bodies."[70] His later observations described the markings in more detail. The "Nakansas" Indians were "tattooed around the eyes and on the nose and have three stripes on the chin."[71] La Clue encountered tattooed Indians living near Mobile. He pointed out that these natives had more elaborate markings: "They have their skins covered with figures of snakes which they make with the point of a needle."[72] Frenchmen generally believed that such markings worsened the Indians' appearance. Pénicaut claimed, "The Nassitoches are handsomer and have better figures than the Colapissas, because the Colapissas' bodies, men's and women's, are all tattooed . . . The arms and faces of the Colaspissas women and girls are tattooed in this way which disfigures them hideously." For this reason, according to Pénicaut, the "Nassitoches" females were "so much better looking; besides they are naturally whiter."[73]

Pénicaut's final comment reveals another key element of French racialization of natives in the Floridas, skin color. From the outset, French explorers and colonists referred to skin color as a way of signifying unchangeable differences between Europeans and Indians. Whether the French perceived this difference as artificial or natural, native skin tones were permanent markers by which they could identify natives. French associations of skin color with other aspects of native appearance and behavior they perceived as pagan and barbaric validated racialized depictions and discriminatory treatment in their minds.

French descriptions of native skin color typically varied. Rochefort labeled the Floridas Indians he encountered as "of an Olive-colour."[74] La Salle's subordinates failed to mention any natural color but commented on the artificial paints Indians wore. Describing the "Corroa" Indians, one chronicler wrote, "Suddenly we saw ourselves surrounded by fifteen to sixteen hundred warriors, all daubed with red and black, with tomahawk and bow in hand."[75] In this case, native coloring was associated with hostility and danger to Europeans. Similar perceptions of both natural and artificial native colorings endured as permanent symbols of the Indians' distinction.

Always the diligent observer, Pénicaut provided many depictions of native skin tones. He noted how skin color played a significant role in encounters between Frenchmen and the Indians of the western Floridas. Referring to his first meeting with the "Biloxi" Indians, he remembered that "they only kept gazing at us, astonished at seeing white-skinned people, some heavily bearded, some bald-headed, for such indeed there were among us. Thus we appeared to be quite different from them, who have very tawny skin and heavy black hair which they groom very carefully."[76] Though Pénicaut's understanding of the Indians' reactions may be inaccurate, his description points out the significance of skin color differences to Europeans.

The author's preference for lighter skin tones surfaced in other observations. Upon entering a native village along the Mississippi River, he commented that females of the "Arcansas" tribes were "quite pretty and white-complexioned."[77] Pénicaut's writings also show that his views regarding Indian skin color were shared by his fellow French immigrants. The observer recorded evidence of this consensus in descriptions of the "Bayagoula" Indians, such as this encounter in 1700: "During the evening they asked M. d'Hyberville in their language whether we had enough to eat and whether we would require as many women as there were men in our party. By showing his hand to them, M. d'Hyberville made them understand that their skin—red and tanned—should not come close to that of the French, which was white."[78] Even prior to widespread French interaction with the Indians of the western Floridas, skin color had become a dividing line that discouraged mixture of the two groups.

Most French commentators on Indian appearance expressed amazement or uncertainty rather than derision. Father Du Ru claimed that "there is one thing prettier than anything I ever saw before, this is the bizarre colors with which they paint their faces."[79] French observers could not agree about which color Indian skin was, however. Levasseur contended that "the skin color of this nation [the "Thomees"] is much darker than that of the Mauvilla."[80] Charlevoix experienced great difficulty in assigning a skin color to natives. Referring to the "Muscogulge" peoples along the gulf coast he wrote, "Their complexion, is of a reddish brown or copper color . . . much darker than any of the tribes to the north of them that I have seen."[81] Yet when he traveled in other areas of the Floridas, he saw Indians with different skin tones. On the west coast of the peninsula, he encountered natives whom he could not identify by name, so instead he resorted to defining them by skin color; they "had a redder skin than any of those I have yet seen."[82]

Some Frenchman attempted to determine the origins of the differences in skin color between Europeans and the natives of the Floridas. La Harpe, after consulting earlier investigations, offered that Indians "are descendants of the Chinese and Tartars . . . based first on the similarity of color, and next on the same bodily form."[83] Not content with this explanation, he also consulted the findings of Henry Martin, "a famous cosmographer." According to Martin, "in the province of Courland, subject to the King of Poland . . . there lived a people greatly resembling Mexicans by their features, color and mannerisms, from which he infers that the Indians of America Issued from them."[84] Le Page du Pratz believed that the differences in skin color emanated from less complex circumstances. According to his view, "The infants of the natives are white when they are born, but they soon turn brown, as they are rubbed with bear's oil and exposed to the sun."[85] Unable to reach a consensus on Indian skin color itself, Europeans had difficulty discovering the origins of color differences.

Despite all this confusion, Indian skin color influenced colonial policies during the first decades of the eighteenth century. Concerned that the population of the province was too low, some officials in France called for more marriages between colonists and Indians, unions that they hoped would lead to greater human reproduction in the region. Colonial administrators vehemently opposed these plans, however. General Commissioner Duclos wrote: "The children that come from such marriages are of an extremely dark complexion, so that in the course of time, if no Frenchmen come to Louisiana, the colony would become a colony of halfbreeds who are *naturally* idlers, libertines and even more rascals as those of Peru, Mexico and the other Spanish colonies give evidence" (emphasis added).[86] The Superior Council of Louisiana, the government department in charge of administering the colony, concurred. Agreeing that French-Indian marriages would produce "only children of a hard and idle character . . . half breeds who are by *nature* idle, loose and even more rogues such as those of the Spanish colonies," the council rejected the proposal (emphasis added).[87] These officials believed that the natives' unusual skin color highlighted or perhaps intensified their inherent lack of civilization.

French Racialization and the Natchez

The evolution of these racialized views helped stimulate the hostility between French settlers and the Natchez during the first half of the eighteenth century. The revolt and subsequent warfare of the 1720s and 1730s was the result of a variety of economic, political, and military factors. Underlying these precursors, however, was the racial antagonism that had developed over the decades. No Indian group living in the western Floridas appeared in French accounts as racially perceived and defined as often as the Natchez. Unable to make the group conform to French dictates, colonists and government officials viewed the Natchez as a principle cause of failure in the region and an impediment to future progress. Racializing these Indians allowed French colonists to pursue a campaign of eradication and justify its consequences for intercultural relationships in the western Floridas.

General patterns of French racialization applied to the Natchez, just as they did with the other native groups. Yet the racialization of this group seems to have set a standard; colonists and officials appeared to evaluate other tribes and their aberrant qualities in comparison with the Natchez model. Father Du Ru declared in 1700 that "probably nowhere in the area of Florida are there more superstitious people than the Taensas and the Natchez."[88] Henri de Tonti, one of Iberville's lieutenants, described the Choctaws by stating that "the men are strongly made and I can compare this nation very favorably with the Natchez."[89] Despite his negative portrayals of other Indian groups, Pénicaut seemed to admire certain attributes of the Natchez. After visiting one of the tribe's villages, he claimed that the Indians did "not at all have the fierce manners of the other savages." He also asserted that "the Natchez men and women are very handsome and quite decently clothed . . . Their speaking voices are quite pleasing, as they do not speak strongly from the throat as the other savages." Yet Pénicaut also witnessed activities practiced by this group that he deemed to be depraved. Commenting on Natchez morality, he wrote:

I should not be at all surprised if these [Natchez] girls are lustful and devoid of restraint because their fathers and their mothers and their religion teach them that, when they leave this world, they have to cross over a narrow and difficult plank before they can enter their Great Village, where they claim they go after death, and that in the Grand Village will be only those who will have made merry indeed with the boys.

He concluded, "From the tenderest age, what detestable lessons are instilled in them—supported by the liberty and idleness in which they are maintained."[90] In light of this situation and similar observations, Pénicaut cautioned other Europeans to be wary of the Natchez. In his mind, it was "always necessary to be suspicious of savages, who are greatly addicted to betrayal of their word."[91]

By the second decade of the eighteenth century, perceptions of the Natchez among the French had worsened. General Commissioner Duclos claimed that the Natchez were "acquainted with no other virtues than vengeance and selfish interest." He argued that the French should treat this tribe differently than European populations. Duclos believed "that to deal with barbarians and Indians as with civilized people is to be willing to be their dupes." The colonial official had determined "that the Indians have peculiar principles and do not behave like Europeans; that mildness accomplishes nothing with them and that to succeed with them it is necessary to treat them with extreme severity."[92]

French missionaries also held low opinions of the Natchez by the 1730s. Father Le Petit claimed that the Natchez "blindly obey the least wish of their great Chief" and consequently indulged in pagan activities.[93] Father Charlevoix agreed, writing that "what distinguishes them more particularly is the form of their government which is entirely despotic." He disapproved of the Indians' veneration of the "grand chief," especially their practice of "raising a cry, or rather a sort of howling" every time they came into his presence. In general, he asserted, "all are in some manner slaves to those who command."[94]

The priests also condemned Natchez morality, especially their treatment and behavior of women. In his journal, Father Charlevoix wrote, "I know no nation on the continent, where the sex [female] is more disorderly than in this. They are even forced by the grand chief and his subalterns to prostitute themselves to all comers."[95] Father Le Petit had similar opinions. He believed that Natchez society, particularly its leadership structures, suffered due to "the licentiousness of their females."[96]

Natchez religious beliefs troubled missionaries as well. Father Le Petit ridiculed the natives' spiritual ceremonies and the men who led them. The "generally old men, who without study or any science undertake to cure all complaints" performed "chants and dances . . . accompanied by contortions so violent, that although they are entirely naked and should naturally suffer from cold . . . are always foaming at the mouth."[97] What made matters worse, in Father Charlevoix's mind, was the failure of efforts to Christianize the Natchez. Though the Indians had been assigned a Catholic missionary, "they once expelled him, on account of his setting their temple on fire." The missionary returned but again departed "on finding they [the Indians] listened to all he was able to say with an indolence which he was unable to get the better of." Father Charlevoix summarized his impressions of the Natchez and their situation by writing that "the dew of heaven has not as yet fallen upon this fine country."[98]

In 1729, the Natchez outraged the French by revolting against Fort Rosalie and the European settlements nearby. Unhappy over ongoing French expansion into the area, leaders of the various Natchez villages agreed to a plan of coordinated attack on the troops and settlers living near the outposts. On 28 November 1729, after deceiving the colonists with gifts of food and furs, Natchez warriors attacked the French garrison, eventually killing over 230 men, women, and children and temporarily ousting the Europeans from surrounding settlements.[99]

Descriptions of the revolt fostered increased racialized animosity. Governor Périer learned that "these barbarians before undertaking this massacre" led local "Negroes to understand that they would be free with the Indians" if the revolt succeeded. The Natchez also allegedly told the black laborers that the French settlers' "wives and children would be their slaves."[100] Périer reported detailed descriptions of how the colonists living near the Natchez villages were killed. The natives captured three groups of Frenchmen; in one group they "burnt two of them while sending us the third to make us proposals of peace, asking us for merchandise and hostages, especially for powder and guns."[101] Missionaries died during the rebellion as well. Périer noted that the Yazoos, allies of the Natchez, shot "Father Doutreleau . . . as he was beginning mass and [he] was left for dead at the foot of the altar by these barbarians."[102] In French accounts, the incident became a slaughter instead of a revolt. Father Le Petit wrote, "Two of our missionaries who were engaged in the conversion of the Indians, have been included in the almost general massacre which this barbarous nation made of the French." Other French observers chose to define all Natchez Indians based on the actions to those who rebelled. An anonymous eyewitness to the event declared, "There had never yet been seen in all America, Indians more insolent, more ferocious, more disgusting, more importunate, more insatiable."[103]

The celebrations of the Natchez and their treatment of prisoners after the revolt also intensified French animosity. One chronicler claimed in 1744 that "the barbarous Nakchas regarded neither Age nor Sex; they burnt . . . all the Men whom they took alive." According to this account, female prisoners were "forced to yield to the brutish Passions of their Masters."[104] The brutality of the Natchez received special attention in most descriptions. Another anonymous witness recorded that the Indians "carried their cruelty so far as to roast some by a slow fire or by making them endure the most barbarous torments."[105] Father Le Petit discovered that after the revolt, "While the brandy lasted . . . they [the Natchez] passed their days and nights in drinking, singing, dancing, and insulting in the most barbarous manner, the dead bodies and the memory of the French." In addition, the Indians "ripped up the belly of every pregnant woman, and killed almost all of those who were nursing their children, because they were disturbed by their cries and tears." Female prisoners were made slaves "and treated . . . with every indignity." The Indians' arrogance and psychological treatment of the slaves disturbed Father Le Petit more than anything else:

> But two things above all, aggravated the grief and hardness of their slavery; it was, in the first place, to have for masters those same persons

whom they had seen dipping their cruel hands in the blood of their husbands; and, in the second place, to hear them continually saying, that the French had been treated in the same manner at all the other posts, and that the country was now entirely freed from them.[106]

In the minds of settlers, the natives' greatest crimes were their rejection of French authority and their interruption of colonial progress.

French reaction to this event revealed the racialized images of the natives many colonists in the western Floridas held. The words used to discuss retaliation indicated that French perceptions of the Natchez differed from their perceptions of European populations. During debates the Superior Council of Louisiana held to determine a response to the incident, one official stated, "My opinion is that we must punish the massacres that this nation commits on the French and the pillagings that it practices on them. These barbarians are not won by presents at all. They must have examples that will make them tremble and exterminate as many of them as possible."[107] This official's attitudes represented those of many French colonists. Commissary Diron D'Artaguiette called for a swift armed invasion of the Natchez lands. He promised that such an expedition would be supported by "a number of colonists" and would allow them to rout "the Natchez and put an end to the embarrassment that this nation will cause us as a consequence."[108]

Racialized attitudes allowed the French to transfer their anger toward the Natchez to other local Indian groups. Father Le Petit warned that neighboring native groups needed to be dealt with cautiously since their "demonstrations of friendship" could not be trusted.[109] Périer agreed with this logic. He reasoned that "one of the great mistakes that we have yet made has been to settle with the Indians themselves." The French would hold a stronger position in segregated outposts, he felt, since the Indians there would interact with Europeans "only for the sake of their affairs and . . . not every day mingling indiscriminately and drinking with the settlers as did those of the Natchez."[110] The governor believed that it was necessary to pacify the Indians living closest to French settlements before they too revolted. He declared that "we must choose our time well to make [the] four little nations who are between here and Natchez retire in order to have the river free and without suspicious people."[111]

French provincial officials immediately put this plan into action. Because "fear has so powerfully taken the upper hand," Périer decided to have the "Chaouchas . . . a nation of thirty men below New Orleans" eradicated. Adding a new dimension to this racialized warfare, the French decided to have the In-

dians "destroyed by our Negroes, which executed [this] with as much prompt-
ness as secrecy."[112] Other smaller tribes suffered too. At Périer's instigation, "the
Yazoos, Corrois and Tioux, were not more fortunate . . . The Akansas fell on
them and made a perfect massacre; of the two former nations, only fifteen Indians remained, who hastened to join the Natchez: the Tioux were all killed
to a man."[113] Though most French colonists in the western Floridas supported
these measures, officials in Paris questioned their wisdom. The comptroller-
general believed that the destruction of these Indians, based only "on a slight
suspicion," was unjustified. Pondering the impact of these actions on future European-Indian relationships, he asked Périer: "What do you expect the natives
will think when they witness the destruction of whole nations who have given
you no offense? What confidence will they have in you? Is it not equivalent to
forcing them to look upon the French as barbarians who must be driven out or
massacred?"[114] Even though the comptroller-general's questions were valid, the
fact that he asked them at all indicated his misunderstanding of how French
settlers perceived the situation in the western Floridas. Périer and other settlers
disregarded the consequences of their actions because they believed they were
correcting a consistent problem. French settlers and colonial officials believed
that they were eliminating a troublesome impediment and ridding colonial society of a useless population.

But this strategy did not work. Even after the French had destroyed small
neighboring tribes as an example to the Natchez, they feared repercussions from
their powerful indigenous neighbors. French Floridians believed that "it was
now an imperious necessity for the colonies to keep themselves on their guard
and wipe out the shame of seeing their wives and daughters enslaved by such
masters."[115] Governor Périer initiated an armed campaign against the Natchez,
but this time the main fighting force consisted primarily of colonial troops and
Choctaw warriors. Claiming that "it is quite necessary that they serve as an example to the other nations," Périer instructed French soldiers to depart for the
Natchez villages.[116]

During the winter of 1730–1731, French colonial troops and their native allies
participated in two military campaigns and countless smaller incursions against
the Natchez. Although they were haphazard and uncoordinated, these efforts
slowly wore down the native group as a unified fighting force and allowed the
French to regain a foothold along the banks of the Mississippi River near Fort
Rosalie. The warfare involved all of the population groups in the region: French
settlers, African American slaves, the Natchez, and various other Indian tribes.

After the winter of 1731, the Natchez never again were an actual military threat to French designs in the western Floridas. Yet the legacy of their resistance lived on in the participants' memory into the future.[117]

Even after the destruction of the Natchez as a coherent society, French settlers and officials continued to discuss their potential threat to the province. As late as 1733, Henri de Louboey, a New Orleans official, reported that "the Indian war is being carried on very slowly, and one hears almost no mention of the Natchez any longer." He added, however, that "there is still a party of about a dozen of these wretches who prowl about between their former forts and the Pointe Coupee."[118] Fear subsided only slowly. Father Charlevoix noted that even though the tribe had been reduced as a military threat, "we were not slow in perceiving that the Natchez could still render themselves formidable."[119] Others complained about the time and expense involved in pursuing the Indians. An anonymous participant reported that "it was not necessary to bear a tenth part of the expense we did; and half our army, composed of eight hundred French and three hundred savages, should have been more than enough to reduce and exterminate all this little nation."[120]

Despite the expenses and the lingering fears, the French essentially had decimated the Natchez. Reports stated that after the fighting, "all these savages, men and women prisoners, were taken to New Orleans and put into a single prison, where a great number died." Those that survived were "sold for the profit of the Company . . . [or] the service of individuals who bought them at four hundred livres each."[121] Other evidence indicated that many of the Natchez were sold to plantation owners in the Caribbean. Father Charlevoix contended that "the Sun [Natchez leader] and all who had been taken with him . . . [were] sold as slaves in St. Domingo."[122] Those who were not captured continued to harass French settlers from time to time on both sides of the Mississippi, remaining a thorn in the imperial administration's side at least until the 1750s. Eventually, most assimilated into the neighboring Chickasaw, Creek, and Cherokee populations, though descendants of the Natchez still maintain their cultural traditions today.[123]

Some Frenchmen in the western Floridas reacted to the Natchez revolt with a determination to resolve "the Indian problem" once and for all. Believing that "Indians as well as other barbarians love and are attached only to the extent that they fear," Périer called for military campaigns against the region's other native groups. He wrote of the Chickasaws, an increasingly troublesome trade partner, that "the present would be the time to get rid of this wretched nation which is the cause of all the evil that has just befallen us."[124] Destruction of the Chickasaws would be further proof of French hegemony in the region. Bienville claimed "that if the Chickasaws were destroyed, the Choctaws would become more tractable . . . The destruction of the Chickasaws and of the Natchez would be an example capable of making these Indians reflect."[125] Decades later, colonial officials were still promoting the destruction of the neighboring Indians by provoking intertribal warfare. Commissary Michel de la Rouvillere proposed to his superiors that factional warfare among the Choctaws presented "a fine opportunity to be rid of all those animals . . . It is prudent for the government to maintain this dissension and to keep them continually occupied in destroying each other themselves without our ever taking part in it."[126] In 1751, Governor Vaudreuil promised that he would "not neglect anything to keep urging the Choctaws to make such frequent incursions upon the Chickasaws that in the end we shall be able to succeed in exterminating them."[127]

By 1763, however, these schemes had failed. Possessing few material or human resources to promote such endeavors, the French gradually lost their influence with Indians in the western Floridas. Instead of providing a point of triumph, the destruction of the Natchez only contributed to French disappointment in the region. In a 1733 report on the status of Louisiana, Bienville found the colony in a much worse condition than thought, "either because of the want of provisions, or merchandise and of money, or because of the considerable decrease in the number of the colonists . . . but especially with reference to the disposition of the Indians in general. Since the slackness with which they saw that the French carried on the war with the Natchez, they have conceived a sovereign contempt for the nation."[128] While they shared this disillusionment, other commentators blamed the colony's problems solely on French conflicts with the Natchez. An anonymous source labeled the events "Fatal" because "after so many useless expenses of the Company, after so many millions that have been spent since by the King during 18 years, the colony has not advanced a step from what it was before that war." He concluded, "If that unfortunate war had not happened, to all appearances the country would today be in the most flourishing condition."[129]

The Natchez revolt and subsequent French campaign of extermination occurred for many reasons. Yet the environment in which these factors united to precipitate conflict emanated from French processes of racialization over a 30–year period. French Americans, like all peoples, viewed "others" subjectively and generated negative opinions about some of their characteristics. In the western Floridas, a combination of failure and disappointment integrated French settlers' negative impressions of native character, religion, and physical appearance into a single racialized image. These perceptions enabled colonists to justify severe reactions to native recalcitrance, including the use of genocidal warfare. Though French racialization generally did not appear in such extreme forms, it influenced European-Indian relationships and crippled any type of mutual accommodation.

Figure 5. Colonial Floridas, 1763–1783.

6

Anglicizing Indians

Great Britain gained control of the Floridas as a result of the Paris peace treaties that ended the Seven Years' War in 1763. British officials soon thereafter divided the Floridas into two administrative districts labeled East Florida and West Florida based on their geographical relationship and boundaries. British imperialists, who had greater human and material resources for colonizing North America than either the French or Spanish, appeared to be in a better position to control the peninsula and its hinterlands. Indeed, even in the decades before Great Britain officially acquired the region, British adventurers infiltrated the Floridas and began transforming economies and cultures. Interaction between the British and natives increased from the 1740s to the 1780s, fostering closer trade relationships, bicultural settlements, and, at times, military alliances. By the dawn of the American Revolution, such forms of compromise seemed to signify the emergence of relationships based on cooperation and mutual consideration, an arrangement that had rarely been apparent in the colonial Floridas.

In reality, intercultural tolerance failed to develop between British immigrants and local natives during the eighteenth century. Economic and military agreements belied the continued existence of opposing world views. British immigrants, like their Spanish and French predecessors, racialized regional Indians on the basis of preconceived ideas, day-to-day experiences, and the ever-present need to justify imperial failures. When British colonists met with disappointments comparable to those of their predecessors, they reacted in a similar fashion. Native differences progressively took on negative connotations to British settlers and officials whose personal and imperial ambitions were stymied. The internal antagonism British Floridians harbored toward Indians prohibited significant growth of intercultural bonds or societal integration. Any accommodation that emerged existed primarily because of subsistence needs and pragmatic associations, not because of true compromise or substantial accommodation.

The process of racialization British immigrants enacted resembled the earlier forms Spanish and French Floridians had initiated. Native ways of life, spiritual beliefs, and physical appearance functioned as markers by which Europeans could distance themselves from the land while formulating negative understandings of indigenous peoples. Visible differences gradually took on unacceptable implications in the minds of settlers and colonial officials. They began to believe that the Indians' cultural and physical differences from them justified their ideas about native incapacity and discriminatory treatment.

New Dynamics

By the 1760s, Great Britain had become the dominant European empire in North America. Spanish and French influence, which was already on the wane, suffered a devastating blow in the Seven Years' War. In the aftermath, both powers were expelled from lands east of the Mississippi River. In the Caribbean, war-related acquisitions translated into the huge profits from sugar plantations that helped generate England's industrialization. The British navy dominated the world's oceanic trade and British markets shaped economic supply and demand from Europe to Asia. Additionally, few nations could match Britain's military strength. Buoyed by the successes of growing colonial populations, diversifying imperial economies, and territorial expansion, Great Britain sometimes overlooked simmering colonial dissent. In most regards, British influence in the New World never had been, and never again would be, as great as it was in the years prior to the American Revolution.

Yet there were areas of eastern North America where British dominance was less clear, and the Floridas stood out as one of these. The region did not become a nominal part of the British empire until the late eighteenth century. Instead of negotiating for the more lucrative Spanish possessions of Cuba or the Philippines, George III's emissaries chose to acquire the less-promising Florida peninsula at the Treaty of Paris in 1763. Few people from the British Isles immigrated to the region and when Spain regained control of the Floridas at the end of the American Revolution, less than 10,000 British colonists lived there. Indians outnumbered settlers from St. Augustine to Natchez, and Britain's vaunted naval and military forces maintained only a minimal presence in the area. Despite the abundant resources at their disposal, British colonialists had little success in populating or prospering from the Floridas, much like the Spanish and French before them. A few planters and some fur traders (of which there was an overabundance) made profits at times, but they rarely did so on a scale that would justify the expense needed to supply and protect them.[1] Therefore, when Spanish forces from Louisiana successfully captured the Floridas during the period 1779-1781, few in Britain lamented the loss, even though most residents in the provinces remained loyal during the American Revolution. To many Britons, the mysterious and problematic colonies were an aberration in a period of hegemony and prosperity. British Floridians in the eighteenth century met fates similar to those of Spanish and French Floridians in previous centuries.

The 1760s also marked a time of new milestones for Indians living in the region. Along the Mississippi River, the Natchez no longer existed in corporate form. Many *petites nations* still survived, but because of warfare, enslavement, disease, and assimilation, they inhabited only a handful of villages and their populations were reduced to the hundreds. While the Chickasaws continued to persist as an influential population to the north, Creeks and Choctaws had become the major native powers in the Floridas. Both groups had grown over the decades, and each had at least 15,000 members by the late eighteenth century. Creeks and Choctaws continued to control the supply of deerskins and to play European powers against each other to ensure that they would be responsive to their needs. These strategies strengthened the diplomatic and military positions of the two native groups.[2] During the 1760s, colonists began to notice for the first time the existence of another Indian group located in the gulf hinterlands and north-central peninsula, a community eventually identified as Seminoles. As the British became the major European power in the Floridas, native peoples enjoyed a prominence in the region that had not been evident for more than a century.

This renaissance of Floridas Indians lasted only briefly, however. The marginalization of France and Spain reduced the effectiveness of the strategy of playing imperial powers against each other and established Britain as the major European power broker in the region. Subsequent expansion of British settlements in the coastal areas and on the east bank of the Mississippi River and the appearance of countless new pelt traders reduced options for indigenous residents both economically and territorially. British pressures on natives to relinquish "sovereignty" increased, and intercultural violence flared on a regular basis. Like most Indians in eastern North America, the *petites nations*, Choctaws, Creeks, and Seminoles participated in the American Revolution, albeit reluctantly. It was not immediately clear to them what the long-term consequences of their participation would be, and it proved divisive in native communities and tended to alienate neighboring colonists, revolutionaries and loyalists alike. By the 1780s, native resurgence in the region appeared to be threatened and Indians faced a new era of European Floridian racialization processes.

British Colonizers and Native Barbarity/Heathenism

Like their other European predecessors, British colonists tended to explain unexpected failures in the Floridas by blaming their Indian neighbors. Indian behavior that settlers labeled barbaric and heathen again functioned as the most frequent symbol of native distinction. Throughout the eighteenth century, British Americans who entered the Floridas commented on the morals, character, and spirituality of the local natives. Significantly, these descriptions mirrored those of Spaniards and Frenchmen in the region 200 years earlier. Such similarities in perception seem absurd, since the region and its native populations had changed radically over the centuries. Yet when we consider the identical expectations and experiences of the various Spanish, French, and British immigrants, the similarity of images becomes more comprehensible.

English visitors to the peninsula at the beginning of the eighteenth century continued to follow earlier precedents regarding images of Indians established by French and Spanish settlers. Jonathan Dickinson, a colonist who was shipwrecked along the eastern coast in 1696, recorded descriptions in his journal of the local natives he encountered. Already bewildered by the shipwreck, Dickinson and the other survivors instantly suspected the indigenous peoples of evil intentions. Their anxiety escalated when the Indians seized the survivors' goods and marched them to their village. The fearful colonists, who were eventually guided overland first to St. Augustine (Spanish) and then to Charles Town (English), spent several weeks with the Floridas natives and developed vivid impressions of their hosts.[3]

Preconceived notions of Indian barbarity influenced Dickinson's initial expectations. When they reached the beach, the survivors "communed together and considered our condition, being amongst a barbarous people such as were generally accounted man-eaters." Feeling defenseless, Dickinson and the others sat down in the sand "expecting cruelty and hard death." Once the local "Hobe"[4] Indians appeared and began seizing the ship's goods, Dickinson's fears increased. Hearing one native headman condemn another passenger in English as a "Son of a Bitch" did little to allay fears and left the observer's mind "with much trouble." Dickinson's greatest concern, however, was not the way the Indians were treating the colonists at the moment but potential future circumstances: "One thing did seem more grievous to me and my wife than any other thing. Which was that if it should so happen that we should be put to death, we feared that our child would be kept alive, and bred up as one of those people; when this thought did arise it wounded us deep."[5] Even before widespread British settlement in the eighteenth century, English immigrants in the Floridas feared the idea of living with, or in the same manner as, the native inhabitants.

Additional comments on native barbarity came from British soldiers invading the Floridas. The founder of colonial Georgia, James Oglethorpe, interacted with regional natives in hope of expanding his province's boundaries. Stimulated in part by the War of Jenkins' Ear, Oglethorpe led a joint Indian-English force against Spanish St. Augustine in May 1740. Though Oglethorpe's army was successful in minor skirmishes north of the city, it failed to breach the walls of the Castillo de San Marcos and eventually splintered because of inadequate supplies and bickering among the soldiers. In 1743, Spain retained control of the Floridas south of the St. Mary's River and Oglethorpe returned to England.[6]

Oglethorpe and his followers commented at length on Indian barbarity before and during their invasions, though most references pertained to allied Indians from the western Floridas. When a Chickasaw warrior brought the head of an enemy native to Oglethorpe as a gift, the commander reacted with disdain, chastising the savagery of the warrior and labeling the Chickasaws "barbarous Dogs."[7] Other Englishmen on the expedition mentioned the activities of their native allies in ways that made it clear they considered them to be base. Edward Kimber complained, "As to their Manners, tho' they are fraught with the greatest Cunning in life, you observe very little in their common Behaviour, above the brute Creation." He based his opinions, at least in part, on Creek eating practices. Kimber claimed that the natives tore their meat "promiscuously with their Fists, and devour it with remarkable Greediness." He also offered his opinions on the historical origins of this behavior. He claimed that observers could perceive in the Creeks, "some Remains of an ancient Roughness and Simplicity, common to all the first Inhabitants of the Earth." According to Kimber, these characteristics had diminished only recently, when the natives had been "made so subservient to the Benefit of the English Nation." Nevertheless, in his view, their barbarity still appeared during military campaigns when "these Creatures" marched in formations and constantly emitted "mournful Howls and Cries."[8]

References to imperfections in the Indian character came from other sources than soldiers and settlers. Colonial officials, many of whom were charged with improving Anglo-Indian relationships, disparaged the natives as well. Edmund Atkin, the first superintendent of the British Indian Department in the Southern District of North America, criticized the behavior of the Choctaws, one of the principle native populations of West Florida. The superintendent believed that "of all Indians, the Chactaws bear the worst Character." He felt that they impeded good Anglo-Indian relationships because "they are Subtle, Decietfull, Insolent, Lucrative, Beggarly, Vicious, and Indolent to such a degree, that for want of Planting Corn sufficient [they live] . . . for the most part miserably." Atkin believed that the Choctaws did not bear full responsibility for their deficiencies; he also blamed the French. He claimed that the Indians' "beggarly Quality is the result of their Poverty, and the Habit they have acquired in making the most out of the French; in like manner as their carnal Vice is the result of their lazy Life."[9]

Once the Floridas officially became part of the British empire, more works concerning regional natives appeared. In 1763, William Roberts published his ideas about Indians, which were based on a variety of traveler and settler accounts of the region.[10] In his report, Roberts indicated general British attitudes toward the spiritual practices of the natives of the Floridas. He asserted that "in point of religion, they are bigotted idolators, worshipping the sun and moon, and bearing an extreme aversion to all Christians." The earlier conversion efforts of Spanish Catholic missionaries contributed to their heathenism, he argued, by inciting the "utmost abhorrence and dread" of Christianity in the Indians. Roberts believed that the Spanish portrayed the Indians "as savage barbarians" in order to justify their treatment of them. Yet even as he criticized the Spaniards' motives, Roberts shared their viewpoints. He admitted that "in the present case, it must nevertheless be allowed, that, from the accounts of all who have had any dealings with them [natives], they are noted for a bold, subtile, and deceitful people."[11]

Less-explicit indications that the British saw indigenous people as unequal also surfaced. West Florida trader Charles Strachan regarded Indian customers much differently than he did European customers. On one occasion when a cask of rum he intended to sell to colonists was partially consumed by sailors in transit, Strachan "filled up the cask with Salt Water." He then proposed to sell it to the natives, since "it was good for nothing but the Indians."[12] Colonial officials made implicit references to the Indians' heathenism in their "talks" to them at congresses, periodic diplomatic gatherings. West Florida governor George Johnstone proclaimed that it was God's plan for the British to obtain control of the Floridas so that they could "Supply the Wants of the Red People, whom he has left more ignorant of those Arts which he has Communicated to us."[13] Johnstone's counterpart in East Florida reinforced British notions that natives were primitive. Governor James Grant claimed that Indians living in "Appalaché" rarely "had much communication with Europeans" prior to British arrival and as a result were "extremely ignorant of Our manners, and Customs."

Consequently, he believed that colonists should engage Indians "with much Delicacy."[14]

Like earlier Spanish and French colonists, British Floridians feared the effects native barbarism would have on the growth of the provinces. Describing the food resources of Pensacola, one British officer complained that supplies were plentiful but always needed to be guarded since the Indians "make a custom of stealing everything" that could be eaten.[15] Another colonist observed that material goods housed at Fort Bute, a British outpost on the lower Mississippi River, had been stolen because the items were "too great a temptation for the Indians to withstand."[16] British accounts also referred to indigenous peoples as bloodthirsty. Governor Johnstone cautioned settlers against attacking the Creeks or the Seminoles in the province because indiscriminant revenge would surely follow. In his mind, natives failed to adhere to European modes of justice and in general "consider and calculate Debts of Blood as exactly as any Banker does his Guineas."[17] The refusal of natives in West Florida to acknowledge Great Britain's supremacy in the region stimulated further apprehension among the colonists. Governor Grant questioned the deference of local Creeks since they had been "Proud, Indolent and overbearing for some Years past." Although he found their conduct unacceptable, he cautioned that "if this Insolence and bad behavior of those Creeks in West Florida is to be resented openly, a war of course must ensue."[18] British Floridians, like Spanish and French Floridians, increasingly saw little reason to tolerate problematic natives.

Surviving records indicate that confusion and misunderstanding influenced colonists' depictions of Indians. Thomas Campbell, a traveler through the Floridas, had difficulty assessing the character of the natives. He believed that the Creeks treated their prisoners "in a very cruel manner," but not because of "their natural disposition." In fact they seemed to be "compationate," assisted each other in times of distress, and were hospitable to strangers. Despite these attributes, however, Campbell still viewed the Creeks as uncivilized because "the customs and superstitions among them are many, the Laws few."[19]

The Indians' apparent lack of laws that derived from European legal standards worried other British Floridians as well. Governor Grant asserted that "Indians have no Idea of any other Rule or law . . . but giving or receiving Blood for Blood."[20] The apparent lack of laws in native cultures took on greater meaning to some colonists. If natives refused to acknowledge *civilized* rules and regulations, logically, they became outlaws. In notes made on his journeys throughout North America, Alexander Cluny emphasized outlaw behavior among the Indians of West Florida. He recorded that the natives were "Enemies principally to be guarded against" since "they act entirely by Surprize, invading in small Parties like Robbers, murdering the People, and destroying all the Effects which they cannot carry off."[21] Provincial officials believed that such behavior threatened British governing policies. Citing accounts "that the Creeks have in Cold blood murdered 138 [settlers] without any Satisfaction being given," Governor Johnstone questioned the wisdom of accommodating Indians through diplomacy and gift-giving. In his opinion, failure to punish natives for what he perceived to be lawlessness meant "that the money distributed on Indian affairs is the Most useless that ever was thrown away by any nation pretending to Independency."[22] The fact that indigenous people seemed to the British to defy both judicial and natural laws transformed their resistance against Europeans into unacceptable acts that threatened the management of the colonies.

Some British immigrants to West Florida maintained hope that the natives' lack of civilization could be rectified. John Stuart, the second superintendent for the Southern District, defended Indian transgressions. He believed that though Indians had minds that were susceptible to "Enmity and Revenge," they also exhibited evidence of "Friendship & gratitude."[23] Stuart felt that the crimes natives committed were similar to the crimes Europeans committed in the social implications they raised. "The Robberies and thefts" the Seminoles or Creeks committed "amounted to little more than killing some cattle to supply their Necessities," in the superintendent's opinion, and they resembled those that were "often practiced by more Civilized Nations."[24] Stuart's viewpoints mirrored the sentiments of other Britons in the region. An anonymous observer discounted Choctaw "Thieving" by contending that "they are a peaceable sort of Indians."[25] Even Cluny, who condemned the crimes of natives, hoped that the "flawed" cultures of the indigenous inhabitants could be reformed. He believed that Britons could most effectively civilize Indians by forming close friendships with them. In this fashion, "they would soon learn our Manners, and incorporating themselves with us, become a Part of our own People." Not only would this help improve the Indians, Cluny reasoned, it would also free British residents "from the Necessity, and Danger of Importing untractable Negroes of Africa."[26]

Despite these opinions, the majority of British immigrants in the Floridas increasingly saw the local natives as irredeemable obstructions to colonial goals. Peter Chester, the last governor of West Florida, contended that no close relationships between settlers and Indians would develop because the latter were too "*naturally* jealous and suspicious in their dispositions" (emphasis added).[27] In other words, nature bestowed different temperaments on natives and settlers. Even John Stuart admitted that difficulties would arise in communities where

Indians and colonists lived together under British laws. Because natives "seldome have Christian Evidences to prove Facts," they rarely gained satisfaction in colonial courts when contesting the actions of settlers. As a result, in the superintendent's view, "when the Savages [met] with disappointments of this kind" they frequently accosted "the white people, with unbound cruelty."[28] Charles Shaw, another British resident of the Floridas, believed natives living in West Florida to be "a most avaricious sort of people, haughty and overbearing, always over-rating their services, and full of their own importance."[29] Charles Stuart, John Stuart's cousin, was an assistant in the Indian Department in the Southern District and saw little promise in the indigenous peoples. "It is well known no People are so jealous of their Liberties or so tenacious of their Property as Indians," he wrote. He also distrusted the overall intentions of the natives because they concealed "their Resentment, till their Schemes for Revenge are brought to Maturity." In light of these behavior patterns, the character of the Indians had few endearing qualities for colonists. Referring to the Creeks, Charles Stuart wrote, "They are a more haughty, stirring, enterprizing, warlike Nation, restless in their Dispositions and relentless, they are so self conceited as to think no other Nation like them."[30] Only when pressured by headmen or community consensus did natives relent in their attacks on colonists. Governor Grant believed that Creek fighters restrained themselves in conflicts with settlers in East Florida primarily due to fears that their "Nation would disapprove of their conduct." Without these fears, in his opinion, the natives "would have left no body alive, & would undoubtedly have carried off the Scalps."[31] Implied in these passages is the core grievance against the Floridas natives held by many British observers—Indians refused to concede Great Britain's domination, militarily or culturally.

Few British residents of the Floridas commented more on native barbarity than the naturalist Bernard Romans. First published in the 1770s, his findings on the region's geography and peoples influenced the way many Europeans and European Americans saw Indians. Romans was extreme in his denunciation of Indian character and culture, and his opinions probably represented the viewpoints of only a small percentage of British Floridians. Nevertheless, since he based many of his conclusions on European-Indian interaction in the region and formed his views after extensive discussions with white residents of the colony, Romans's works offer valid insight into the racialization process in the Floridas.[32]

Romans strongly disagreed with opinions on native civilization held by individuals such as John Stuart and Alexander Cluny. "I must contradict them," Romans announced. He believed Indians to be a "Treacherous, Cruel, deceitful, Faithless and thieving Race, not in the least to be trusted, but by all means much to be watched against." He argued that Britons should not offer friendship to the natives, "for they have a thousand Arts of low Cunning . . . They will not scruple to commit Violence, which they do with Impunity even in our Towns and the best Settlements."[33]

This self-proclaimed "scientist" rejected the label "Indians" for the natives and supported "the French name of savage as a more proper one." He believed the French term more appropriate since "the manners of red men are in every respect such as betray that disposition." Romans saw no hope for the Indians' improvement. They were "not only rude and uncultivated, but incapable of civilization." The typical native "is cunning and designing, knows no fear . . . is very deliberate and careful in his mischief and cruelty . . . and his gazing and staring always end in sovereign contempt." According to Romans, the natives did not have spiritual belief systems, even in terms of superstitions, and "no religion of any kind can we trace among them." Like many Europeans in the Americas, Romans thought the Indians to be exceedingly lazy. "A savage has the most determined resolution against laboring or tilling the ground," according to Romans, "and was impatient and incapable of bearing labour."[34]

Romans concluded his remarks on Indian barbarism by illustrating what he argued was the apparent uselessness of the natives' existence. In his mind, they were "brutal and have not the most distant idea of decorum; without taste." Their main contributions to the colony were negative, he felt. "There is not villany nor crime, they will not commit" he wrote, "and when they recover their senses, throw the blame on the liquor, holding themselves entirely excused." In addition, the Indians seemed to hold themselves in little regard; "possessed of indifference and want of sentiment, they drag themselves through a kind of life which would make us [Europeans] pass our days very irksomely, and tire us in a short time with the disagreeable similitude of our hours." Romans summarized his views of native civilization in the following way: "In a word, they have nothing in their way of life to tempt a man of the least reflection, to envy them in their miserable state of nature."[35]

British Colonizers and Native Physical Appearance

British settlers and officials continued the practice of emphasizing the physical appearance of Indians to support their ideas about native barbarity. References to size, features, attire, skin color, and so-called inhuman behavior appeared alongside commentaries on the uncivilized ways of life of native peoples. Together these remarks strengthened the process of racialization and justified condemnatory attitudes.

Dickinson and his followers, who were on the peninsula against their will after their shipwreck, pointed out the Indians' physical differences from themselves. The first natives the group encountered were "naked" for the most part, "running fiercely and foaming at the mouth." Dickinson's depictions of the Indians' appearance were often interspersed with comments on their animal-like characteristics. "Their countenance was very furious and bloody" to Dickinson and his companions. Even when the Indians stood around chatting, they exhibited what the Britons perceived as a "wild, furious countenance." Unnerved by the situation, Dickinson offered the natives some tobacco and pipes at one point. In response, the Indians "greedily snatched" the offerings from the Europeans, "and making a snuffing noise like a wild beast, turned their backs upon us and run away."[36] Later that day, members of the "Hobe" tribe returned to the ship to seize the remaining supplies. Petrified by the "bloody minded creatures," Dickinson was further appalled when they began to strip the Europeans of their clothing.

> They came in the greatest rage that possibly a barbarous people could . . . They tore all from my wife, and espying her hair-lace, some were going to cut it hair and (all) away to get it, but, like greedy dogs, another snatched and tore it off . . . After they had taken all from us but our lives, they began to talk with one another, vehemently, foaming at mouth, like wild boars.[37]

Dickinson and his fellow passengers, one of the earliest groups of English colonists in the Floridas, quickly associated native activities with their physical appearance.

Members of Oglethorpe's expedition against St. Augustine also were frightened by the physical appearance of the natives they encountered. Upon attending a ceremony at a Creek village in preparation for the conflict, one soldier recorded his impressions of the Indian dancers he saw: "Their dress is very wild and frightful their Faces painted with several sorts of Colours . . . They paint their Short Hair and stick it full of feathers." He used animal imagery in his elaborate description of the dancers' hairstyles, noticing their hair was close cropped "except three Locks one of wch hangs over their Forehead like a horse fore Top." The observer ended his description of the ceremonies by noticing that "their dancing is of divers Gestures and Turnings of their Bodies in a great many frightfull Postures."[38]

Another member of the expedition commented on the size and skin color of the Indians he met. Kimber believed that "these Sons of Earth" were "generally of the largest Size, well proportion'd, and robust, as you can imagine Persons nurs'd up in manly Exercises can be." He continued, "Their Colour is swarthy, copper Hue, their Hair generally black, and shaven, or pluck'd off by the Roots, all round their Foreheads and Temples." Unlike earlier commentators, Kimber made distinctions between the Indians' natural skin tone and the shades they intentionally applied. "They paint their Faces and Bodies, with Black, Red, or other Colours, in a truly diabolic Manner" he wrote, adding that most wore very little other than a blanket or animal skin and "a Shirt which they never wash, and which is consequently greasy and black to the last Degree."[39]

British descriptions of the natives' physical form closely resembled earlier Spanish and French descriptions. Roberts echoed Soto, Charlevoix, and others when he noted that "the native Indians of Florida are of an olive complexion, their bodies are robust, and finely proportioned; both sexes go naked, excepting that they fasten a piece of deer-skin about their middle." The author went on to note that the natives' hair was black, long, and "very graceful and becoming." Roberts also remarked that the "women are very handsome and well-shaped" and could swim exceptionally well and "climb, with surprising swiftness, to the tops of the highest trees." The climate of the Floridas seemed to promote Indian fitness. As evidence, the observer pointed out the "size, firmness, strength of constitution, and longevity of the Floridian Indians: in all these particulars they far exceed the Mexicans."[40]

Remarks on native physical characteristics continued to surface in accounts written by settlers and officials during the 1760s and 1770s. A British officer in Pensacola stated that neighboring Indians were "a hardy well made set of people, calculated seemingly to bear fatigue" and then added, "Their feathers are manly and expressive." After observing the Indians at length, the officer offered explanations for their skin color. "They early rub themselves over with grease and some juice of an Herb, which render their faces & bodies of a dim copper tint," he conjectured. In addition, the natives were "fond of having their faces painted with vermillion & black in strange manners."[41] Other commentators described the attractiveness of the indigenous peoples of the Floridas. Thomas Campbell claimed that native "men are in general middle size well limd and clean, made with features serious, manly and agreeable." The females also pleased him; he described them as "short thick and strong in proportion, and some of them very handsome."[42] Unlike most commentators, traveler Edward Mease noticed differences in the appearance of different native groups. He considered the "Arkansa" Indians "very gaily drest after their manner and were reckon'd as fine & well made Indians as any in America." Other tribes he encountered in his journeys did not impress him in the same way. Referring to a group of Choctaw hunters, he complained, "They were[,] as they generally are[,] extremely dirty."[43]

Romans provided the most vivid descriptions of Indian physical appearance and its meaning to British immigrants in the Floridas. His account was more comprehensive than those of others, and he reached conclusions about the physical features, origins, subhuman characteristics, and inherent differences from Europeans of indigenous Floridians. His findings on these topics, like his views about barbarism, probably reflect the beliefs of only a small segment of British Floridians. Nevertheless, they bear investigation because of the methods he used to reach his conclusions and the widespread influence of his accounts.

Despite his condemnation of the Floridas natives in general, Romans admired their physical features. "All savages, with whom I have been acquainted, are, generally speaking, well made, of a good stature, and neatly limbed," he wrote. Europeans rarely saw deformed or disabled natives. According to Romans, most Indians had long black hair, insignificant beards, "lively and piercing" black eyes, and good teeth. Indian females were "handsome, well made" and industrious. As physical specimens, the natives of the Floridas appeared to be quite impressive to the self-styled naturalist.[44]

Nevertheless, Romans found the skin color of the local people to be unattractive. "Their colour resembles that of cinnamon, with a copperish cast," claimed the author, and "they are born white, but retain that hue a very short time." For Romans, skin color was one of the few imperfections in the appearance of native females. Romans believed that Indian women lacked "the colour and clenliness of our ladies, to make them lovely in every eye."[45]

Romans's views on skin color emanated from his theories about the origins of the Floridas Indians. He emphatically asserted "that from one end of America to the other, the red people are the same nation and draw their origin from a different source from either Europeans, Chinese, Negroes, Moors, Indians, or any other different species of the human genus." Thus, Native Americans had different origins from every other human species. Dismissing theories about prehistoric migrations from Asia, Romans declared, "I am firmly of opinion, that God created an original man and woman in this part of the globe, of different species from any in the other parts." Rather than provide empirical evidence for this statement, Romans challenged those who disagreed with him to provide evidence that his theory was not sound. Convinced that none could refute his assertions, he proclaimed, "What can now be said against this my argument for a separate origins of the savages? Nothing that will amount to an absolute proof of the contrary."[46]

We do not know whether British Floridians accepted Romans's theory of origins. However, general settler commentary did not contradict his circumstantial evidence for proving the innate differences between Europeans and Indians. Romans listed a variety of distinctions that colonists had observed in their interactions with natives. He reported:

> Our women carry their children with their faces towards their own, a she savage puts the back of hers towards her own back . . . We make war in an open brave way, a savage by hiding himself surprises: our prisoners are sure of life, the prisoner of a savage is sure to die by cruel tortures . . . A savage either buries none of his dead, or if he does he puts the body in a sitting or standing position.

Colonists accustomed to denigrating barbarity and physical differences rarely disagreed with such evidence. Although they might have disagreed with much of what Romans said about native peoples, many colonists would have agreed with his conclusions on the subject: "In a word, if they [Indians] had always studied to be in contrast with us, they could not be more so, than *nature* has made them" (emphasis added).[47]

The Ambiguous Language of Racialization: William Bartram and James Adair

Other observers of natives in the British Floridas publicized their findings during the 1770s. The most prominent among them were William Bartram and James Adair. Unlike Romans, these two authors openly acknowledged their admiration of the Indians and wanted to provide accounts of them that did not use demeaning rhetoric. Bartram and Adair often downplayed, refuted, or romanticized distinctions between natives and Europeans in their writing. Though they had different perspectives with which they viewed natives, neither man condemned indigenous inhabitants as innately inferior or argued that their divine or genetic origins were different from those of other population groups. In this regard, their works offer a strong counterpoint to that of Romans and indicate an alternative British understanding of Indians in the Floridas.

Yet these works also contain many indications that the process of racialization in the Floridas continued uninterrupted during the British period. In their descriptions and defenses of the natives, both Bartram and Adair resorted to the same racialized language earlier Spanish, French, and British observers had used. In their attempts to explain and justify native differences, the two authors often reinforced racialized understandings or contributed new condemnations of the

Indians on the basis of their culture or physical form. In many ways, the works of Bartram and Adair encapsulate the basis of European racialization of Indians in the Floridas. Though it may have been offhand and obscure, the language they used to describe the natives helped generate negative images of the Indians in the European mind. British Floridians who read these works might have derived conclusions far different from those intended by the authors. During times of turmoil, hardship, and disappointment, colonists tended to synthesize isolated negative images to create a damning racialized definition of the indigenous peoples that could be used to justify a variety of nefarious activities.

No observer openly admired the region's indigenous peoples more than Bartram. As the son of a prominent Philadelphia scientist and a noted colonial intellectual in his own right, Bartram was well versed in theories about the native peoples of North America. After the American Revolution, Bartram frequently corresponded with individuals such as George Washington, Alexander Hamilton, and James Madison on a variety of topics including settler relations with Indians. Until his death in 1823, he was a devoted defender of the capacities of Indians and an opponent of the use of the military to displace the tribes living within the United States.[48]

Bartram reinvigorated the "noble savage" depiction of natives in North America that had first been established during the earliest explorations. "How happily situated is this retired spot on earth! What an Elysium it is!" he wrote, "where the wandering Siminole, the naked red warrior, roams at large, and after the vigorous chase retires from the scorching heat of the meridian sun." Bartram alluded to European mythology to impress this image on his readers. The typical Indian rested "under the odoriferous shades of Zanthoxylon, her verdant couch guarded by the Deity; Liberty and the Muses inspiring him with wisdom and valour." This occurred while "balmy zephyrs fan him to sleep."[49]

Like other commentators, Bartram associated character traits with the physical appearance of Indians. Unlike his fellow writers, however, he believed that the native form represented only positive qualities. The indigenous peoples of the Floridas were "tall, erect, and moderately robust; their limbs well shaped, so as generally to form a perfect human figure." In Bartram's mind, the natives had "features regular, and countenance open, dignified and placid; yet the forehead brow so formed, as to strike you instantly with heroism and bravery."[50]

Bartram believed that Indian societies closely resembled European states in the civility of the behavior of their members. "I cannot find, upon the strictest inquiry," he wrote, "that their bloody contests at this day are marked with deeper stains of inhumanity or savage cruelty, than what may be observed amongst the most civilized nations."[51] Bartram saw little distinction between native, British, Spanish, or French justifications for warfare: "Thus we see that war or the exercise of arms originates from the same motives, and operates in the spirits of the wild red men of America, as it formerly did with the renowned Greeks and Romans, or modern civilized nations."[52] Indians also resembled Europeans in their social transgressions. He wrote, "They are given to adultery and fornication, but, I suppose, in no greater excess than other nations of men."[53] In his opinion, Indians "stand as examples of reproof to the most civilized nations, as not being defective in justice, gratitude, and good standing . . . As moral men they certainly stand no need of European civilization."[54]

Bartram provided effective counterarguments to those supplied by Romans and other deriders of native culture and physique. Yet laced throughout his assertions are many of the same depictions of natives that were the basis for the racialization process. Though they appeared infrequently in Bartram's writing, these descriptions and their implications undercut his primary arguments. Evidence that the author himself racialized the Floridas Indians weakened his overall conclusions.

Despite his stated admiration for the Indians' character and culture, Bartram made various references to the contrary in his writings. Like many commentators before him, he criticized their obstinacy and work ethic. Describing one of his encounters with an Indian laborer in the Floridas, he wrote, "I readily complied with his desire [to cease working], knowing the impossibility of compelling an Indian against his own inclinations, or even prevailing upon him by reasonable arguments, when labour is in question."[55] This statement reinforced the stereotype perpetuated by earlier colonists that Indians lacked a vigorous work ethic. In addition, Bartram alluded to the laborer's failure to be swayed by reason in the matter of work.

Bartram also emphasized differences between Europeans and Indians. He claimed that the Muscogulges, or Creeks, were "a proud, haughty and arrogant race of men."[56] Bartram implied that the Indian race was separate from the European race, an idea European Floridians discussed with greater frequency during the eighteenth century. Though the term "race" had different meanings in the eighteenth century than it does today, it referred to "category" or "strata" even during that period.[57] The language Bartram used indicated that he viewed natives as part of a group that was distinctly separate from Europeans.

On other occasions, Bartram reinforced already-established notions regarding native skin color. Like earlier writers, he believed that the Indians had a "complexion of a reddish brown or copper colour; their hair long, lank, coarse, and black as a raven, and reflecting the like luster at different exposures to light."[58] Though this was a relatively benign statement, the underlying senti-ment strengthened ideas about the innate differences between Europeans and Indians. He took this observation one step further in his romanticized praise of the motives for warfare of "the wild red men."[59] Even though he meant to laud them, the idea he conveyed was that "red" Indians were wild or uncivi-lized.

A more revealing example of how Bartram's evidence for his conclusions belied his actual statements involves his depiction of a fictionalized personal encounter with a Seminole while traveling through East Florida. In his descrip-tion of the initial meeting, Bartram indicated that the native planned to kill him. However, once the scientist extended his hand and offered friendship, the Seminole's attitude changed. Allowing the author to live, the native, in "the si-lent language of his soul," stated "'go to thy brethren, tell them thou sawest an Indian in the forests, who knew how to be humane and compassionate.'" Bar-tram used this fictional example as an opportunity to comment extensively on the Indians' civility. "Can it be denied," he wrote, "but that the moral principle, which directs the savages to virtuous and praiseworthy actions is natural or in-nate?" He argued that this "episode" provided further evidence of the natives' high level of civilization.[60]

But the actual words Bartram used leave a different impression on the reader. During the initial meeting of the author and Indian, "the intrepid Siminole stopped suddenly . . . and silently viewed me [Bartram] his countenance angry and fierce." This statement appears to contradict his conclusions about native character and demeanor. When Bartram first extended his hand in friendship, the Seminole "hastily jerked back his arm, with a look of malice, rage, and dis-dain, seeming very discontented." Bartram conveyed the image of an arrogant, intolerant Indian who unjustifiably rejected an offer of friendship from a Euro-pean. His wording of the Seminole's imagined response promoted the disdain-ful image of indigenous peoples that European Floridians commonly harbored. According to Bartram, the Indian said, "White man, thou art my enemy, and thou and thy brethren may have killed mine; yet it may not be so, and even were that the case, thou art now alone, and in my power."

Once more, the author emphasized that Indians and white settlers were different. He implied that these differences caused the two populations to be enemies embroiled in ongoing efforts to kill one another. Finally, the phrase "thou art alone, and in my power" resonated deeply with British Floridians, who believed that they too, like Bartram in this fictional situation, were alone and dependent on the goodwill of neighboring Indians.[61]

Similar patterns are apparent in the writing of James Adair. Adair, who was one of the earliest English traders in the Gulf South, had accompanied factor caravans throughout the region since the 1730s. Unlike many frontier merchants, Adair could read and write, had a rudimentary knowledge of classical theorists (Homer, Cicero, Herodotus), and understood a smattering of Latin, Hebrew, and Cherokee. He became relatively prosperous in the fur trade, and at various times also served as a British agent among the local tribes. By the 1770s, however, he, like many other colonists, had become disenchanted with royal administration of the North American provinces, especially the British government's handling of Indian affairs.[62]

Like Bartram, Adair provides evidence intended to show the Indians' similarity with Europeans.[63] In the dedication of his 1775 book *History of the American Indians*, he complained about the "fictitious and fabulous, or very superficial and conjectural accounts of the Indian natives" then available to the public. He provided his own investigation to clear up any misconceptions. "My intentions were pure when I wrote, truth hath been my standard, and I have no sinister or mercenary views in publishing," contended Adair. Unlike other works, Adair's investigation was based on firsthand evidence: "I sat down to draw the Indians on the spot—had them many years standing before me,—and lived with them as a friend and brother." For this reason, "fiction and conjecture" had no place in his work. Adair assured his readers that they could " depend on the fidelity of the author" and noted that his descriptions were "genuine though perhaps not so polished and romantic as other Indian histories and accounts."[64]

While he was not an admirer of the civilization of the Indians of the Floridas, Adair asserted that the natives were capable of attaining European levels of character and society. The author believed that most Indians "led a plain simple" existence but were increasingly growing "fond of the ornaments of life, of raising live stock, and using a greater industry than formerly, to increase wealth." Because of their interactions with British traders, Indians were making great steps in "being civilized," he wrote.[65] He believed that within a short time, they would be able to embrace Christianity and better integrate into white society.

Adair disagreed with previous assertions that the Indians' skin color emanated from inherent differences from Europeans. His explanation centered on environmental factors. "The hotter, or colder the climate is, where the Indians have long resided," he wrote, "the greater proportion have they either of the red, or white, colour." Adair dismissed biology as a determiner of skin tone. He asserted, "Many incidents and observations lead me to believe, that the Indian colour is not natural; but the external difference between them and the whites, proceeds entirely from their customs and methods of living." According to Adair, native skin tone could not possibly have resulted "from any inherent spring of nature."[66] Furthermore, contrary to the opinions of Romans and others, Adair stated that Indians did not constitute a different "species" than Europeans. Except for skin color, Adair believed that "the American Indians neither vary from the rest of mankind, in their internal construction, nor external appearance." Most differences were "either entirely accidental, or artificial." Based on this evidence, Adair concluded that "the Indians have lineally descended from Adam, the first, and the great parent of all the human species."[67]

Yet, like Bartram, Adair's defenses of Indians were peppered with racialized language. In contrast to Bartram, however, Adair's contentions seem to have been deliberate. While Adair attempted to stress similarities between indigenous peoples and Europeans in certain regards, he denounced the natives' character and physical appearance. While Bartram's presentation of his racialized understandings of the Floridas Indians was inadvertent, Adair openly displayed his beliefs. Adair's views probably correspond to the sentiments of British Floridians more accurately. Bartram visited the region for only a few months, whereas Adair lived among the region's Indians for several decades. Adair's writing provides a significant window into the British American process of racialization.

The author-trader condemned native character. He deemed Indians to be "cunning, and deceitful; very faithful indeed to their own tribes, but privately dishonest, and mischievous to the Europeans and christians." Above all, he felt, Europeans could not trust indigenous peoples. Adair believed that natives were "retentive of their secrets," that they never forgot injuries, and that they were "revengeful of blood, to a degree of distraction." Additionally, he argued, natives were "very jealous of encroachments from their christian neighbours . . . and can form surprisingly crafty schemes, and conduct them with equal caution, silence, and address." The author believed Indians to be at their worst when intoxicated by alcohol. At these times, "they often transform themselves by liquor into the likeness of mad foaming bears."[68]

Despite other indications that Adair saw potential for improvement in the Indians, he at times questioned their purpose in the world. "They seem quite easy, and indifferent, in every various scheme of life, as if they were utterly divested of passions, and the sense of feeling," he recorded. The only time he felt that indigenous peoples applied themselves was in the context of violence and warfare. Adair sensed that "martial virtue, and not riches, is their invariable standard for preferment."[69] Indeed, for the most part the natives were "artful ambuscaders" and "wolfish savages" who "cannot live without shedding blood." Adair also focused on the Indians' alleged penchant for criminal activities. The Choctaw were "in the highest degree, of a base, ungrateful, and thievish disposition." Adair wrote that the natives were "such great proficients in the art of stealing, that in our store-houses, they often thieve while they are speaking to, and looking the owner in the face."[70]

Many of Adair's descriptions of the Indians contained references to their hostile or violent tendencies. In the context of a discussion of their spiritual beliefs, he proclaimed "that the Indians in general, are guided by their dreams when they attend their holy ark of war."[71] Even their perceived laziness receded during violent pursuits. "They are a very dilatory people, and noted for procrastinating every thing that admits of the least delay," he wrote, "but they are the readiest and quickest of all people in going to shed blood." Paraphrasing local traders, Adair concluded "that an Indian is never in haste, only when the devil is at his arse."[72]

Adair's attitudes regarding native skin color and physical appearance further enhanced common stereotypes British Floridians promoted. Despite his refutation of its innate origins, Adair emphasized Indian skin tone in his writings and at times connected it to aberrant behavior. He claimed that the Floridas indigenous peoples were "of a copper or red-clay colour—and they delight in every thing, which they imagine may promote and increase it." Adair asserted that the Indians were themselves racists. "All the Indians are so strongly attached to, and prejudiced in favour of, their own colour," the author claimed, "that they think as meanly of whites, as we possibly do of them."[73]

Adair explored this topic further by examining the origins of North America's indigenous populations. He bolstered his argument that the natives' skin color was artificial by pointing out that they had originally lived in Asia. Much like those of Asians, in Adair's opinion, "the lips of the Indians, in general, are thin. Their eyes are small, sharp, and black; and their hair is lank, coarse, and darkish." These facts, in addition to "their rites, customs, &c . . . prove them to be orientalists." Interestingly, and seemingly in contradiction to his earlier statements, Adair also pointed out biological factors that contributed to the Indians' apparent "copper or red-clay colour." Citing the work of North American physicians, he claimed that the natives had "discerned a certain fine cowl, or web, of a red gluey substance, close under the outer skin, to which it reflects the colour." He continued: "This corpus mucosum, or gluish web, is red in the Indians, and white in us; the parching winds, and hot-sun-beams, beating upon their naked bodies, in their various gradations of life, necessarily tarnish their skins with the tawny red colour." These factors, along with the natives' use of bear grease and "a certain red root" apparently produced "the Indian colour in those who are white born." Adair claimed to have personally witnessed such a transformation on several occasions.[74]

Among his many racialized depictions of the natives, none is more significant than the last. In spite of his other statements, Adair asserted that there were distinct cultural and physical differences between Europeans and Indians. In addition, he believed that for whatever reason, the natives' skin color had degenerated from its original state. Although it was initially white, like that of Europeans, it had been transformed after being "tarnished." More important, the factors responsible for this transformation were environmental. The environment of the Floridas reduced the appearance of the natives, much like it impeded European goals in the region. According to Adair, the same factors that contributed to colonial failure in the Floridas also molded the natives of the region.

Racialization and Cultural Divergence

The racialized descriptions of Adair, Bartram, Romans, and others reflected general British American attitudes in the Floridas and influenced the colonists' views of Indians. Alexander Cameron, deputy superintendent of the Indian Department in the Southern District, remarked that European Americans in the provinces generally had little respect for the natives and "affect to despise" the "dastardly Indians."[75] Military officials sometimes based their planning and deployment of troops on racialized expectations rather than on actual native activities. On at least one occasion, Lieutenant Colonel Augustine Prevost, initially the highest-ranking British military commander in East Florida, disregarded native assurances of peace and the extension of "white feathers in token of Friendship" in his decisions. Instead, because he had "since learn[ed] of the Crueltys lately committed in America and [put] no great confidence in their promises," the commander prepared his troops for hostilities "to prevent any Surprise."[76] Except for isolated skirmishes, no large-scale fighting occurred between Indians and British forces in the Floridas during the two decades before the American Revolution, though fears of such uprisings persisted among settlers. In correspondence with provincial officials, trader George Galphin conveyed how these fears often took on racialized undertones. Settlers told him in 1770 of rumors that Creek and Choctaw Indians, despite their many differences, were plotting to "joyne against the white people" in war.[77] Galphin admitted that little evidence existed to validate the rumors of this alliance but said that the idea remained plausible among colonists, who were perpetually concerned about their security. Governor Grant's letters to other colonial officials illustrated the ultimate fears of many Europeans. He concluded that the "Indians can with great ease stop the Settlement of this Province." If they succeeded, "the Floridas would cease to have an existence."[78]

British immigrants illustrated the effect of racialization on their perceptions of the indigenous population in petitions to officials in London. In 1766, a memorial from the West Florida legislature requested that officials take stronger measures against local Indians. They believed that it was necessary to "[reduce] the Indians to some subjection" to forestall further violence in the backcountry settlements. Failure to do so would decrease settler immigration to the region. The legislators asked, "What man will venture his property or the credit of his friend in erecting habitations or establishing sawmills . . . when not only his all but his life depends on the wanton fury of those barbarians?"[79] Later petitions elaborated on the natives' "uncivilized" behavior. In 1768, the West Florida government implored colonial officials to rescind an order that removed regular army troops from the region. "This unexpected order has justly alarmed the inhabitants who apprehend that being left exposed to the cruel and savage disposition" of the neighboring Indians would cause them to be "ruined and exposed to want and misery." Colonists predicted widespread butchery in the outlying settlements. They believed that the Indians would demand exorbitant gifts and supplies for their restraint and that if the natives were not "immediately gratified to their utmost wishes, they [would] instantly attack our settlers, and commit the most horrid cruelties, insults, and barbarities on them." British colonists believed that only the vigorous use of military force could withstand the predations of the "treacherous and faithless" Indian warriors.[80]

The way British immigrants actually treated the Indians of the Floridas further revealed the impact of racialization. Most colonists believed that deficiencies among indigenous peoples could be rectified only with the assistance of Europeans. Governor Grant believed that even when Indians' grievances against colonists were justified, they "must be taught to behave more temperately."[81] In a congress with Choctaw Indians, Major Robert Farmar, the first British military leader in West Florida, stated in a speech to the natives, "As you are freemen [you] . . . ought to have learn't to think, since you have frequented the white Peoples." His implication was that they were limited in intellectual ability before contact with Europeans. Farmar went on to warn the Indians not to molest the remaining French settlers in the province or, in other words, any European Floridians. In order to convince the natives, he said, "Do no harm to the French, remember always, that they have taught you to become Men."[82] According to Farmar and other colonists, the indigenous population attained true manhood, or humanity, only with the assistance of the Europeans.

British racialized understandings of the natives also appeared in the laws they passed. In 1767, the West Florida government passed "An Act for the Regulation and Government of Negroes and Slaves." Though the act did not specifically apply to Indians, its provisions stated that in matters relating to witness testimony, evidence at trials, and committing of crimes, the same punishments and privileges that applied to slaves also applied to any "free Negro, mulatto, mustee or Indian." Similar provisions were included in a subsequent act titled "An Act for the Order and Government of Slaves."[83] Increasingly, natives were given the same status and treatment as other racially defined groups, including chattel slaves.

The way British officials and traders in the Floridas viewed Indians fostered greater misunderstanding and intercultural strife. General John Campbell, British military commander in charge of West Florida's defenses during the American Revolution, failed to comprehend the expectations of the allied Indians who helped defend Mobile and Pensacola from Spanish invasion. Many natives refused to return during later engagements after Campbell repeatedly refused to provide them with supplies and dismissed them without compensation.[84] According to Deputy Superintendent Alexander Cameron, Campbell did "not understand any thing of Indians or their affairs he thinks they are to be used like slaves or a people void of *natural* sence" (emphasis added).[85] In Cameron's opinion, Campbell regarded natives as inherently lacking the ability to reason. The general's attitudes probably reflected those of many European settlers he was attempting to defend. According to Governor Chester, most disputes between natives and Europeans in the Floridas revolved around the frontier merchants' continuous "imposing and cheating" of "the poor ignorant Indians."[86] Although the governor did not record the beliefs that, in the traders' minds, would sanction such behavior, Adair helps us fill in the gap: "The general observation of the traders among them is just, who affirm them [Indians] to be divested of every property of a human being, except shape and language."[87]

Modern concepts of racism did not appear in the Floridas until after the American Revolution. Yet the basis for such differentiation was firmly established by British Floridians during the eighteenth century. Settlers and officials commonly described, identified, and condemned the natives on the basis of their behavior and appearance. British contributions to the process closely resembled those of the French and Spanish of earlier periods. Three centuries of association and experience had done little to alter how Europeans assessed their native neighbors in the Floridas. Misunderstanding, disappointment, failure, and insecurity persisted, reinforcing a chasm between native and European cultures that would only deepen in the years to come.

7

Conclusion

Even today, it is difficult to decipher the racialization process that emerged in the colonial Floridas. Few settlers recorded its development or acknowledged its existence in written materials. Definitive empirical evidence documenting the impact of racialization in legal or social hierarchies remains available only through descriptions of obscure laws or isolated practices. In past and contemporary narratives and analyses, the process continues to be largely hidden behind depictions of warfare and bicultural antagonism, peace treaties and harmonious trade relationships. Ambiguous in most of its forms, racialization appears in the historical record primarily as scattered comments, offhand remarks, and backhanded compliments.

Yet nothing confirms the existence of this phenomenon more than the consistency of these miscellaneous observations. Spaniards, Frenchmen, and Britons who colonized the region under vastly different circumstances over a 300-year period delivered a remarkably similar collective commentary on the natives they encountered. Often casually and, for the most part, unintentionally, European colonists constructed a negative image of Indians based on morality, behavior, spirituality, and physical appearance. Sparked by disappointments associated with a general misunderstanding of the environment of the colonial Floridas, this process resulted in gradual ethnic divergence, occasional violence and brutality, and the erosion of any substantial mutual accommodation.[1]

But perhaps more important in terms of a comprehensive understanding of human interaction in the region was the impact of this process on the development of a European Floridian identity. Soldiers, missionaries, traders, and settlers from varied ethnic, cultural, spiritual, and economic backgrounds forged bonds through racialization of the natives that they were unable to achieve through any other method. Ordinarily contentious and disparaging in their descriptions of one another, Spaniards, Frenchmen, and Britons achieved common ground through their intellectual conceptualizations of the Indians. Hernando de Soto, Pedro Menéndez de Avilés, Luís Cancer, René de Laudonnière, Paul Du Ru, Jonathan Dickinson, and James Adair, to name but a few, reached consensus in radically varied settings on little else besides their differences from the natives. Though perhaps unforeseen, these bonds created a European Floridian identity that would intensify racialization, racial categorization, and racist ideology following the American Revolution.

The culmination of this process is clearly represented by the Spanish settlers who entered the region after the expulsion of British colonizers during the American Revolution. Among the first Spaniards to visit the provinces and record his impressions following the war was Francisco de Saavedra, an adventurer keenly interested in observing the transfer of power in the Floridas. Saavedra, like many of his fellow countrymen, condemned most of the aspects of British colonization he witnessed upon entering the peninsula in 1781. In his journals, the Spaniard criticized British goals, attitudes, and practices on multiple occasions. At times, he indicated a disdain for the French and their settlement endeavors in the Americas as well. Nonetheless, in at least one important regard, his attitudes mirrored those of the colonists the Spanish had recently displaced. Echoing Garcilaso's words published almost 200 years previously, Saavedra noted that despite British attempts to reform them, the various native groups in the Floridas still were primitive. He believed that "the customs of all are almost identical because they all lead the same kind of life, their needs are the same, and they have the same method of satisfying those needs."[2] Like his European predecessors, the recent emigrant denigrated the various qualities the Indians exhibited. He wrote, "Their moral character is a monstrous and almost irreconcilable aggregate of good and bad qualities."[3] Spiritually, the Indians also erred: "The religion of these nations is far from perfect. It is limited for the most part to certain superstitious practices inspired in them by precognition or fear."[4] Saavedra's descriptions of the natives' physical appearance resembled those of his Anglo-American contemporaries, Bartram and Adair. Though they were "of the same race as the rest of the indigenous people of the New World," he insisted that the original Floridians differed from Europeans because they "lack[ed] beards, their eyes are small and lively their features heavy, their color red with a copper cast, and their hair black and straight."[5] Although he admitted that both cultural groups had common origins, Saavedra cautioned that many differences existed between Europeans and natives. Summarizing the viewpoints of the explorers, soldiers, missionaries, traders, and settlers who had inhabited the colonial Floridas for three centuries, the Spaniard wrote, "The advancements in civilization made up to now by the Indians are so few that the nations present a clear idea of the infancy of the human race."[6]

Colonist racialization of natives in the Floridas would continue into the Second Spanish Period and beyond, as would native resistance to that process. But both endeavors took on different forms during the nineteenth century. New laws, population growth, scientific theories, spiritual movements, modes of warfare, and policies based on the theory of manifest destiny transformed old practices. Racialization evolved into racism, the identity formation of settlers inspired U.S. patriotism, and native resistance led to new forms of genocidal conflict. Nevertheless, the origins of these two traditions, settler identity formation and racialization, remained the same. Much like their ancestors, European Americans in the postcolonial Gulf South understood their environment, natural obstacles, and collective identity in relation to their indigenous neighbors. Like their forebears, natives in the region sought to preserve their cultures and coherence. Images continued to play a dominant role in both European American and Native American exercises. Providing continuity from past to present, the perpetual idea of an unexploited Florida influenced intercultural relationships within the peninsula and its hinterlands into the modern era.

Notes

Chapter 1. Introduction

1. The plural term "Floridas" is used throughout the text in order to take account of the varied geographies of "Florida" during the colonial period. At different times between the sixteenth and nineteenth centuries, Europeans used derivations of "Florida" to describe both specific areas such as St. Augustine and broader geographic locales such as the entire present-day southeastern United States. Unless otherwise stated, "Floridas" refers to the territory immediately south of the 32° 28' latitude adjacent to the Atlantic Ocean, the Mississippi River, and Gulf of Mexico.

2. In this sense, Europeans in the colonial Floridas resembled Christopher Columbus. Stephen Greenblatt has characterized Columbus's emphasis on the "marvelous" setting and peoples of the New World as a rhetorical device to divert attention from his settlement failures and inability to provide expected riches for Spain. "The marvelous stands for the missing caravels laden with gold; it is—like the ritual of possession itself—a word pregnant with the imagined, desired, promised"; Stephen Greenblatt, *Marvelous Possessions: The Wonder of the New World* (Chicago: University of Chicago Press), 73, 75–78.

3. Though significantly influenced by New Indian History paradigms, this study is not a traditional tribal or ethnohistorical assessment of natives in the colonial Floridas. Rather, it is an analysis of how Europeans incorporated Indians into the construction of a European Floridian identity. The words and activities of Indians, as depicted mostly through European documents, are analyzed primarily through this perspective in an attempt to reveal subtle native voices previously overlooked in pre–eighteenth-century writings dealing with the Floridas. Consequently, a major goal of this study is to facilitate further study of identity formation in the region from the native point of view.

4. The most notable exceptions include Michael G. Gannon, ed., *The New History of Florida* (Gainesville: University Press of Florida, 1996); Robert L. Gold, *Borderland Empires in Transition: The Triple Nation Transfer of Florida* (Carbondale: Southern Illinois University Press, 1969); Jerald T. Milanich, *Florida Indians and the Invasion from Europe* (Gainesville: University Press of Florida, 1995). In addition, a variety of works dealing with broader subjects often include important information pertaining to the Floridas.

5. See Charles E. Bennett, *Laudonnière and Fort Caroline: History and Documents* (Gainesville: University Press of Florida, 1964); Mark F. Boyd, Hale G. Smith, and John W. Griffin, *Here They Once Stood: The Tragic End of the Apalachee Missions* (Gainesville: University Press of Florida, 1951); Amy T. Bushnell, *The King's Coffer: Proprietors of the Spanish Florida Treasury, 1565–1702* (Gainesville: University Press of Florida, 1981); Kathleen Deagan, *Spanish St. Augustine: The Archaeology of a Colonial Creole Community* (New York: Academic Press, 1983); Robin F. A. Fabel, *The Economy of British West Florida, 1763–1783* (Tuscaloosa: University of Alabama Press, 1988); Michael V. Gannon, *The Cross in the Sand: The Early Catholic Church in Florida, 1513–1870* (Gainesville: University Press of Florida, 1965); Maynard Geiger, *The Franciscan Conquest of Florida (1573–1618)* (Washington, D.C.: Catholic University of America, 1937); John H. Hann, *History of the Timucua Indians and Missions* (Gainesville: University Press of Florida, 1996); Eugene Lyon, *The Enterprise of Florida: Pedro Menéndez de Avilés and the Spanish Conquest of 1565–1568* (Gainesville: University Press of Florida, 1976); Bonnie G. McEwan, ed., *The Spanish Missions of La Florida* (Gainesville: University Press of Florida, 1993); V. F. O'Daniel, *Dominicans in Early Florida* (New York: United States Catholic Historical Society, 1930); Martha C. Searcy, *The Georgia-Florida Contest in the American Revolution*, 1776–1778 (Tuscaloosa: University of Alabama Press, 1985); J. Barton Starr, *Tories, Dons, and Rebels: The American Revolution in British West Florida* (Gainesville: University Press of Florida, 1976); John J. TePaske, *The Governorship of Spanish Florida, 1700–1763* (Durham, N.C.: Duke University Press, 1964); J. Leitch Wright, Jr., *Florida in the American Revolution* (Gainesville: University Press of Florida, 1975).

6. See John H. Hann, *Apalachee: The Land between the Rivers* (Gainesville: University Press of Florida, 1988); Clinton N. Howard, *The British Development of West Florida*, 1763–1769 (Berkeley: University of California Press, 1947); Cecil Johnson, *British West Florida, 1763–1783* (New York: Archon Books, 1971); Charles L. Mowat, *East Florida as a British Province, 1763–1784* (Gainesville: University Press of Florida, 1964).

7. In addition to many of the works listed above, see Charles W. Arnade, *Florida on Trial, 1593–1602* (Coral Gables, Fla.: University of Miami Press, 1959). An important exception is Paul E. Hoffman, *Florida's Frontiers* (Bloomington: Indiana University Press, 2002).

8. John Elliott, "Introduction: Colonial Identity in the Atlantic World," in *Colonial Identity in the Atlantic World, 1500–1800* edited by Nicholas Canny and Anthony Pagden (Princeton, N.J.: Princeton University Press, 1987), 3.

9. Transnational approaches to North American history are examined in Joyce E. Chaplin, "Expansion and Exceptionalism in Early American History," *Journal of American History* 89, no. 4 (2003): 1431–55; David Thelen, "The Nation and Beyond: Transnational Perspectives on United States History," *Journal of American History* 86, no. 3 (December 1999): 965–76; and Jeremy Adelman and Stephen Aron, "From

Borderlands to Borders: Empires, Nation-States, and the Peoples in Between in North American History," *American Historical Review* 104, no. 3 (October 1999): 814–42.

10. For similar assessments, see Patrick Riordan, "Seminole Genesis: Native Americans, African Americans, and Colonists on the Southern Frontier from Prehistory through the Colonial Era" (Ph. D. diss., Florida State University, 1996), 3; Claudio Saunt, *A New Order of Things: Property, Power, and the Transformation of the Creek Indians, 1733–1816* (Cambridge, England: Cambridge University Press, 1999), 3–5.

11. Most attempts to investigate racial distinctions in the colonial Floridas pertain exclusively to white-black relationships. See David Colburn and Jane Landers, eds., *The African American Heritage of Florida* (Gainesville: University Press of Florida, 1995); Jane Landers, "An Examination of Racial Conflict and Cooperation in Spanish St. Augustine: The Career of Jorge Biassou, Black Caudillo," *El Escribano* 25 (December 1988): 85–100; and Kevin Mulroy, *Freedom on the Border: The Seminole Maroons in Florida, the Indian Territory, Coahuila, and Texas* (Lubbock: Texas Tech University Press, 1993). A broader analysis of race relations is available in Theodore G. Corbett, "Migration to a Spanish Imperial Frontier in the Seventeenth and Eighteenth Centuries: St. Augustine," *Hispanic American Historical Review* 54, no. 3 (August 1974): 414–30.

12. Over the past century, scholars have continuously revised the definition of "race" as it relates to North American Indians in the seventeenth and eighteenth centuries. In addition to the works mentioned in the text, see Theodore Allen, *The Invention of the White Race*, 2 vols. (London: Verso, 1994–1997); David Bidney, "The Idea of the Savage in North American Ethnohistory," *Journal of the History of Ideas* 15 (April 1954): 322–27; Franz Boas, ed., *Race, Language, and Culture* (New York: The Free Press, 1940); T. H. Breen, "Creative Adaptations: Peoples and Cultures," in *Colonial British America: Essays in the New History of the Early Modern Era*, edited by Jack P. Greene and J. R. Pole (Baltimore: Johns Hopkins University Press, 1984); Marvin Harris, *Patterns of Race in the Americas* (New York: W.W. Norton, 1964); Nicholas Hudson, "From 'Nation' to 'Race': The Origin of Racial Classification in Eighteenth-Century Thought," *Eighteenth-Century Studies* 29, no. 3 (spring 1996): 247–64; Annette M. Jaimes, "American Racism: The Impact on American-Indian Identity and Survival," in *Race*, edited by S. Gregory and R. Sanjek (New Brunswick, N.J.: Rutgers University Press, 1994); Mangus Morner, *Race Mixture in the History of Latin America* (Boston: Little, Brown, 1967); Ronald Sanders, *Lost Tribes and Promised Lands: The Origins of American Racism* (Boston: Little, Brown, 1978); G. E. Thomas, "Puritans, Indians and the Concept of Race," *The New England Quarterly* 48, no. 1 (March 1975): 3–27; Richard White, "Race Relations in the American West," *American Quarterly* 38, no. 3 (1986): 400–401.

13. For similar interpretations, see Robert H. Jackson, *Race, Caste, and Status: Indians in Colonial Spanish America* (Albuquerque: University of New Mexico Press, 1999), 9, 51; Karen O. Kupperman, *Indians & English: Facing Off in Early America*

(Ithaca, N.Y.: Cornell University Press, 2000), 10–11; Jane T. Merritt, "Metaphor, Meaning, and Misunderstanding: Language and Power on the Pennsylvanian Frontier," in *Contact Points: American Frontiers from the Mohawk Valley to the Mississippi, 1750–1830,* edited by Andrew R. L Cayton and Fredrika J. Teute (Chapel Hill: University of North Carolina Press, 1998), 67; Philip D. Morgan, "Encounters between British and 'Indigenous' Peoples, c. 1500–c. 1800," in *Empire and Others: British Encounters with Indigenous Peoples, 1600–1850,* edited by Martin Daunton and Rick Halpern (Philadelphia: University of Pennsylvania Press, 1999), 62.

14. Though not the subject of this study, gender and its application to the colonial Floridas merit further research. In her works on the Chesapeake region during the seventeenth and eighteenth centuries, Kathleen M. Brown asserts that race and gender should be conceptualized "as overlapping and related social categories, not as variables competing for analytical supremacy." See Kathleen M. Brown, *Good Wives, Nasty Wenches, and Anxious Patriarchs: Gender, Race, and Power in Colonial Virginia* (Chapel Hill: University of North Carolina Press, 1996), 4–7, 57–61; quote on page 4.

15. Audrey Smedley, *Race in North America: Origin and Evolution of a Worldview,* 2nd ed. (Boulder, Colo.: Westview, 1999), 18.

16. For a synopsis of the "othering" process, see Eve Kornfeld, "Encountering 'the Other': American Intellectuals and Indians in the 1790s," *William and Mary Quarterly* 52 (1995): 287–91; Mechal Sobel, "The Revolution in Selves: Black and White Inner Aliens," in *Through a Glass Darkly: Reflections on Personal Identity in Early America,* edited by Ronald Hoffman, Mechal Sobel, and Fredrika Teute (Chapel Hill: University of North Carolina Press, 1997), 171.

17. Jill Lepore, *The Name of War: King Philip's War and the Origins of American Identity* (New York: Knopf, 1998), 11.

18. Ronald Takaki, "The Tempest in the Wilderness: The Racialization of Savagery," *Journal of American History* 79, no. 3 (December 1992): 899.

19. Smedley, *Race in North America,* 79.

20. Gary B. Nash, "The Image of the Indian in the Southern Colonial Mind," *William and Mary Quarterly* 29, no. 2 (April 1972): 201.

21. European perceptions that native residents were barbarous and the significance of such ideas for intercultural relationships are discussed in James H. Merrell, *Into the American Woods: Negotiators on the Pennsylvania Frontier* (New York: Norton, 1999), 129.

22. Smedley, *Race in North America,* 61.

23. Takaki, "The Tempest in the Wilderness," 906.

24. Thomas C. Holt, "Of Blood and Power: An Introduction," *William and Mary Quarterly* 61, no. 3 (July 2004): 436.

25. Joyce Chaplin, "Natural Philosophy and an Early Racial Idiom in North America: Comparing English and Indian Bodies," *William and Mary Quarterly* 54, no. 1 (January 1997): 252. Chaplin further elaborated on these ideas in *Subject Matter:*

Technology, the Body, and Science on the Anglo-American Frontier, 1500–1676 (Cambridge, Mass.: Harvard University Press, 2001).

26. Smedley, *Race in North America*, 28.

27. Audrey Smedley, "'Race' and the Construction of Human Identity," *American Anthropologist* 100, no. 3 (September 1998): 693–94.

28. Lepore, *The Name of War*, 80.

29. Thomas D. Matijasic, "Reflected Values: Sixteenth-Century Europeans View the Indians of North America," *American Indian Culture and Research Journal* 11, no. 2 (1987): 38.

30. Smedley, Race in North America, 76, 83, 103.

31. Takaki, "The Tempest in the Wilderness," 908–9. For a similar assessment of a different region in North America, see Merrell, *Into the American Woods*, 22, 152.

32. Nicholas P. Canny, "The Ideology of English Colonization: From Ireland to America," *William and Mary Quarterly* 30, no. 4 (October 1973): 597–98; Kornfeld, "Encountering 'the Other,'" 287–91; Sobel, "The Revolution in Selves," 171–72.

33. Philip Deloria, *Playing Indian* (New Haven, Conn.: Yale University Press, 1998), 4–5.

34. Eric Hinderaker, *Elusive Empires: Constructing Colonialism in the Ohio Valley, 1673–1800* (New York: Cambridge University Press, 1997), 256–59.

35. Elizabeth Perkins, "Distinctions and Partitions amongst Us: Identity and Interaction in the Revolutionary Ohio Valley," in *Contact Points: American Frontiers from the Mohawk Valley to the Mississippi, 1750–1830*, edited by Andrew R. L. Cayton and Fredrika J. Teute (Chapel Hill: University of North Carolina Press, 1998), 233.

36. Smedley, *Race in North America*, 7. For similar perspectives see Elliott, "Introduction: Colonial Identity in the Atlantic World"; Jack P. Greene, *Imperatives, Behaviors, and Identities: Essays in American Cultural History* (Charlottesville: University of Virginia Press, 1995); and Patricia Seed, *Ceremonies of Possession in Europe's Conquest of the New World, 1492–1640* (New York: Cambridge University Press, 1995).

Chapter 2. Imagining an Idyllic Environment

1. Bernard Bailyn, *Voyagers to the West: A Passage in the Peopling of America on the Eve of the Revolution* (New York: Vintage Books, 1986), 435, 431.

2. European perceptions of the North American environment are evaluated in William Cronon, *Changes in the Land: Indians, Colonists, and the Ecology of New England* (New York: Hill and Wang, 1983), 22–25, 34–37, 168–70; Timothy Silver, *A New Face on the Countryside: Indians, Colonists, and Slaves in South Atlantic Forests, 1500–1800* (Cambridge, England: Cambridge University Press, 1990), 33–34.

3. Europeans' association of Indians with nature and the environment has been a contentious topic among scholars for centuries. Examples of the most recent treatments of the subject are Robert F. Berkhofer, Jr., *The White Man's Indian: Images of the*

American Indian from Columbus to the Present (New York: Knopf, 1978; reprint, New York: Vintage Books, 1979); Chaplin, *Subject Matter*; Greenblatt; Shepard Krech, *The Ecological Indian: Myth and History* (New York: W. W. Norton, 1999); Silver, *A New Face on the Countryside.*

4. See Benjamin Keen, trans., *The Spanish Character: Attitudes and Mentalities from the Sixteenth to the Nineteenth Century by Bartolomé Bennassar* (Berkeley: University of California Press, 1979), 127–28; Lyle N. McAlister, *Spain and Portugal in the New World, 1492–1700* (Minneapolis: University of Minnesota Press, 1984), 109–10; Anthony Pagden, *Lords of All the World: Ideologies of Empire in Spain, Britain, and France,* c. 1500–c. 1800 (New Haven, Conn.: Yale University Press, 1995), 67, 115; Linda F. Stine, "Mercantilism and Piedmont: Colonial Perceptions of the Southern Fur Trade, circa 1640–1740," in *Volumes in Historical Archaeology,* edited by Stanley South (Columbia: University of South Carolina, 1990), XIV:5.

5. W. J. Eccles, *France in America* (East Lansing: Michigan State University Press, 1990), 2; David J. Weber, *The Spanish Frontier in North America* (New Haven, Conn.: Yale University Press, 1992), 88.

6. Among the many works that address Spain's formative period, the most recent and comprehensive is Henry Kamen, *Empire: How Spain Became a World Power, 1492–1763* (New York: HarperCollins, 2003).

7. Though Martyr was Italian, he frequently resided in Spain and associated with the Spanish court; see McAlister, *Spain and Portugal in the New World,* 92.

8. John F. Scarry, "The Late Prehistoric Southeast"; and Paul E. Hoffman, "Lucas Vázquez de Ayllón's Discovery and Colony," in *The Forgotten Centuries: Indians and Europeans in the American South, 1521–1704,* edited by Charles Hudson and Carmen C. Tesser (Athens: University of Georgia Press, 1994), 1, 39.

9. "Peter Martyr on Ponce de León's first voyage," in *New American World: A Documentary History of North America to 1612,* 5 vols., edited by David B. Quinn (New York: Arno Press, 1979), 1:234.

10. See Wayland D. Hand, "The Effect of the Discovery on Ethnological and Folklore Studies in Europe," in *First Images of America: The Impact of the New World on the Old,* 2 vols., edited by Fredi Chiappelli (Berkeley: University of California Press, 1976), 1:46–47; McAlister, *Spain and Portugal in the New World,* 473–74.

11. "La provincial de Apalache es muy fertile e abundantísima de mantenimientos, de mucho maíz, e fésoles, e calabazas, e fructas diversas, e muchos venados, y muchas disversidades de aves, y cerca de la mar para pescados que hay muschos y Buenos, e es tierra aplacible aunque hay ciénegas; pero son tiesas por ser sobre arena," Gonzalo Fernández de Oviedo, *Historia general y natural de las Indias,* 5 vols. (Madrid: Ediciones Atlas, 1959), 2:162; "The official narrative of the expedition of Hernando de Soto, by Rodrigo Rangel, his secretary, as rendered by Gonzalo Fernández de Oviedo, 1539–1541," in Quinn, *New American World,* 2:166.

12. Richard Hakluyt, *Divers Voyages Touching the Discoerie of America* (London:

Thomas Woodcoke, 1582; reprint, Ann Arbor, Mich.: University Microfilms, 1966), 11–12, 169–70.

13. "Que era a mais rica terra que no mundo avia," Gentleman of Elvas, *True Relation of the Hardships Suffered by Governor Fernando de Soto & Certain Portuguese Gentlemen During the Discovery of the Province of Florida. Now Newly Set Forth by a Gentleman of Elvas*, 2 vols., translated and edited by James A. Robertson (Deland: Florida State Historical Society, 1932), 2:9.

14. "& por ysso lhe pos o tal nome, & por lhe parecer q'acharia nella ouro, prata, & grade riq'za, a pedio a el rey do Fernado, q' foy causa de sua morte & dano, como muitos na tal empresa te recibido," Antonio Galvão, *The discoveries of the world from their original unto the year of Our Lord 1555* (Lisbon, 1563; English translation, London, 1601; reprint, London: Hakluyt Society, 1862), 123; António Galvão, *The Discoveries of the World by Antonie Galvano*, translated by Richard Hakluyt (London: Impensis G. Bishop, 1601; reprint, New York: Da Capo Press, 1969), 47.

15. "Las islas de las marinas estan llenas de arboles y caza: Al Rededor dellas ay mucho marisco, pescado, lenguados, ostras . . . parras siluestres, seruales . . . palmitos Como los de El Andalucia . . . abia mucha brea y alquitran, porque ay muchos pinares: Abia grandes Aparejos para Edificar casas, hacer nauios y naos, que son cosas que bienen de alemania . . . y se pueden lleuar a españa Con gran facilidad y poca Costa . . . qüentas de corales . . . turquesas y esmeraldas . . . toda la tierra es de muy buen temple y cielo saludable," Bartolomé Barrientos, *Pedro Menéndez de Avilés, Founder of Florida*, translated by Anthony Kerrigan (Gainesville: University Press of Florida, 1965), Section I, 24–26, Section II, 24–27; "Bartolomé Barrientos on Pedro Menéndez' Successful Attack on the French Colony, 1565," in Quinn, *New American World*, 2:456–58.

16. "De cuya fertilidad también hemos dicho que es mucha, porque es abundante de zara o maíz y otras muchas semillas de frisoles y calabaza . . . y otras legumbres de diversas especies, sin las frutas que hallaron de las de España como son ciruelas de todas maneras . . . Sin esta fertilidad de la cosecha tiene la tierra muy buena d'sposición para criarse en ella toda suerte de ganados, porque tiene Buenos montes y dehesas con buenas aguas, ciénegas y lagunas con mucha juncia y enea para ganado prieto que se cría muy bien con ella," Garcilaso de la Vega, *Obras completas del Inca Garcilaso de la Vega*, 4 vols. (Madrid: Ediciones Atlas, 1960–1965), 1:367–68; Garcilaso de la Vega, *The Florida of the Inca: A History of the Adelantado, Hernando de Soto, Governor and Captain General of the Kingdom of Florida, and of Other Heroic Spanish and Indian Cavaliers, Written by the Inca, Garcilaso de la Vega, An Officer of His Majesty, and a Native of the Great City of Cuzco, Capital of the Realms and Provinces of Peru*, translated and edited by John G. Varner (Austin: University of Texas Press, 1962), Book 2, Chapter 25, 259–60.

17. Frederick T. Davis, "History of Juan Ponce de León's Voyages to Florida: Source Records," *Florida Historical Quarterly* 14, no. 1 (July 1935): 17.

18. "La Tierra es fria, con buenos Pastos para Ganados . . . con grandes Arboledas . . . que traìa los Hijos en una bolsa, que tiene en la barriga," Antonio de Herrera y Tordesillas, *Historia general de los hechos de los castellanos en las islas I tierra firme del mar oceano,* 8 vols. (Madrid: Imprento Real de Nicolas Rodiguez Franco, 1726–1728), 4:65; Antonio de Herrera, *The General History of the Vast Continent and Islands of America Commonly Call'd, the West Indies, From the First Descovery Thereof,* 6 vols., translated by John Stevens (Madrid, 1601–1605; reprint, London: Printed for J. Batley, 1725–1726) 4:30–31.

19. Eccles, *France in America,* 1–12.

20. Colin G. Calloway, *New Worlds for All: Indians, Europeans, and the Remaking of Early America* (Baltimore: Johns Hopkins University Press, 1997), 10–11; James J. Cooke, "France, The New World and Colonial Expansion," in *La Salle and His Legacy: Frenchmen and Indians in the Lower Mississippi Valley,* edited by Patricia K. Galloway (Jackson: University of Mississippi Press, 1982), 81–92.

21. "Souvent qu'elle est frappee des rayons de son haut soleil, reçoit en elle force challeur: laquelle toutesfois est temperee: non seulement de la fraischeur de la nuit où de la rosee du ciel, mais aussi de gracieuses pluyes en abondance, dont le gazon en devient fertile, voire, de sorte que l'herbe forte y croist en hauteur admira ble: qu'elle est riche d'or et de toutes sortes d'animaux: qu'ayant les champs plains et spacieux: ce neantmoins aussi ses montagnes sont assez hautes, les fleuves plaisans à merveilles, arbres divers, rendans la gomme odoriferante," in *Le Français en Floride. Textes de Jean Ribault, René De Laudonnière, Nicolas Le Challeux et Dominique de Gourges,* edited by Suzanne Lussagnet (Paris: Presses Universitaires de France, 1958), 207; Nicolas Le Challeux, "Discours e l'histoire de la Floride," in Quinn, *New American World,* 2:371.

22. Bennett, *Laudonnière and Fort Caroline,* 74.

23. "Que tout cela consideré, ne pouvoit autrement advenir que l'homme ne trouvast là grand plaisir et singuliere delectation," in Lussagnet, *Le Français en Floride,* 207; Challeux, "Discours e l'histoire de la Floride," 2:371.

24. "Ou pource qu'elle est toute verte & florissante, & que même les eaux y sont couvertes d'herbes verdoyantes . . . Pour la qualité de la terre, il ne se peut rien voir de plus beau, car elle étoit toute couverte de hauts chenes & cedres en infinité, & au dessus d'iceux de lentisques de si suave odeur, que cela seul rendoit le lieu desirable," Marc Lescarbot, *Histoire de la Nouvelle France,* 3 vols., translated and edited by H. P. Biggar and W. L. Grant (Paris, 1618; reprint, New York: Greenwood, 1968), 1:55, 63, 243, 247.

25. "Quoy que lesdites provinces soyet sans hiver, & jouïssent d'vne verdure perpetuelle . . . Mais aussi ceux de la Floride ont ils eu de l'heur en ce qu'ils étoiet en vn païs doux, fertile, & plus ami de la saté humaine que la Nouvelle-France Septentrionale," ibid., 2:190, 284, 480, 529.

26. Myron P. Gilmore, "The New World in French and English Histories of the

Sixteenth Century," in *First Images of America: The Impact of the New World on the Old*, 2 vols., edited by Fredi Chiappelli (Berkeley: University of California Press, 1976), 2:520, 525–26.

27. "Qui sont excellentes pour la culture de l'Indigo de Tabac, du Ris, du Bled d'Inde, & des Cannes à sucre . . . Ce pays est peuplé de Marchands, d'Artisans, & d'Estrangers; c'est un séjour enchanté par la salubrité de son air, la fécondité de son terroir, & la beauté de sa position," J. B. Bossu, *Nouveaux Voyages en Louisiane, 1751–1768*, edited by Philippe Jacquin (Paris: Aubier-Montaigne, 1980), 46; Bossu to Marquis de l'Estrade, 1 July 1751, in *Jean Bossu, Travels in the Interior of North America, 1751–1762*, translated and edited by Seymour Feiler (Norman: University of Oklahoma Press, 1962), 24.

28. "Le sol des environs de la Mobile, est un sable gros, néanmoins le bétail y vient très-bien, & les troupeaux y multiplient beaucoup," Bossu, *Nouveaux Voyages en Louisiane*, 125; Bossu to Monsieur de Moras, 6 January 1759, in Bossu, Travels in the Interior of North America, 127.

29. Bossu, *Travels in the Interior of North America*, [?] January 1760, 195.

30. Ibid., 194.

31. "The True and last discouerie of Florida made by Captaine John Ribault in the yeere 1562," in Hakluyt, *Divers Voyages*, n.p.

32. Richard Hakluyt, *The Principal Navigations, Voyages, Trafiques & Discoveries of the English Nation Made by Sea or Over-Land to the Remote and Farthest Distant Quarters of the Earth at Any Time Within the Compasse of These 1600 Yeeres*, 12 vols., vol. 8 (London, 1589; reprint, Glasgow: J. Maclehose and Sons, 1903–1905), 451–52.

33. "John Sparke's Report on Florida, July 1565," in Quinn, *New American World*, 2:365, 369–70.

34. Richard Blome, *A Geographical Description of the Four Parts of the World, Taken from Notes & Workes of the Famous Monsieur Sanson, Geographer to the French King, and Other Eminent Travellers and Authors* Microform (London: Printed by T. N. for R. Blome, 1670), 10.

35. Thomas Jefferys, *A Description of the Spanish Islands and Settlements on the Coast of the West Indies. Compiled from Authentic Memoirs, Revised by Gentlemen Who Have Resided Many Years in the Spanish Settlements. Illustrated with Thirty-two Maps and Plans, Chiefly from Original Drawings Taken from the Spaniards in the Last War* (London: Printed for T. Jefferys, 1762), 68–69.

36. *The American Gazetteer. Containing a Distinct Account of All the Parts of the New World; Their Situation, Climate, Soil, Produce, Former and Present Condition; Commodities, Manufacturers, and Commerce. Together with an Accurate Account of the Cities, Towns, Ports, Bays, Rivers, Lakes, Mountains, Passes, and Fortifications*, 3 vols. (London: Printed for A. Millar, 1762), 1:n.p.

37. Entry for January 1763, in *The Scots Magazine*, 55 vols. (Edinburgh: Sands, Brymer, Murray, and Cochran, 1739–1793), 24:696.

38. See Bailyn, *Voyagers to the West*, 411–68; Charles L. Mowat, "The First Campaign of Publicity for Florida," *Mississippi Valley Historical Review* 30, no. 3 (December 1943): 359–76; James H. O'Donnell, "Armchair Adventurers and Horseback Botanists: Explorations of Florida's Natural History, 1763–1800," *Gulf Coast Historical Review* 8, no. 1 (Fall 1992): 85–93; Pagden, Lords of All the World, 116–17; George C. Rogers, "The East Florida Society of London, 1766–1767," *Florida Historical Quarterly* 54, no. 4 (April 1976): 479–96.

39. William Stork to Charles, Marquis of Rockingham, in *William Stork, An Account of East Florida; with a Journal Kept by John Bartram of Philadelphia, Botanist of His Majesty for the Floridas; Upon a Journey from St. Augustine up the River St. Johns* (London: Sold by Nicol, 1765; reprint, Fernandina: The Florida Mirror, 1881), n.p.

40. Ibid., 5.

41. Ibid., 6.

42. Ibid., 10.

43. Ibid., 11, 13–14.

44. Entry for January 1766, in *The Scots Magazine*, 28:50. In reality, Rolle's plantation produced little wealth and functioned as a virtual death camp for its European inhabitants. See Bailyn, Voyagers to the West, 447–61.

45. When they gained control of the Floridas from Spain following the Seven Years' War, British officials divided the region into two distinct provinces for administrative purposes. East Florida consisted of all lands east of the Apalachicola River while West Florida was comprised of lands west of the river to Spanish New Orleans and the Mississippi River. See Fabel, *Economy of British West Florida*, 1–3.

46. Entry for May 1766, in *The Scots Magazine*, 28:271.

47. Entry for June 1766, in ibid., 28:322–23.

48. Entry for January 1767, in ibid., 29:50.

49. Philip Pittman, *The Present State of the European Settlements of the Missisippi* introduction by and edited by John F. McDermott (1770; reprint, Gainesville: University Press of Florida, 1973), vi, 37.

50. John Gerar William De Brahm, *Report of the General Survey in the Southern District of North America*, edited by Louis De Vorsey, Jr. (Columbia: University of South Carolina Press, 1971), 210.

51. Letter of 27 September 1773, *New York Gazette*, in Robin Fabel, "The Letters of R: The Lower Mississippi in the Early 1770s," *Louisiana History* 1983 (24): 419.

52. Letter of 13 September 1773, ibid., 408.

Chapter 3. The Origins of Disillusionment

1. For analysis of Garcilaso de la Vega and his work, see Charles Hudson, "The Hernando de Soto Expedition, 1539–1543," in *The Forgotten Centuries: Indians and Europeans in the American South, 1521–1704*, edited by Charles Hudson and Carmen C. Tesser (Athens: University of Georgia Press, 1994), 100; Juan Marichal, "The New

World from Within: The Inca Garcilaso," in *First Images of America: The Impact of the New World on the Old*, 2 vols., edited by Freda Chiappelli (Berkeley: University of California Press, 1976), 1:57–61; Jerald T. Milanich and Charles Hudson, *Hernando de Soto and the Indians of Florida* (Gainesville: University Press of Florida, 1993), 6–7.

2. "Como toda su tierra sea casi de una misma suerte y calidad, llana y con muchos ríos que corren por ella, así todos sus naturals pueblan, visten, comen y beben casi de una misma manera . . . en sus ídolos, ritos y cermonias . . . y en sus armas, condición y ferocidad, difieren poco o nada unos de otros," Garcilaso, Obras completas del Inca Garcilaso de la Vega, 1:319; Garcilaso, *The Florida of the Inca*, Book 3, Chapter 30, 170.

3. John H. Hann, *Indians of Central and South Florida, 1513–1763* (Gainesville: University Press of Florida, 2003), 17–60; Jerald T. Milanich, *Laboring in the Fields of the Lord: Spanish Missions and Southeastern Indians* (Washington, D.C.: Smithsonian Institution Press, 1999), 41–45, 50–54.

4. See David Armitage, "The New World and British Historical Thought: From Richard Hakluyt to William Robertson," in *America in European Consciousness, 1493–1750*, edited by Karen O. Kupperman (Chapel Hill: University of North Carolina Press, 1995), 63–64; James Axtell, *The European and the Indian: Essays in the Ethnohistory of Colonial North America* (New York: Oxford University Press, 1981), 282–83; Berkhofer, *The White Man's Indian*, 15–16, 24; Canny, "The Ideology of English Colonization," 580–98; Ivan Hannaford, *Race: The History of an Idea in the West* (Baltimore: Johns Hopkins University Press, 1996), 149–50, 178, 202; Francis Jennings, *The Founders of America: From the Earliest Migrations to the Present* (New York: W. W. Norton, 1993), 82–83, 172–73; Smedley, *Race in North America*, 185.

5. Jerald T. Milanich, *Florida Indians and the Invasion from Europe* (Gainesville: University Press of Florida, 1995), 115–25.

6. Weber, *The Spanish Frontier in North America*, 376.

7. "Relation that Alvar Nunez Cabeca de Vaca gave of what befell the armament in the Indies whither Panfilo de Narvaez went for Governor from the year 1527 to the year 1536 [1537] when with three comrades he returned and came to Sevilla," in Quinn, *New American World*, 2:163.

8. Milanich, *Florida Indians and the Invasion from Europe*, 127–36.

9. "Tan bravos, fuertes y diestros son en tirar las flechas comúnmente los naturales de este gran reino de la Florida. Mas no hay de qué espantarnos, si e advierte al perpetuo ejercicio que en ellas tienen en todas edades, porque los niños de tres años, y de menos, en pudiendo andar en sus pies, movidos de su natural inclinación y de lo que continuamente ven hacer a sus padres, les piden arcos y flechas, y, cuando no se las dan, ellos mismos las hacen de los palillos que pueden haber, y con ellos andan desfenecidos tras las sabandijas que topan en casa . . . Con este ejercicio tan continuo, y por el hábito que en él tienen hecho, son tan diestos y feroces en el tirar las flechas, con las cuales hicieron tiros extrañísimos," Garcilaso, *Obras completas del Inca Garcilaso de la Vega*, 1:346–47; Garcilaso, *The Florida of the Inca*, Book 2, Chapter

2, 234. Chaplin asserts that English colonists in New England and Virginia had similar opinions about natives and child-rearing. See Chaplin, *Subject Matter*, 255, 257–59.

10. For European viewpoints on Native Americans and warfare, see Calloway, *New Worlds for All*, 92–114; Matijasic, "Reflected Values," 41–42; Daniel K. Richter, "War and Culture: The Iroquois Experience," in *American Encounters: Natives and Newcomers from European Contact to Indian Removal, 1500–1850*, edited by Peter C. Mancall and James H. Merrell (New York: Routledge, 2000), 284–85; Ian K. Steele, *Warpaths: Invasions of North America* (New York: Oxford University Press, 1994), 3–36, 151–70.

11. Luis Hernández de Biedma, *Narratives of the Career of Hernando Soto in the Conquest of Florida, as Told by a Knight of Elvas and in a Relation by Luys Hernández de Biedma, Factor of the Expedition*, 2 vols., translated by Buckingham Smith, edited by Edward G. Bourne (New York: Allerton, 1922), 1:66–67.

12. For European attitudes on Native Americans and clothing, see Matijasic, "Reflected Values," 36–38; Weber, *The Spanish Frontier in North America*, 314–15; Timothy J. Shannon, "Dressing for Success on the Mohawk Frontier: Hendrick, William Johnson, and the Indian Fashion," in *American Encounters: Natives and Newcomers from European Contact to Indian Removal, 1500–1850*, edited by Peter C. Mancall and James H. Merrell (New York: Routledge, 2000), 352–76.

13. "Es Caluza una provincia de más de noventa pueblos (no subjecta a nadie), de gente feroz, muy belicosa y muy temida," Oviedo, *Historia general y natural de las Indias*, 2:176; "The official narrative of the expedition of Hernando Soto, by Rodrigo Rangel, his secretary, as rendered by Gonzalo Fernández de Oviedo, 1539–1541," in Quinn, *New American World*, 2:178.

14. "El governador, oída la respuesta del indio, se admiró de ver que con tanta soberbia y altivez de ánimo acertase un bárbaro a decir cosas semejantes," Garcilaso, *Obras completas del Inca Garcilaso de la Vega*, 1:297; Garcilaso, *The Florida of the Inca*, Book 2, Chapter 16, 119. This text refers to the Acuera Indians, a Timucuan chiefdom located near present-day Ocala. See Milanich, *Laboring in the Fields of the Lord*, 48.

15. "Vitachuco respondió extrañisimamente, con una bravoisidad nunca jamás oída ni imaginada en indio," Garcilaso, *Obras completas del Inca Garcilaso de la Vega*, 1:303; Garcilaso, *The Florida of the Inca*, Book 2, Chapter 20, 133.

16. "Vitachuco para haber de morir, de donde se coligió que los fieros y amenazas tan extrañas que de principio había hecho, habían nacido de esta bravosidad y fiereza de ánimo, la cual, por haber sido rara, no había admitido consigo la consideración, prudencia y consejo que los hechos grandes requieren," Garcilaso, *Obras completas del Inca Garcilaso de la Vega*, 1:317; Garcilaso, *The Florida of the Inca*, Book 2, Chapter 28, 163–64.

17. Paul E. Hoffman, *A New Way to Andalucia and a Way to the Orient: The American Southeast During the Sixteenth Century* (Baton Rouge: Louisiana State University Press, 1990), 100–101.

18. "Sabe Nuestro Señor quanto nos holgamos de verlos en tanta paz como nos mostravan, que de tantos abrazados estava bien almagrado, y aque ello i mas sufriera en los avitos porque dejasen la carne segura: yo por ver si estava libre i me dejarian ir a la chalupa, use desia cautela que les dije que tenia mas que les dar i que iva por ello, i en la verdad ya yo lo tenia en la manga, sino lo quise dar todo porque tenia intento de hacer esto: fui i bolvi i halle tantos que me venian abrazar, que no me podia apartar dellos: su amor i amicia cierto de creer es que era mas por lo que pensavan haver que por nosotros, en pero como esto es camino destotro, segun todos esperimentamos i decimos que obras son amores i dadivas quebrantan peñas, holgue que nos hiciesen buen recivimiento por aquello temporal," Buckingham Smith, *Coleccion de varios documentos para la historia de la Florida y tierras adyacentes* (Londres, Argentina: Trübner, 1857), 193–94; "The mission of Fray Luís Cancer to Florida as told by Beteta, 1549," in Quinn, *New American World*, 2:192.

19. Eugene Lyon, "Settlement and Survival," in *The New History of Florida*, edited by Michael Gannon (Gainesville: University Press of Florida, 1996), 40–46.

20. "Ills sont grands dissimulateurs et traistres . . . Ces Prestres . . . ils portent tousjours avec eux un plein sac d'herbes et de drogues, pour medeciner les maladies qui sont la p uspart de verole: car ils aiment fort les femmes et les filles qu'ils appellent filles du Soleil: toutesfois quelques uns sont Sodomites," Lussagnet, *Le Français en Floride*, 42–44; René de Laudonnière, *Histoire Notable de la Floride. A Foothold in Florida: The Eye-Witness Account of Four Voyages Made by the French to that Region and Their Attempt at Colonization, 1562–1568*, translated by Sarah Lawson (East Grinstead, N.Y.: Antique Atlas 1992), 7–8. For analysis of European attitudes toward natives and gender during the colonial period see Linda L. Sturtz, "Spanish Moss and Aprons: European Responses to Gender Ambiguity in the Exploration and Colonization of South-eastern North America," *Seventeenth Century* 11 (1996): 125–40.

21. "Et proposerent lors à tous leurs subjets, la briefve diligence dont il convenoit user à bastir une autre maison, leur monstrans que les François leur estoient affectionnez amys, et qu'ils leur avoient fait paroistre par les dons et presens qu'ils en avoient receuz: protestant que celuy qui de tout son pouvoir n'y tiendroit la main, seroit tenu comme inutile, et comme n'ayant rien de bon en luy (ce que ces Barbares craignent entre toutes autres choses). Cela fut cause qu'un chacun commença á s'esvertuer," Lussagnet, *Le Français en Floride*, 74; Laudonnière, *Histoire Notable de la Floride*, 39.

22. "Copy of a Letter Coming from Florida, Sent to Roen and then to M. D'Everon, Together with the Plan and Picture of the Fort Which the French Build There, 1564," in Bennett, *Laudonniére and Fort Caroline*, 67.

23. "Quant aux moeurs, ils sont dissolus, ils n'enseignent point leurs enfans et ne les corrigent aucunement, ils prennent sans conscience, et s'attribuent tout ce que ils peuvent secrettement emporter," Lussagnet, *Le Français en Floride*, 211–12; "Discours de l'histoire de la Floride, 1566," in Quinn, *New American World*, 2:373.

24. Hoffman, *A New Andalucia and a Way to the Orient*, 222.

25. "John Sparke's report on Florida, 2 July 1565," in Quinn, *New American World*, 2:365–66.

26. Lyon, "Settlement and Survival," 43–59.

27. "Ni los indios por ser Muy gerreros no consentillos ni querer trauar Amistad Con los xpistianos . . . de los indios, que no tienen ningun genero de aspereza, sino yrse tras sus sensualidad y deleytes bestiales," "Of the Reasons Furnished His Majesty by Pedro Menéndez for not Allowing Florida to Fall into the Hands of Lutherans or Other Foreigners, 1567," in Barrientos, *Pedro Menéndez de Avilés*, Section I, 27–28; Section II, 28–29.

28. "Pedro Menéndez' Letter to Philip II, Describing French in Florida and Their Relationships to Local Indians, 15 October 1565," in Eugene Lyon, *Pedro Menéndez de Avilés* (New York: Garland, 1995), 165.

29. "El estilo y horden que se puede otener Con ellos para hacer que cumplan sus palabras, porq son muy grades mentirosos y traydores para hacerles Rendir, es yr a buscar sus pueblos, quemalles las casas, Cortarles las sementeras y tomarles las canoas y de Rocar las pesqueras: Entonces les Es forzado, o dejar la tierra, o hacer lo que los christianos hicieren. . . son indios de mal arte y traydores Estos de los puertos de S Matheo y sant agustin, porq se hacen amigos de los xpistianos por los intereses q pretenden dellos: ban a los fuertes, y si no les dan de comver, bestidos, hachas de hierro y Rescates, banse muy enojados, Rompen la guerra, matan los xpistianos q hallan," "Of the Adelantado's Departure from Guale to San Mateo and St. Augustine, 1567," in Barrientos, *Pedro Menéndez de Avilés*, Section I, 107; Section II, 112–13.

30. "Son los indios de muy buen Entendim y no tan Rusticos y saluages como los demas, y ansí tienen costumbres: conforme a su justicia, Castigan al que miente, Aunque todos los indios son grandes mentirosos, y abominan de los ladrones," in Barrientos, *Pedro Menéndez de Avilés*, Section I, 26; Section II, 27; "Bartolomé Barrientos on Pedro Menéndez' successful attack on the French colony, 1565," in Quinn, *New American World*, 2:458.

31. "Los indios, de ver el desastre que nos avía venido y el desastre en que estávamos con tanta desventura y miseria, se sentaron entre nosotros. Y con el gran dolor y lástima que huvieron de vernos en tanta fortuna, començaron todos a llorar rezio y tan de verdad que lexos de allí se podía oír. Y esto les duró más de media ora, y cierto ver que estos hombres, tan sin razón y tan crudos a manera de brutos, se dolían tanto de nosotros, hizo que en mí y en otros de la compañía cresçiesse más la passión y la consideración de nuestra desdicha," Rolena Adorno and Patrick Charles Pautz, eds., *Álvar Núñez Cabeza de Vaca: His Account, His Life, and the Expedition of Pánfilo de Narváez*, 3 vols. (Lincoln: University of Nebraska Press, 1999), 1:98, 100; "Relation that Alvar Núñez Cabeca de Vaca gave of what befell the armament in the Indies whither Pánfilo de Narváez went for Governor from the year 1527 to the year 1536 when with three Comrades he returned and came to Sevilla," in Quinn, *New American World*, 2:29.

32. "Les voilles furent incontinent appareillez, et navigasmes vers la grande riviere.

Mais ces deux Indiens, voyans que ne faisions aucun semblant de mettre pied en terre, ains seulement que poursuyvre le meilleu du courant, commencerent un peu à se fascher, et à toute force se vouloient jetter en l'eau: car ils sont si accords à nager, que tout incontinent ils eussent gaigné les forests. Toutefois cognoissans leur humeur, nous y prismes garde de pres, et essayasmes par tous moyens de les contenter: ce qu'il ne nous estoit possible pour lors, jaçoit qu'on leur presentast choses qu'ils estimoient beaucoup: lesquelles ils desdaignoient prendre, et rendoient à l'opposite tout ce qu'on leur avoit donné, pensans que tels dons les eussent du tout obligez, et qu'en les rendant, la liberté leur seroit octroyee," Lussagnet, *Le Français en Floride*, 58; Laudonnière, *Histoire Notable de la Floride*, 27–28.

33. Michael Gannon, "First European Contacts," in *The New History of Florida*, edited by Michael Gannon (Gainesville: University Press of Florida, 1996), 20; "Antonio de Alaminos guides Hernández de Cordoba's fleet to Florida, 1517," in Quinn, *New American World*, 1:243.

34. "La gente que allí hallamos son grandes y bien dispuestos . . . Tienen los hombres la una teta horadada de una parte a otra y algunos ay que las tienen ambas . . . Traen también horadado el labio de abaxo y puesto en él un pedaço de la caña delgada como medio dedo," Adorno and Pautz, *Álvar Núñez Cabeza de Vaca*, 1:106, 108; "Herrera's account of the breakup of the Narváez expedition, 1528," in Quinn, *New American World*, 2:11–13.

35. "Quantos indios vimos desde la Florida aquí todos son flecheros, y como son crescidos de cuerpo y andan desnudos, desde lexos paresçen gigantes. Es gente a maravilla bien dispuesta, muy enxutos y de muy grandes fuerças y ligereza," Adorno and Pautz, *Álvar Núñez Cabeza de Vaca*, 1:62; Fanny Bandelier, trans. and ed., *The Journey of Alvar Núñez Cabeza de Vaca and His Companions from Florida to the Pacific* (New York: A. S. Barnes, 1905), 31–32. Also see "Relation that Alvar Núñez Cabeca de Vaca Gave of what befell the armament in the Indies whither Pánfilo de Narváez went for Governor from the year 1527 to the year 1536 when with three comrades he returned and came to Sevilla," in Quinn, *New American World*, 2:23.

36. "Os indios sam bè propozcionados: os vas terras chèas lam mais altos o corpos y milboz des poltos q os vas ferras os do sartam sam mais abastados de mays y roupa va terra q os . . . costa;" Gentleman of Elvas, *True Relation of the Hardships Suffered by Governor Fernando de Soto & Certain Portuguese Gentlemen*, 2:312–13, n.p.

37. "Alonso de Carmona . . . nota particularmente la ferocidad de los inidios de la provincia de Apalache, de los cuales dice estas palabras que son sacadas a la letra: 'Estos indios de Apalache son de grande estatura y muy valientes y animosos . . . no les estorban los aderezos de las ropas, antes les ayuda mucho el andar desnudos,'" Garcilaso, *Obras completas del Inca Garcilaso de la Vega*, 1:357; Garcilaso, *The Florida of the Inca*, Book 2, Chapter 25, 258–59.

38. "Ils n'ont aucun accoustrement, non plus les hommes que les femmes: mais la femme ceint un petit voile de pellisse de Ciof ou d'autre animal, le noeud batant le

costé gauche sur la cuisse, pour couvrir la partie de sa nature la plus honteuse . . . ils ne sont ne camus ne lippus, ains ont le visage rond et plain, les yeux aspres et vigoureux," Lussagnet, *Le Français en Floride*, 211; "Discours de l'histoire de la Florida, 1566," in Quinn, *New American World*, 2:372–73.

39. "Copy of a Letter Coming from Florida, Sent to Roen and then to M. D'Everon, Together with the Plan and Picture of the Fort Which the French Build There, 1564," in Bennett, *Laudonniére and Fort Caroline* 67.

40. "Les homes . . . de grande corporance, beaux sans aucune difformité et bien proportionnez . . . Ils portent les cheveux fort noirs et longs jusques sur la hanche, toutesfois ils les troussent d'une façon qui leur est bien senate . . . qui est un des plus hauts hommes et des mieux formez qui se puisse trouver . . . l'Indienne beauté," Lussagnet, *Le Français en Floride*, 42, 94; Laudonnière, *Histoire Notable de la Floride*, 8.

41. "Ils sont entièrement nus et d'une belle stature, puissants, beaux, et aussi bien bâtis et proportionnés qu'aucun peuple au monde, très doux, courtois et de bon naturel," Lussagnet, *Le Français en Floride*, 9; Jean Ribault, *The Whole and True Discovery of Terra Florida* (1563; reprint, Deland: Florida Historical Society, 1927), 69; Hoffman, *A New Andalucia and a Way to the Orient*, 206–15.

42. "Ils se peignent fort le visage, et s'emplissent les cheveux de dumel pour apparoistre plus effroyables," Lussagnet, *Le Français en Floride*, 45; Laudonnière, *Histoire Notable de la Floride*, 8.

43. "John Sparke's report on Florida, 2 July 1565," in Quinn, *New American World*, 2:365.

44. "Es grande de cuerpo y muy flechera, Enjuta y de grandes fuerzas y ligereza," Barrientos, *Pedro Menéndez de Avilés*, Section I, 24; Section II, 25.

45. "Y que todos andauan desnudos hechos saluages como los mesmos indios," Barrientos, Pedro Menéndez de Avilés, Section I, 81; Section II, 85; "Gonzalo Solis de Meras on the achievements of Menéndez de Avilés in Florida," in Quinn, *New American World*, 2:479.

46. "Que de tantos abrazados estava bien almagrado, y aque ello I mas sufriera en los avitos porque dejasen la carne segura," Smith, *Coleccion de varios documentos para la historia de la Florida y tierras adyacentes*, 193; "The mission of Fray Luís Cancer to Florida as told by Beteta, 1529," in Quinn, *New American World*, 2:192.

47. Hernández de Biedma, *Narratives of the Career of Hernando Soto*, 1:66–67.

48. "Fueron a otra sabana, donde tenían los indios fecha una albarrada muy fuerte, y dentro della muchos indios de Guerra muy embijados y pintados todos de colores que parescían muy bien (y aun parescían mal, o a lo menos les eran dañosos a los cristianos)," Oviedo, Historia general y natural de las Indias, 2:177–78; "The official narrative of the expedition of Hernando de Soto, by Rodrigo Rangel, his secretary, as rendered by Gonzalo Fernández de Oviedo, 1539–1541," in Quinn, *New American World*, 2:160.

49. For assessments on how Native American skin color became identified as red during the colonial period, see Jack D. Forbes, *Africans and Native Americans: The*

Language of Race and the Evolution of Black Peoples (Chicago: University of Illinois Press, 1993), 239–64; Nancy Shoemaker, "How Indians Got to Be Red," *American Historical Review* 102, no. 3 (June 1997): 625–44.

50. "Ils sont de couleur tannée," Lussagnet, *Le Français en Floride*, 10; Ribault, 69.

51. "Et d'un taint tirant au rouge," Lussagnet, *Le Français en Floride*, 211; "Discours de l'histoire de la Floride," in Quinn, *New American World*, 2:372–73.

52. "Les hommes sont de couleur olivastre . . . La pluspart d'eux sont peints par le corps, par les bras et cuisses de fort beaux compartimens, la peinture desquels ne se peut jamais oster, à cause qu'ils sont picquez dedans la chair," Lussagnet, *Le Français en Floride*, 42; Laudonnière, *Histoire Notable de la Floride*, 7.

53. "Copy of a Letter Coming From Florida, Sent to Rouen and Then to M. D'Everon, Together with the Plan and Picture of the Fort Which the French Built There," in Bennett, *Laudonniére and Fort Caroline* 67.

54. "Porque comúnmente son tenidos por gente simple, sin razón ni entendimiento, y que en paz y en guerra se han poco más que bestias, y que, conforme a esto, no pudieron hacer ni decir cosas dignas de mermoria y encarecimiento," Garcilaso, *Obras completas del Inca Garcilaso de la Vega*, 1:314; Garcilaso, *The Florida of the Inca*, Book 2, Chapter 27, 2:157–58.

55. "Et d'autant que le desir de se venger est naturellement planté au coeur de l'homme, mesmes aussi l'appetit commun à tous animaux de se deffendre, son corps et sa vie, et de destourner les choses qui semblent apporter quelque nuisance, il ne faut douter que ce sauvage ne complota et practiqua avec l' Espagnol, comme il se pourroit delivrer de ceste gent," Lussagnet, *Le Français en Floride*, 215; "Discours de l'histoire de la Floride, 1566," in Quinn, *New American World*, 2:374.

56. "Y en disparando El soldado El arcabuz; sale El indio como a nadon en el agua A diferente parte de aquella a donde le hicieron la punteria: y son En esto tan Mañosos y diestros y industriosos, q pone Espanto: pelean escaramuzando y saltando por encima de las matas Como corzos . . . y como andan desnudos y nadan como peces . . . pasados de la otra parte gritan y se Rien de los xpistianos," "Of the Adelantado's Departure from Guale to San Mateo and St. Augustine," in Barrientos, *Pedro Menéndez de Avilés*, Section I, 107; Section II; 113.

57. Gannon, "First European Contacts," 17–21.

58. "Pero el temple de la región era muy diferente e desconviniente a lo que él llevaba imaginado, e los naturales de la tierra gente muy áspera e muy salvaje e belicosa, e feroz e indómita . . . de pensar es que no era Dios servido ni el tiempo llegado de la conversión de aquella tierra e provincia a nuestra sancta fe católica, pues permite que el diablo aún los tenga engañados e por suyos a aquellos indios, e que se aumente la población infernal con sus ánimas," Oviedo, *Historia general y natural de las Indias*, 4:321; "Oviedo on Juan Ponce de León's second voyage, 1521," in Quinn, *New American World*, 1:247.

59. "Nosotros, vista la pobreza de la tierra y las malas nuevas que de la poblaçión . . . y como los indios nos hazían continua Guerra . . . acordamos de partir de allí e

ir a buscar la mar," Adorno and Pautz, *Álvar Núñez Cabeza de Vaca*, 1:60; "Relation that Alvar Núñez Cabeca de Vaca gave of what befell the armament in the Indies whither Pánfilo de Narváez went for Governor from the year 1527 to the Year 1536 when with three comrades he returned and came to Sevilla," in Quinn, *New American World*, 2:23.

60. "Con tales nuevas. . .concluirian. . .todos estos Infieles dignos de muerte i merecedores que los viniesen a hacer Guerra," Smith, *Coleccion de varios documentos para la historia de la Florida y tierras adyacentes*, 196; "The mission of Fray Luís Cancer to Florida as told by Beteta, 1529," in Quinn, *New American World*, 2:194.

61. "Là ils apportoient leur poisson dans leurs petites almadies, jusques ausquelles nos pauvres soldats estoient contraints aller, et le plus souvent (ainsi que j'ay veu) se despouiller de leur propre chemise pour avoir un poisson. Que si quelque fois ils remonstroient aux sauvage, le pris excessif qu'ils prenoient, ces meschans leur respondirent brusquement: Si tu fais si grand cas de ta merchandise, mange là, et nous mangerons nostre poisson, puis ils s'esclatoient de rire, et se mocquoient de nous à gueule bee. Dont nos soldats perdans toute patience, eurent souvent envie de les mettre en pieces, et leur faire payer le tribut de leur folle arrogance," Lussagnet, *Le Français en Floride*, 144–45; Laudonnière, *Histoire Notable de la Floride*, 105–6.

62. "The Adelantado, Pedro Menéndez, Reports the Damages and Murders Caused by the Coast Indians of Florida, 1573–1574," in *Colonial Records of Spanish Florida: Letters and Reports of Governors and Secular Persons*, edited and translated by Jeannette T. Connor (Deland: Florida State Historical Society, 1925), 35–36; "Pedro Menéndez de Avilés provides detailed plans for the disposal of the enslaved Florida Indians, 1573," in Quinn, *New American World*, 2:589–90.

Chapter 4. Paradoxical Images

1. For detailed examinations of Spanish efforts to Christianize the Floridas, see Amy Turner Bushnell, *Situado and Sabana: Spain's Support System for the Presidio and Mission Provinces of Florida* (Athens: University of Georgia Press, 1994); Michael V. Gannon, *The Cross in the Sand: The Early Catholic Church in Florida, 1513–1570* (Gainesville: University Press of Florida, 1965); Maynard J. Geiger, *The Franciscan Conquest of Florida (1573–1618)* (Washington, D.C.: Catholic University of America, 1937); Hann, *Apalachee*; Kathleen Hoffman, "Cultural Development in La Florida," *Historical Archaeology* 31, no. 1 (spring 1997): 24–35; McEwan, *The Spanish Missions of La Florida*; Milanich, *Laboring in the Fields of the Lord*; David J. Weber, "Blood of Martyrs, Blood of Indians: Toward a More Balanced View of Spanish Missions in Seventeenth Century North America," in *Columbian Consequences*, 3 vols., edited by David Thomas Hurst (Washington, D.C.: Smithsonian Institution Press, 1990), 2:429–48.

2. Bushnell, *Situado and Sabana*, 121–24; Hoffman, *Florida's Frontiers*, 146–47; Weber, *The Spanish Frontier in North America*, 100–21.

3. Weber, *The Spanish Frontier in North America*, 141–45.

4. For a concise overview of historiographical debates regarding missionization in the Floridas, see Bushnell, *Situado and Sabana*, 20–28.

5. Milanich, *Laboring in the Fields of the Lord*, 160, 189.

6. For European views on native paganism/heathenism, see Berkhofer, *The White Man's Indian*, 34–38; Matijasic, "Reflected Values," 32–36; Gregory H. Nobles, *American Frontiers: Cultural Encounters and Continental Conquest* (New York: Hill and Wang, 1997), 29; Michael L. Oberg, *Dominion and Civility: English Imperialism and Native America, 1585–1685* (Ithaca, N.Y.: Cornell University Press, 1999), 20; Roy H. Pearce, *Savagism and Civilization: A Study of the Indian and the American Mind* (Berkeley: University of California Press, 1988), 4–8; Weber, *The Spanish Frontier in North America*, 20–24.

7. "De quelques circonstances que facilement on les pourroit dresser, non seulement a civilité et honnesteté, mais aussi a sainteté et religion, si le decret du Seigneur le permettoit," Lussagnet, *Le Français en Floride*, 213–14; "Discours de l'histoire de la Floride, 1566," in Quinn, *New American World*, 2:373.

8. "Gonzalo Solis de Mera's account of Pedro Menéndez de Avilés' attack on the French fort in Florida, 1565," in Quinn, *New American World*, 2:426.

9. Milanich, *Laboring in the Fields of the Lord*, 93–97.

10. Father Juan Rogel to Father Jerónimo Ruiz del Portillo, 25 April 1568, in *Missions to the Calusas*, translated and edited by John Hann (Gainesville: University Press of Florida, 1991), 259.

11. "Autos of Don Juan García de Palacios, Bishop of Santiago de Cuba, August-December 1682," in ibid., 52, 56.

12. "Account of Father Fray Alonso de Posada, Representative of Viceroy of New Spain, Report of 14 March 1686," in *Alonso de Posada, Alonso de Posada Report, 1686: A Description of the Area of the Present Southern United States in the Late Seventeenth Century*, translated and edited by Barnaby Thomas (Pensacola, Fla.: Perdido Bay Press, 1982), 49.

13. Don Diego Ebelino de Compostela, Bishop of Santiago de Cuba, to the Dean and Chapter of Holy Cathedral Church of Santiago de Cuba, 2 January 1690, in Hann, *Missions to the Calusas*, 87–88.

14. Comparable situations emerged in other areas colonized by the Spanish. See Miguel Leon-Portilla, *Endangered Cultures*, translated by Julie Goodson-Lawes (Dallas: Southern Methodist University Press, 1990), 55–64, 81–83.

15. Themes of disillusionment and dedication to duty characterized Spanish missionary writings throughout North America. Such expressions educated skeptical church and government officials in Spain while emphasizing the unwavering sacrifice and dedication of missionaries. Racialized depictions further illustrated the obstacles priests faced among Indians and justified their claims of day-to-day symbolic martyrdom and potential literal martyrdom. Thus, racialization and its extended impact provided added incentive for missionaries to continue their efforts instead of dis-

couraging them. See Weber, *The Spanish Frontier in North America*, 106–7, 120–21; and Ramón A. Gutiérrez, *When Jesus Came, the Corn Mothers Went Away: Marriage, Sexuality, and Power in New Mexico, 1500–1846* (Stanford, Calif.: Stanford University Press, 1991), 128–30.

16. Hernández de Biedma, *Narratives of the Career of Hernando de Soto* , 1:29–30; "Como elles sam ser vos do diabo tem poz cuitume ose recer lbe almas y fangue de seus indios, ou doutra qualquer gente que podè aver," Gentleman of Elvas, *True Relation of the Hardships Suffered by Governor Fernando de Soto & Certain Portuguese Gentlemen*, 2:42, n.p.

17. "Padilla's account of Coosa, 1560," in Quinn, *New American World*, 2:243.

18. "Ils n'ont cognoissance de Dieu ny d'aucune religion, sinon, que ce qui leur apparoist comme le Soleil et la Lune. Ils ont leurs Prestres ausquels ils croient fort, pour autant qu'ils sont grands magiciens, grands devins et invocateurs de Diables," in Lussagnet, *Le Français en Floride*, 43; Laudonnière, *Histoire Notable de la Floride*, 8.

19. "Customs of the Indians in Florida, 1566," in Quinn, *New American World*, 2:539; "Memorial of Juan Lopez de Velasco, 1569(?)," in Hann, *Missions to the Calusas*, 316.

20. "Florida Indians Customs," in Lyon, *Pedro Menéndez de Avilés*, 324.

21. Pedro Menéndez de Avilés to a Jesuit, 15 October 1566, in Quinn, *New American World*, 2:536–37.

22. Fray Feliciano Lopez to Fray Pedro Taybo, 1697, in Hann, *Missions to the Calusas*, 159–61.

23. "Capitulations between Charles V and Pánfilo de Narváez for the conquest of the land between the Rio de las Palmas and Florida, 11 December 1526," in Quinn, *New American World*, 2:7–9.

24. " Indigno de haber nacido y de vivir en la bárbara gentilidad de aquella tierra," Garcilaso, *Obras completas del Inca Garcilaso de la Vega*, 1:279; Garcilaso, *The Florida of the Inca*, Book 2, Chapter 4, 73–74.

25. "Estos indios son gentiles de nación e idólatras. Adoran al Sol y a la Luna pro principales dioses . . . Andan desnudos. Solamente traen unos pañetes de gamuza . . . que les cubre honestamente todo lo necesario por delante y atrás," Garcilaso, *Obras completas del Inca Garcilaso de la Vega*, 1:255–56; Garcilaso, *The Florida of the Inca*, Book 1, Chapter 4, 13–18.

26. "Pedro Menéndez' Letter to a Jesuit Friend at Cadiz, 15 October 1566," in Lyon, *Pedro Menéndez de Avilés*, 324.

27. "No conociendo ni temiendo a dios ni sabiendo . . . por esto los luteranos facilmente, Con su mala seta, tiranizararian todas aquellas prouincias, por ser los naturales dellas saluajes y sin lumbre de fe," "Of the Reasons Furnished His Majesty by Pedro Menéndez for Not Allowing Florida to Fall into the Hands of Lutherans or Other Foreigners, 1567," in Barrientos, *Pedro Menéndez de Avilés*, Section I, 28; Section II, 29. At the time, the term *Lutheran* was commonly used in reference to all Protestants.

28. Father Juan Rogel to Father Jerónimo Ruiz del Portillo, 25 April 1568, in Hann, *Missions to the Calusas*, 235–36, 250, 258–59.

29. Lyon, "Settlement and Survival," 56–57.

30. Father Luis Hieronimo de Ore, "An Account of the Martyrs of the Provinces of Florida: Twelve Religious of the Society of Jesus, Who Suffered in Jacan, and Five of the Order of Our Seraphic Father Saint Francis, in the Province of Guale. Offered Also, is a Description of Jacan Where the English Have Fortified Themselves; and of Other Matters Relative to the Conversion of the Indians," in *Spanish Borderlands Sourcebooks: The Missions of Spanish Florida*, edited by David H. Thomas (New York: Garland, 1991), 23:72, 91–92.

31. James W. Covington and A. F. Falcones, eds., *Pirates, Indians, and Spaniards: Father Escobedo's "La Florida"* (St. Petersburg, Fla.: Great Outdoors Publishing, 1963), 22, 28.

32. Other possible reasons for the revolt include the resistance of natives to Spanish demands for tribute, the restrictions missionaries placed on movement of natives between villages, and the interference of priests in traditional leadership structures. See Hoffman, *Florida's Frontiers*, 82–83.

33. Thomas, *Spanish Borderlands Sourcebooks*, 23:121–22, 136.

34. "Inquiry by Gonzalo Méndez de Canzo into the Indian uprising of 1597 and his actions in regard to the Indians Who took part in it, 7 October 1597 to 12 January 1598," in Quinn, *New American World*, 5:78.

35. "Report of Juan Menéndez Marquéz to the King, 5 January 1608," in *The Unwritten History of St. Augustine, Copied from the Spanish Archives in Seville, Spain*, edited by Abbie M. Brooks (St. Augustine: The Record Co., 1909), 77.

36. Letter of Alonso de Alas to the King, 23 November 1609, in "Translation of the Ecija Voyages of 1605 and 1609 and the Gonzalez Derrotero of 1609," in John H. Hann, *Spanish Translations: The History of Florida's Spanish Mission Period* (Tallahassee: Bureau of Archaeological Research, 1986), 20.

37. The Franciscans of Florida to Phillip III, 16 October 1612, in Quinn, *New American World*, 5:138–40.

38. Letters of Apalachee Friars, 10 May 1657, in *Visitations and Revolts in Florida, 1656–1695*, edited by John H. Hann (Tallahassee: Florida Bureau of Archaeological Research, 1993), 17.

39. "Characteristics of the Christianized Indians," in Gabriel Díaz Vara Calderón, *A Seventeenth-Century Letter of Gabriel Díaz Vara Calderón, Bishop of Cuba, Describing the Indians and Indian Missions of Florida*, translated and edited by Lucy L. Wenhold (Washington, D.C.: Smithsonian Institution, 1936), 12–14.

40. Governor Laureano de Torres y Ayala to the King, 3 February 1697, in Hann, *Missions to the Calusas*, 143.

41. "Notes by the Council of the Indies, 8 August 1698," in ibid., 210–11.

42. "Memorial to the King Our Lord and His Royal and Supreme Council of the

Indies in which a Report is Given of the State in which the Presidio of St. Augustine Happens to Be. . . ., 1700?," in Hann, *Spanish Translations*, 199–200.

43. Governor Zuniga to the King, 15 September 1704, in *Here They Once Stood: The Tragic End of the Apalachee Missions*, edited by Mark F. Boyd, Hale G. Smith, and John W. Griffin (Gainesville: University Press of Florida, 1952), 68.

44. Fray Joseph de Bullones to the King, 5 October 1728, in Hann, *Missions to the Calusas*, 377.

45. "Report on the Indians of Southern Florida and Its Keys by Joseph Maria Monaco and Joseph Javier Alana Presented to Governor Juan Francisco de Güermes y Horcasitas, 1760," in ibid., 419.

46. Ibid., 422–24, 427.

47. "Ni en election de aquellos frailes e clérigos de que iba acompañado para el ejercicio del culto divino e servicio de la iglesia, aunque predicasen cuanto quisiesen, ni pudieran ser entendidos con la brevedad que se les figuraba a ellos e al que allá los llevó, si Dios, de poder absoluto, no los hiciera ser entendidos de aquellas gentes barbarísimas e salvajes idólatras, e colmadas de delictos e vicios," Oviedo, *Historia general y natural de las Indias*, 4:321; "Oviedo on Juan Ponce de León's second voyage, 1521," in Quinn, *New American World*, 1:247.

48. "Capitulations between Charles V and Panfilo de Narváez for the conquest of the land between the Rio de las Palmas and Florida, 11 December 1526," in Quinn, *New American World*, 2:8.

49. Covington, 87.

50. "Sin quererlos oir . . . que gente tan bárbara e inhumana no quiere oir sermons," Garcilaso, *Obras completas del Inca Garcilaso de la Vega*, 1:255; Garcilaso, *The Florida of the Inca*, Book 1, Chapter 4, 13–18.

51. "Letters from the Licenciado Gonzalo de Esquivel to Cardinal Espinosa about the Florida Mission of the Jesuit Order," in Lyon, *Pedro Menéndez de Avilés*, 411.

52. Father Juan Rogel to Father Didacus Avellaneda, November 1566 to January 1567, in Hann, *Missions to the Calusas*, 280–81.

53. Father Juan Rogel to Father Jerónimo Ruiz del Portillo, 25 April 1568, in ibid., 239.

54. "The Discovery of Jacan, and the Martyrdom of Twelve Religious of the Society of Jesus," in Thomas, *Spanish Borderlands Sourcebooks*, 23:70.

55. "The Appointment of Pedro Menéndez Marquéz; the Religious of St. Francis Who Set Out for the Conversion of the Natives; and an Account of Jacan," in ibid., 91–92.

56. "Porque en su platica los entendi que no fuera lijitimo el bautismo en ellos que fueran herejes como se an alsado," Fontaneda Hernando D'Escalante, *Memoire of D'Escalante Fontaneda Respecting Florida. Written in Spain, About the Year 1575*, translated by Buckingham Smith, edited by David O. True (Coral Gables, Fla.: University of Miami Press, 1944), 17, 70.

57. "Los cojan A Buena manera conbidandoles la pas y metellos debajo de las cubiertas A mari dos y mugeres y Repartillos por Vasallos A las yslas y avn en tierra firme por dineros como Algunos señores en españa conpran Al Rei basallos y desta manera Abria maña y amenguandolos y esto digo que seria cosa Asertada," in ibid., 21, 74.

58. Milanich, *Laboring in the Fields of the Lord*, 112–14.

59. "Inquiry by Gonzalo Méndez de Canzo into the Indian Uprising of 1597 and his Actions in regard to the Indians who took part in it, 7 October 1597 to 12 January 1598," in Quinn, *New American World*, 2:85–86.

60. "Bartolomé de Argüelles' reports to the king and to the Council of the Indies on the situation in Florida, 3 August 1598," in ibid., 2:90.

61. "Patron Letter from Fray Francisco Pareja, of the San Franciscan Order to the King, 1600," in Brooks, *The Unwritten History of St. Augustine*, 49.

62. "Report on the Florida Missions by Father Juan Rogel, 1608–1611," in Hann, *Missions to the Calusas*, 287.

63. The Franciscans of Florida to Philip III, 16 October 1612, in Quinn, *New American World*, 5:138–40.

64. "Council of the Indies, 15 June 1657," in Hann, *Spanish Translations*, 133–34.

65. "Letter of the Religious of the Province of Santa Elena to H. M. in Complaint About the Evil Conduct and Affronts Done to Those Natives by the Governor of Florida Don Diego de Rebolledo, 10 September 1657," in Hann, *Visitations and Revolts in Florida*, 13.

66. "Letter of the Apalachee Friars, 15 July 1657," in ibid., 23.

67. Milanich, *Laboring in the Fields of the Lord*, 166.

68. Governor Hita Salazar to Queen, 24 August 1675, in Hann, *Visitations and Revolts in Florida*, 42.

69. Governor Diego de Quiroga y Losada to the King, 1 April 1688, in Hann, *Missions to the Calusas*, 79–80.

70. Diego Ebelino de Compostela, Bishop of Santiago de Cuba, to the King, 10 February 1689, in ibid., 76.

71. Milanich, *Laboring in the Fields of the Lord*, 168.

72. Governor Laureano de Torres y Ayala to the King, 3 February 1697, in Hann, *Missions to the Calusas*, 144.

73. Fray Feliciano Lopez to Fray Pedro Taybo, 1697, in ibid., 158–59.

74. "Testimony about the Calusa Mission's Failure, 1698"; "Notes by the Council of the Indies, 8 August 1698," both in ibid., 165–67, 209–10.

75. "Memorial to the King our Lord and His Royal and Supreme Council of the Indies . . .," in Hann, *Spanish Translations*, 177–78.

76. Fray Joseph de Bullones to the King, 5 October 1728, in Hann, *Missions to the Calusas*, 374–75.

77. Governor Dioniso Martines de la Vega to the King, 7 July 1732, in ibid., 382–83.

78. "Report on the Indians of Southern Florida and Its Keys by Joseph Maria Monaco and Joseph Javier Alana presented to Governor Juan Francisco de Güemes y Horcasitas, 1760," in ibid., 424–25, 430–31.

Chapter 5. Reevaluating the Western Floridas

1. Notable works on French colonization in this region include Mathé Allain, *"Not Worth a Straw": French Colonial Policy and the Early Years of Louisiana* (Lafayette: The Center for Louisiana Studies, 1988); Patricia Galloway, ed., *La Salle and His Legacy: Frenchmen and Indians in the Lower Mississippi Valley* (Jackson: University Press of Mississippi, 1982); John R. Swanton, *Indian Tribes of the Lower Mississippi Valley and the Adjacent Coast of the Gulf of Mexico, Bureau of American Ethnology Bulletin* 43 (Washington, D.C.: Government Printing Office, 1911); Daniel H. Usner, Jr., *American Indians in the Lower Mississippi Valley: Social and Economic Histories* (Lincoln: University of Nebraska Press, 1998); and Patricia D. Woods, *French-Indian Relations on the Southern Frontier, 1699–1762* (Ann Arbor, Mich.: University Microfilms International Research Press, 1980).

2. This perspective originates in part from a thesis offered by Daniel H. Usner, Jr. in his paradigm-shifting study *Indians, Settlers, & Slaves in a Frontier Exchange Economy: The Lower Mississippi Valley before 1783* (Chapel Hill: University of North Carolina Press, 1992). In this work, Usner challenged the marginalization of the Gulf South in colonial historiography and historians' emphasis on imperial competition in the region to the neglect of social, cultural, and economic interaction. Claiming that frontiers in the area were "networks of cross-cultural interaction," he called for a new focus on the Gulf borderlands that minimized constantly changing colonial demarcations. Specifically, the "persistence of frontier exchange across the political boundary can too easily be overlooked when Louisiana and West Florida are treated separately" (2–8). Using Usner's premise, the present study treats the Gulf South east of the Mississippi River as culturally influenced by peninsular Florida regardless of imperial borders, especially in terms of social development and historical continuity.

3. Works supporting this theory include Colin G. Calloway, "Neither White Nor Red: White Renegades on the American Indian Frontier," *Western Historical Quarterly* 17, no. 1 (January 1986): 46; Eccles, *France in America*, 41; John M. Faragher, "'More Motley than Mackinaw': From Ethnic Mixing to Ethnic Cleansing on the Frontier of the Lower Missouri, 1783–1833," in *Contact Points: American Frontiers from the Mohawk Valley to the Mississippi, 1750–1830*, edited by Andrew R. L. Cayton and Fredrika J. Teute (Chapel Hill: University of North Carolina Press, 1998), 305; Richard White, *The Middle Ground: Indians, Empires, and Republics in the Great Lakes Region, 1650–1815* (New York: Cambridge University Press, 1991), 341–42.

4. It is important to note that French treatment of the Natchez neither refutes nor supports the racialization processes of settlers as depicted in this study. The efforts of

colonists to exterminate this particular native group took place in the context of an uncommon situation in the colonial Floridas: France was a European power with the resources necessary to militarily dominate Indian adversaries. French racialization of the Natchez should not be perceived differently from racialization of other native peoples based solely on the consequences of specific incidents. Much like African and African American slaves in the Atlantic seaboard colonies (who were racialized by the eighteenth century), some native individuals and groups in the western Floridas experienced a wide range of treatment from Europeans depending on their perceived docility and contributions to colonial endeavors. Racialization rarely resulted in uniform European actions toward natives. Nevertheless, as will be seen, French racialized understandings of the Natchez and the warfare the French waged against that group set a precedent for attitudes and strategies regarding other native groups in the region.

5. Richard S. Dunn, *Sugar and Slaves: The Rise of the Planter Class in the English West Indies, 1624–1713* (New York: Norton, 1972), 19, 21–24; Eccles, *France in America*, 27–28, 32–33, 58–60, 93–94.

6. Usner, *Indians, Settlers, & Slaves*, 1–29.

7. The term *petites nations* refers to the dozens of small Indian communities inhabiting the lands along the Lower Mississippi River and Gulf of Mexico coastline that were not affiliated with larger groups such as the Creeks or Choctaws. Descendants of Mississippian culture populations that had been dominant in the region prior to European arrival, each of these smaller groups numbered in the hundreds or less by the late seventeenth century and constantly struggled to maintain their independence from larger native groups and European settlers. See Robin F. A. Fabel, *Colonial Challenges: Britons, Native Americans, and Caribs* (Gainesville: University Press of Florida, 2000), 88–90; Usner, *Indians, Settlers, & Slaves*, 45, 60, 63.

8. Ibid., 45–49; Peter H. Wood, "The Changing Population of the Colonial South: An Overview by Race and Region, 1685–1790," in *Powhatan's Mantle: Indians in the Colonial Southeast*, edited by Peter H. Wood, Gregory A. Waselkov, and M. Thomas Hatley (Lincoln: University of Nebraska Press, 1989), 56, 57, 59, 67–69, 75–77.

9. César de Rochefort, *The History of the Caribby-Islands*, Viz, *Babados, St Christophers, St Vincents, Martinico, Dominico, Barbouthos, Monserrat, Mevis, Antego, &c,* translated by John Davies (London: J. M. for Thomas Dring and John Starkey, 1666), 2:235.

10. Father de Montigny to Anonymous, 2 January 1699, in Robert Calhoun, "The Taensa Indians: The French Explorers and Catholic Missionaries in the Taensa Country," *Louisiana Historical Quarterly XVII*, nos. 3–4 (July and October 1934): 648.

11. "Ces Sauvages sont les plus gueux que j'aye encore veus, n'ayant aucune commodité chez eux ny aucun ouvrage," Pierre Margry, *Découvertes et établissements, des Français dans l'ouest et dans le sud de l'Amérique Septentrionale, 1614–1754*, 6 vols. (Paris: D. Jouaust, 1876–1786), 4:171; entry for 15 March 1699 in "Iberville's Journal,"

in *A Comparative View of French Louisiana, 1699 and 1762: The Journals of Pierre Le Moyne d'Iberville and Jean-Jacques-Blaise d'Abbadie*, translated and edited by Carl A. Brasseaux (Lafayette: Center for Louisiana Studies, 1981), 50.

12. "Ils ne vivent que de chasse . . . parce qu'alors il y a beaucoup de gibier dans leur pays. C'est la cause qu'ils ne sont pas laborieux et très peu adonnés à la culture des terres," Margry, *Découvertes et établissements*, 5:402; Richebourg G. McWilliams, trans. and ed., *Fleur de Lys and Calumet: Being the Pénicaut Narrative of French Adventure in Louisiana* (Baton Rouge: Louisiana State University Press, 1953), 35.

13. "J'ose me flatter que les Sauvages feront aveuglément ce que nous voudrons, quoyque bien paresseux," Margry, *Découvertes et établissements*, 5:460; entry for January 1700 in *The Journal of Sauvole*, translated and edited by Jay Higginbotham (Mobile, Ala: Colonial Books, 1969), 40.

14. Entry for 5 March 1700, in Paul du Ru, *Journal of Paul du Ru* (Chicago: Caxton Club, 1934), 27.

15. Entry for 6 March 1700, in ibid., 28.

16. Entry for 6 March 1700, in ibid., 29.

17. Entry for [?] March 1700, in ibid., 52.

18. Ibid., 52–53.

19. Father James Gravier to Father Delamberville, 14 November 1700, in Calhoun, "The Taensa Indians," 666.

20. Entry for 28 May 1701, in journal of Charles Levasseur, in Vernon J. Knight and Sheree L. Adams, "Voyage to the Mobile and Tomeh in 1700 with Notes on the Interior of Alabama," *Ethnohistory* 28, no. 2 (spring 1981): 182.

21. "Elles me faisoient pasmer de rire avec leur prononciation sauvage . . . il faut avouer qu'ils n'ont rien de sauvage que le langage," Margry, *Découvertes et établissements*, 5:470, 5:487; McWilliams, *Fleur de Lys and Calumet*, 113, 133–35.

22. King Louis XIV to Lamothe Cadillac, 13 May 1710, in *Mississippi Provincial Archives: French Dominion*, 3 vols., translated and edited by Dunbar Rowland and A. G. Sanders (Jackson: Mississippi Department of Archives and History, 1927–1932), 3:147. (Hereafter cited as MPAFD1.)

23. Memoir of D'Artaguiette to Pontchartrain, 8 September 1712, in ibid., 2:72.

24. Duclos to Pontchartrain, 25 December 1715, in ibid., 2:207.

25. Duclos to Pontchartrain, 9 October 1713, in ibid., 2:96–97.

26. Bienville to Hubert, 25 June 1718, in ibid., 3:223.

27. Entry of 16 July 1720, in Jean-François Bertet de la Clue, *A Voyage to Dauphin Island to 1720: The Journal of Bertet de la Clue*, translated and edited by Francis Escoffier and Jay Higginbotham (Mobile, Ala: Museum of the City of Mobile, 1974), 63–64.

28. Entry of 25 December 1721, in "Historic Journal of Father Pierre François Xavier de Charlevoix in Letters Addressed to the Duchess of Lesdguieres," in Benjamin F. French, *Historical Collections of Louisiana and Florida Including Translations*

Relating to Their Discovery and Settlement, 5 vols. (New York: AMS Press, 1976), 3:128–29.

29. "State of the Colony of Louisiana in 1724," in Jean Baptiste Bénard de la Harpe, *The Historical Journal of the Establishment of the French in Louisiana*, translated and edited by Joan Cain and Virginia Koenig, edited by Glenn R. Conrad (Lafayette: Center for Louisiana Studies, 1971), 171.

30. "Memoir, Designed to Make Known the Importance of the Colony of Louisiana and the Necessity of Continuing Its Settlement, 1723?," in ibid., 162–63.

31. "Treatise on the Origins of the Indians of America, 1724?," in ibid., 176.

32. "Memoir on Louisiana, 1725?," in Dawson A. Phelps, "The Chickasaw, the English, and the French: 1699–1744," *Tennessee Historical Quarterly XVI* (1957): 123.

33. "Continuation of the Memoir of Bienville, 1725–1726?," in MPAFD1, 3:527.

34. Ibid., 3:529, 531–32.

35. Périer to the Abbé Raguet, 12 May 1728, in MPAFD1, 2:574. Périer's statement obscures the fact that French colonizers along the Gulf Coast and Mississippi River enslaved hundreds, if not thousands, of Indians during the colonial period. See Alan Gallay, *The Indian Slave Trade: The Rise of the English Empire in the American South, 1670–1717* (New Haven, Conn.: Yale University Press, 2002), 308–31.

36. Despite Salmon's assertions, Choctaws and most native groups in the region consistently allied themselves militarily with the French or other European colonizers throughout the eighteenth century. See Salmon to Maurepas, 8 February 1733, in *Mississippi Provincial Archives, French Dominion*, Vols. 4 and 5, edited by Patricia K. Galloway (Baton Rouge: Louisiana State University Press, 1984), 4:125–26. (Hereafter cited as MPAFD2.)

37. Bienville to Maurepas, 30 September 1734, in MPAFD1, 1:240.

38. Bienville to Maurepas, 10 February 1736, in ibid., 1:277.

39. "Les femmes & filles Naturelles font plus heureufes étant efclaves des François qu'étant mariées chez elles," Antoine Le Page du Pratz, *Histoire de la Louisiane, contenant la decouverte de ce vaste pays; sa description geographique coutumes & religion des naturels, avec leurs origins; deux voyages dans le nord du nouveau Mexique, don't un jusqu'a la mer du Sud* 3 vols. (Paris: De Bure, l'aine, 1758), 3:423; Antoine S. Le Page du Pratz, *History of Louisiana or the Western Parts of Virginia and Carolina* (London: T. Becket, 1774; reprint, Claitor's Publishing Division, 1972), 94.

40. Le Page du Pratz, *History of Louisiana*, 340.

41. Rochefort, *The History of the Caribby-Islands*, 2:235.

42. "Narrative of La Salle's Voyage Down the Mississippi, by Father Zenobious Membré, Recollect, May 1682," in John G. Shea, *Discovery and Exploration of the Mississippi Valley* (New York: Redfield, 1852), 173.

43. Ibid., 182.

44. "Journal of Thaumur de la Source, 1699?," in Calhoun, "The Taensa Indians," 645.

45. "Il s'éleva tout d'un coup un orage espouvantable; le tonnerre tomba sur leur temple, brusla toutes leurs idoles et réduisit leur temple en cendres. Aussitost ces Sauvages accourent devant leur temple, en faisant des hurlemens terribles, s'arrachant les cheveux et levant les bras en haut. Le visage tourné du costé de leur temple, ils invoquèrenr leur grand Esprit, en criant comme des possédés d'esteindre le feu; puis ils prenoient de la terre dont ils s'en frottoient le corps et le visage. Les pères et les mères apportoient leurs enfans et, après les avoir estranglez, ils les jetoient dans le feu. M. d'Iberville eut horreur d'un si cruel spectacle, et il commanda d'arrester ce spectacle si affreux," Margry, *Découvertes et établissements*, 5:397–98; McWilliams, *Fleur de Lys and Calumet*, 29.

46. Entry for 6 March 1700, in Du Ru, *Journal of Paul du Ru*, 29.

47. Entry for [?] March 1700, in ibid., 52.

48. Entry for 2 May 1700, in ibid., 66–67.

49. "Je crois que c'est le diable qu'ils invoquent, puisqu'ils sortent de cette cabane furieux comme des possédez et qu'alors ils font des sortilèges, comme de faire marcher la peau d'une loutre morte depuis plus de deux ans, et qui est pleine de paille . . . Ceux qui font ces sortes de tours, qu'ils soient magiques ou autrement, sont fort estimés des autres Sauvages," Margry, *Découvertes et établissements*, 5:427–28; McWilliams, *Fleur de Lys and Calumet*, 64.

50. "Father Poisson to Father Patouillet, 18 July 1721," in "Excerpt of a Letter Written by Mr. Faucond du Manoir, Director General of the Colony of Ste Catherine, to Those Interested in the Said Colony at the Natchez, July 18th 1721," *Louisiana Historical Quarterly II* (1919): 170–73.

51. Father Raphael to the Abbé Raguet, 15 September 1725, in MPAFD1, 2:509.

52. Le Page du Pratz, *History of Louisiana*, 331.

53. Rochefort, *The History of the Caribby-Islands*, 2:231.

54. "The Minet Relation," in *La Salle, the Mississippi, and the Gulf: Three Primary Documents*, edited by Robert S. Weddle, translated by Ann Linda Bell and Robert S. Weddle (College Station: Texas A&M University Press, 1987), 57.

55. "Tous les Sauvages y estoient nuds comme la main, les hommes et les garcons; les femmes et les filles avoient seulement un peu de mousse qui leur passoit entre les jambes et couvroit leur nudité," Margry, *Découvertes et établissements*, 5:388; McWilliams, *Fleur de Lys and Calumet*, 18.

56. Father Montigny to Anonymous, 2 January 1699, in Calhoun, "The Taensa Indians," 648.

57. "Tous les hommes sont nuds, sans s'apercevoir de l'estre. Les femmes n'ont qu'une braye faite d'escorce d'arbre . . . Elles sont avec cela suffisamment cachées, les cordons estans tousjours en movement," Margry, *Découvertes et établissements*, 4:171; entries for 16 February and 15 March 1699, in "Iberville's Journal," in Brasseaux, *A Comparative View of French Louisiana, 1699 and 1762*, 33, 50.

58. Entry for 16 July 1720, in La Clue, *A Voyage to Dauphin Island to 1720*, 63–64.

59. Entry for 27 February 1700, in Du Ru, *Journal of Paul du Ru*, 21–22.

60. Letter XXXIV, 5 June 1722, in Pierre François Xavier de Charlevoix, *Journal of a Voyage to North America*, 2 vols. (Ann Arbor, Mich.: University Microforms, 1966), 2:322.

61. For analysis of native skull-altering practices, see Charles Hudson, *The Southeastern Indians* (Knoxville: University of Tennessee Press, 1975), 31; and Fred B. Kniffen, Hiram F. Gregory, and George A. Stokes, *The Historic Indian Tribes of Louisiana: From 1542 to the Present* (Baton Rouge: Louisiana State University Press, 1987), 182.

62. "The Minet Relation," in Weddle, *La Salle, the Mississippi, and the Gulf*, 59–60.

63. "Narrative of La Salle's Voyage Down the Mississippi, by Father Zenobius Membré, Recollect, May 1682," in Shea, *Discovery and Exploration of the Mississippi Valley*, 182.

64. "Je n'en ay veu aucune de jolie . . . C'est un agréement aux femmes de se noircir les dents, ce qu'elles font avec une herbe pilée en mastic; elles durent noires du temps et redeviennent blanches," Margry, *Découvertes et établissements*, 4:171–72; entry for 15 March 1699, in "Iberville's Journal," in Brasseaux, *A Comparative View of French Louisiana, 1699 and 1762*, 50.

65. "Ce chef est un homme de cinq pieds trois ou quatre pouces de haut, assez maigre . . . Il m'a paru le Sauvage le plus absolu que j'aye veu, aussi gueux que les autres . . . tous grands hommes bien faits, for desœuvrés," Margry, *Découvertes et établissements*, 4:412; entry for 11 March 1699, in "Journal of the Voyage of the Chevalier D'Iberville. . .," in *Iberville's Gulf Journals*, translated and edited by Richebourgh G. McWilliams (Tuscaloosa: University of Alabama Press, 1981), 126.

66. "Les homes sont la pluspart gros et trapus," Margry, *Découvertes et établissements*, 5:402; McWilliams, *Fleur de Lys and Calumet*, 35.

67. "Ces Sauvages n'ont pas du tout d'autres poils que leurs cheveux. Ils se les arrachent tant au visage qu'ailleurs; ils se pèlent avec de la cendre de coquilles et de l'eau chaude, comme on feroit un cochon de lait, tant les hommes que les femmes et les filles," Margry, *Découvertes et établissements*, 5:468–69; McWilliams, *Fleur de Lys and Calumet*, 112.

68. Entry for 25 December 1721, in "Historic Journal of Father Pierre François Xavier de Charlevoix," in French, *Historical Collections of Louisiana and Florida*, 3:128–29.

69. Le Page du Pratz, *History of Louisiana*, 307.

70. "Se matachant le visage et le corps," Margry, *Découvertes et établissements*, 4:172; entry for 15 March 1699, in "Iberville's Journal," in Brasseaux, *A Comparative View of French Louisiana, 1699 and 1762*, 50.

71. "Tous les Sauvages d'icy ont le tour des yeux piqué et sur le nez, et trois raies sur le menton," Margry, *Découvertes et établissements*, 4:440; entry for 19 April 1699, in "Journal of the Voyage of the Chevalier D'Iberville," in McWilliams, *Iberville's Gulf Journals*, 153.

72. Entry for 16 July 1720, in La Clue, *A Voyage to Dauphin Island to 1720*, 63–64.

73. "C'est pourquoy les femmes sont bien plus belles, outre qu'elles sont naturellement plus blanches," Margry, *Découvertes et établissements*, 5:467; McWilliams, *Fleur de Lys and Calumet*, 110.

74. Rochefort, *The History of the Caribby-Islands*, 2:231.

75. "The Minet Relation," in Weddle, La Salle, *the Mississippi, and the Gulf*, 59–60.

76. "Ils n'estoient occupez que de nous regarder, estonnés qu'ils estoient de voir des gens, dont la peau estoit blanche avec de grandes barbes, et d'autres sans cheveux, comme il y en avoit parmi nous, ce qui nous rendoit fort dissemblables à eux qui ont la peau fort basanée et une grande chevelure noire qu'ils ont fort soin de conserver," Margry, *Découvertes et établissements*, 5:378; McWilliams, *Fleur de Lys and Calumet*, 4.

77. "Elles sont fort jolies et blanches," Margry, *Découvertes et établissements*, 5:402; McWilliams, *Fleur de Lys and Calumet*, 35.

78. "Le soir ils demandèrent en leur langue à M. d'Iberville, si nous avions assés mangé et s'il nous falloit autant de femmes que nous estions d'hommes. M d'Iberville, en leur montrant sa main, leur fit comprendre que leur peau rouge et bazanée ne devoit point s'approcher de celle des François, qui estoit blanche," Margry, *Découvertes et établissements*, 5:394; McWilliams, *Fleur de Lys and Calumet*, 24.

79. Entry for 27 February 1700, in Du Ru, *Journal of Paul du Ru*, 22.

80. Knight, 28 May 1701, 182.

81. Entry for 25 December 1721, in "Historic Journal of Father Pierre François Xavier de Charlevoix," in French, *Historical Collections of Louisiana and Florida*, 3:128–29.

82. Charlevoix, *Journal of a Voyage to North America*, Letter XXXIV, 5 June 1722, 2:322.

83. "Treatise on the Origins of the Indians of America, 1724," in La Harpe, *The Historical Journal of the Establishment of the French in Louisiana*, 178–79.

84. Ibid.

85. Le Page du Pratz, *History of Louisiana*, 308.

86. Duclos to Pontchartrain, 25 December 1715, in MPAFD1, 2:208. The original translators of this letter into English used the term "halfbreed" as a synonym for the French word *mulastres* (mulatto). See Guillaume Aubert, "'The Blood of France': Race and Purity of Blood in the French Atlantic World," *William and Mary Quarterly* 61, no. 3 (July 2004): 469–70.

87. "Minutes of the Superior Council of Louisiana, 1 September 1716," in MPAFD1, 2:218–19.

88. Du Ru, *Journal of Paul du Ru*, 19 March 1700, 42.

89. Jay Higginbotham, "Henri de Tonti's Mission to the Chickasaw, 1702," *Louisiana History XIX* (1978): 289.

90. "Cette nation qui n'a point les manières farouches des autres Sauvages . . . Les hommes et les femmes de Natchez sont très bien faits et assez proprement vestus . . .

Ils ont le parler assez agréable, ne parlent pas du gosier si fortement que les autres Sauvages . . . Je ne suis point estonné si ces filles sont lubriques et qu'elles n'ayent aucune retenue, puisque leurs père et mère et leur religion leur enseignent qu'au sortir de ce monde il y a une planche très estroite et difficile à passer pour entrer dans les grands villages, où ils prétendent qu'ils vont après leur mort, et il n'y aura que celles qui se seront bien diverties avec les garcons qui passeront facilement ceste planche. On voit la suite de ces détestables leçons, qu'on leur inspire dès leur bas âge, appuyées de la liberté et de l'oysiveté où elles sont entretenues," Margry, *Découvertes et établissements*, 5:444–48; McWilliams, *Fleur de Lys and Calumet*, 84–87.

91. "Nous arrivasmes au village des Natchez avec nos armes en bon estat, parce qu'il faut tousjours se méfier des Sauvages, qui sont fort sujets à trahir leur parole," Margry, *Découvertes et établissements*, 5:524; McWilliams, *Fleur de Lys and Calumet*, 181.

92. Duclos to Pontchartrain, 7 June 1716, in MPAFD1, 3:207, 210.

93. Father Le Petit to Father D'Avaugour, 12 July 1730, in *The Early Jesuit Missions in North America; Compiled and Translated from the Letters of the French Jesuits*, 2 vols., compiled and translated by William I. Kip (New York: Wiley and Putnam, 1847), 2:271.

94. Letter XXX, 25 December 1721, in Charlevoix, *Journal of a Voyage to North America*, 2:259–65.

95. Ibid.

96. Father Le Petit to Father D'Avaugour, 12 July 1730, in Kip, *The Early Jesuit Missions in North America*, 2:272–73.

97. Ibid., 2:280.

98. Letter XXXI, 10 January 1723, Charlevoix, *Journal of a Voyage to North America*, 2:277, 280–81.

99. Usner, *American Indians*, 26–27; Woods, *French-Indian Relations on the Southern Frontier*, 95–96.

100. Périer to Maurepas, 18 March 1730, in MPAFD1, 1:63.

101. Ibid., 1:68.

102. Ibid., 1:76.

103. Book XXII, 1730?, in *Charlevoix's Louisiana: Selections from the History and the Journal*, edited by Charles O'Neill (Baton Rouge: Louisiana State University Press, 1977), 107.

104. Anonymous, *The Present State of the Country and Inhabitants, Europeans and Indians, of Louisiana, on the North Continent of America, Containing the Garrisons, Forts and Forces, Prices of All Manner of Provisions. . .to Which Are Added Letters from the Governor of that Province on the Trade of the French and English with the Natives . . . /By an Officer at New Orleans to His Friends at Paris* (London: J. Millan, 1744), 22.

105. "Anonymous to M. Faneuil, September 25, 1748," *Louisiana Historical Quarterly VI* (1923): 550–51.

106. Father Le Petit to Father D'Avauguor, 12 July 1730, in Kip, *The Early Jesuit Missions in North America*, 2:287–88.

107. Minutes of the Superior Council of Louisiana, 16 May 1723, in MPAFD1, 3:365.

108. Diron d'Artaguiette to Maurepas, 20 March 1730, in ibid., 1:80.

109. Father Le Petit to Father D'Avauguor, 12 July 1730, in Kip, *The Early Jesuit Missions in North America*, 289.

110. Périer to Maurepas, 10 April 1730, in MPAFD1, 1:119.

111. Ibid.

112. Périer to Maurepas, 18 March 1730, in ibid., 1:64.

113. Book XXII, 1730?, in O'Neill, *Charlevoix's Louisiana*, 108.

114. Comptroller-General to Périer, 1731[?], in Jean Delanglez, "The Natchez Massacre and Governor Périer," *Louisiana Historical Quarterly XVII* (1934): 640–41.

115. "Anonymous to M. Faneuil, September 25, 1748," 552–54.

116. Périer to Maurepas, 10 April 1730, in MPAFD1, 1:120.

117. Ian Brown, "An Archaeological Study of Culture Contact and Change in the Natchez Bluffs Region," in *La Salle and His Legacy: Frenchmen and Indians in the Lower Mississippi Valley*, edited by Patricia K. Galloway (Jackson: University of Mississippi Press, 1982), 181; John R. Swanton, *The Indians of the Southeastern United States* (1946; reprint, Washington, D.C.: Smithsonian Institution Press, 1979), 160; Usner, *American Indians*, 28–31; Woods, *French-Indian Relations on the Southern Frontier*, 98–103.

118. Louboey to Maurepas, 8 May 1733, in MPAFD1, 1:215.

119. Book XXII, 1731?, in O'Neill, *Charlevoix's Louisiana*, 121–22.

120. John A. Green, "Governor Périer's Expedition against the Natchez Indians, December 1730–January 1731," *Louisiana Historical Quarterly* 19 (1936): 558.

121. Ibid., 559. "The Company" refers to the Company of the Indies, the dominant trade organization in the region.

122. Book XXII, 1731?, in O'Neill, *Charlevoix's Louisiana*, 121–22.

123. Louis LeClerc Milfort, *Memoirs, or a Quick Glance at My Various Travels and My Sojourn in the Creek Nation*, translated by Ben C. McCary (Savannah: Beehive Press, 1972), 116; Swanton, *Indians of the Southeastern United States*, 160; Usner, *American Indians*, 30–31; Woods, *French-Indian Relations on the Southern Frontier*, 103–9.

124. Périer to Maurepas, 18 March 1730, in MPAFD1, 1:73.

125. Bienville to Maurepas, 26 August 1734, in ibid., 1:234.

126. Michel to Rouillé, 2 July 1750, in MPAFD2, 5:52.

127. Vaudreuil to Rouillé, 10 October 1751, in ibid., 5:108.

128. Bienville to [?], 15 May 1733, in MPAFD1, 1:193.

129. "Anonymous to M. Faneuil, September 25, 1748," 552–54.

Chapter 6. Anglicizing Indians

1. During this period, immigrants established dozens of plantations along the peninsula's Atlantic coast and the eastern bank of the Mississippi River that produced a variety of foodstuffs and the major cash crop of the region, indigo. The trade in deerskins proved to be the major economic endeavor, however. The Floridas as a whole exported skins valued at almost £40,000 between 1773 and 1775, an amount similar to that exported by neighboring Georgia during the same period. Nevertheless, an ongoing trade deficit (more imports to the colonies than exports to England) along with the need for annual royal subsidies to pay for government, defense, and diplomacy negated the economic benefits from the Floridas. See Fabel, *Economy of British West Florida*, 55–57, 110–13; Hoffman, *Florida's Frontiers*, 221–25.

2. Richter, *Facing East from Indian Country*, 169–70, 177–78; Usner, *Indians, Settlers, & Slaves*, 124–25, 168–69; Wood, "The Changing Population of the Colonial South," 59–60, 72.

3. Milanich, *Florida Indians and the Invasion from Europe*, 56–60.

4. Other than Dickinson's account, little historical evidence exists on the Hobe, or Jobe, Indians, a nonagricultural group that inhabited the southeastern coast of peninsular Florida (present-day Martin County) during the early colonial period. Archaeologists speculate that the Hobe functioned as a subordinate group of the larger Ais Indian community that lived to the north near Cape Canaveral. See Hann, *Indians of Central and South Florida*, 2–4, 16, 61–62, 167; Milanich, *Florida Indians and the Invasion from Europe*, 40, 56–60.

5. "With the Indians at Hoe-Bay, 23 June 1696," in Jonathan Dickinson, *Jonathan Dickinson's Journal or God's Protecting Providence. Being the Narrative of a Journey from Port Royal Jamaica to Philadelphia between August 23, 1696 and April 1, 1697*, edited by Charles Andrews and Evangeline Andrews (New Haven, Conn.: Yale University Press, 1945), 29, 31, 37, 59.

6. Charles W. Arnade, "Raids, Sieges, and International Wars," in *The New History of Florida*, edited by Samuel Proctor (Gainesville: University Press of Florida, 1996), 110–14.

7. *An Impartial Account of the Late Expedition Against St. Augustine Under General Oglethorpe*, introduction and index by Aileen M. Topping (1742; reprint, Gainesville: University Press of Florida, 1978), 44.

8. Edward Kimber, *A Relation or Journal of a Late Expedition to the Gates of St. Augustine, on Florida*, edited by Samuel Proctor (1744; reprint, Gainesville: University Press of Florida, 1976), 17–18.

9. Edmund Atkin, *Indians of the Southern Colonial Frontier: The Edmund Atkin Report and Plan of 1755*, introduction by and edited by Wilbur R. Jacobs (Columbia: University of South Carolina Press, 1954), 71–72.

10. O'Donnell, "Armchair Adventurers and Horseback Botanists," 87.

11. William Roberts, *An Account of the First Discovery, and Natural History of Florida: With a Particular Detail of the Several Expeditions and Descents Made on That Coast*, introduction and index by Robert L. Gold (1763; reprint, Gainesville: University Presses of Florida, 1976), 5.

12. Charles Strachan to Mr. Johnson & Wylly, 28 May 1764, in *Letterbooks of Charles Strachan*, 5, MS 119, National Library of Scotland, Edinburgh.

13. Chactaw Congress, 26 March 1765, in *Mississippi Provincial Archives, 1763–1766, English Dominion Letters and Enclosures to the Secretary of State from Major Robert Farmar and Governor George Johnstone*, vol. 1, edited by Dunbar Rowland (Nashville: Brandon Printing, 1911), 224. (Hereafter cited as MPAED.)

14. James Grant to Denys Rolle, 14 September 1764, in *Papers of James Grant of Ballindalloch, 1740–1819*, Reel 1, Library of Congress, Washington, D.C. (Hereafter cited as James Grant Papers.)

15. "Journal of an Officer Who Travelled Over a Part of the West Indies, and of South America in the Course of 1764 and 1765," 14, Kings MS 213, The British Library, London. (Hereafter cited as "Journal of an Officer.")

16. John Lindsay to James Grant, 1 October 1768, *James Grant Papers*, Reel 16.

17. Governor Johnstone's Report to Mr. Conway, 23 June 1766, MPAED, 511.

18. James Grant to the Board, State of Indian Affairs in the Southern Province of America from 1755 to 1766, 30 August 1766, in Transcriptions of the British Colonial Office Records. Copied from the Library of Congress Collections of the Files of Florida Writers' Project, Works Project Administration, 2 vols. (N.p.: 1939), 1:260. Copy available in Strozier Library, Florida State University. (Hereafter cited as WPA.)

19. Thomas Campbell to Lord Deane Gordon, 14 June 1767, in "Thomas Campbell to Lord Dean Gordon: An Account of the Creek Nation, 1764," *Florida Historical Quarterly* 8, no. 3 (January 1930): 161–62.

20. James Grant to [?], 20 June 1768, WPA, 2:747.

21. Alexander Cluny, *The American Traveller: Containing Observations on the Present State, Culture and Commerce of the British Colonies in America* (London: E. and C. Dilly, 1769), 111. Also see James Grant to William Knox, 30 October 1767, *James Grant Papers*, Reel 2.

22. George Johnstone to James Grant, [?] September 1766, *James Grant Papers*, Reel 10.

23. John Stuart to Secretary Hillsborough, 2 December 1770, in *Colonial Office Class 5*, vol. 72, Public Records Office, United Kingdom (microfilm reproductions of correspondence). (Hereafter cited as CO5.)

24. John Stuart to Secretary Hillsborough, 7 January 1772, CO5, vol. 73.

25. "R" to the New York Gazette, 18 October 1773, in Fabel, "The Letters of R," 421–23.

26. Cluny, *The American Traveller*, 112.

27. Peter Chester to the Earl of Hillsborough, 9 March 1771, in Eron O. Rowland, "Peter Chester, Third Governor of the Province of British West Florida under British Dominion 1770–1781," in *Publications of the Mississippi Historical Society*, edited by Dunbar Rowland (Jackson: Mississippi Historical Society, 1925), 5:38.

28. John Stuart to Board of Trade, 1764, *James Grant Papers*, Reel 7.

29. Charles Shaw to Secretary Germain, 7 August 1779, CO5, vol. 80.

30. Charles Stuart to Peter Chester, 15 April 1771, in Rowland, *Publications of the Mississippi Historical Society*, 46, 49.

31. James Grant to John Gordon, 5 November 1767, *James Grant Papers*, Reel 2.

32. Romans was a royal land surveyor in both Georgia and the Floridas during the 1760s, eventually obtaining land grants in both locations before the American Revolution. He hoped to stimulate further British settlement with his descriptions of the region. See Lincoln Diamant, *Bernard Romans: Forgotten Patriot of the American Revolution* (Harrison, N.Y.: Harbor Hill Books, 1985), 15, 21–22; Fabel, *The Economy of British West Florida*, 15; O'Donnell, "Armchair Adventurers and Horseback Botanists," 91–92.

33. "An Attempt towards a Short Description of West Florida, 22 July 1773," in Rowland, *Publications of the Mississippi Historical Society*, 180.

34. Bernard Romans, *A Concise Natural History of East and West Florida* (1775; reprint, Gainesville: University Press of Florida, 1962), 37–44.

35. Ibid.

36. "With the Indians at Hoe-Bay, 23 June 1696," in Dickinson, *Jonathan Dickinson's Journal or God's Protecting Providence*, 28–29.

37. Ibid., 29, 43.

38. Entry for 8 August 1739, in "A Ranger's Report of Travels with General Oglethorpe, 1739–1742," in *Travels in the American Colonies*, edited by Newton D. Mereness (New York: Macmillan, 1916), 220–21.

39. Entry for 11 March 1744, in Kimber, *A Relation or Journal of a Late Expedition to the Gates of St. Augustine*, 16.

40. Roberts, *An Account of the First Discovery, and Natural History of Florida*, 3–5.

41. "Journal of an Officer," 15–16.

42. Thomas Campbell to Lord Deane Gordon, 17 June 1767, in "Thomas Campbell to Lord Dean Gordon: An Account of the Creek Nation, 1764," 161.

43. "Narrative of a Journey Through Several Parts of the Province of West Florida in the Years 1770 and 1771 by Edward Mease, 2 March 1771," in Rowland, *Publications of the Mississippi Historical Society*, 80–81.

44. Romans, *A Concise Natural History of East and West Florida*, 37–54.

45. Ibid.

46. Ibid.

47. Ibid.

48. Kathryn E. H. Braund and Gregory A. Waselkov, eds., *William Bartram on the*

Southeastern Indians (Lincoln: University of Nebraska Press, 1995), 2–23; Edward J. Cashin, *William Bartram and the American Revolution on the Southern Frontier* (Columbia: University of South Carolina Press, 2000), 1–4, 253; Kornfeld, "Encountering 'the Other,'" 298, 308, 313; Charlotte M. Porter, "William Bartram's Travels in the Indian Nations," *Florida Historical Quarterly* 70, no. 4 (April 1992): 434–50.

49. William Bartram, *Travels of William Bartram*, edited by Mark Van Doren (New York: Dover, 1955), 107.

50. Ibid., 380.

51. Ibid., 183.

52. Ibid., 315–16.

53. Ibid., 183–84.

54. Ibid., 385–86.

55. Ibid., 113.

56. Ibid., 382–83.

57. Smedley, *Race in North America*, 16–18.

58. Bartram, *Travels of William Bartram*, 380.

59. Ibid., 315–16.

60. Ibid., 44–46.

61. Ibid.

62. Charles Hudson, "James Adair as Anthropologist," *Ethnohistory* 24, no. 4 (Autumn 1977): 312; J. Leitch Wright, Jr., *Creeks and Seminoles: The Destruction and Regeneration of the Muscogulge People* (Lincoln: University of Nebraska Press, 1986), 131–32.

63. Adair argued that Native Americans were the lost tribes of Israel, thus sharing a religious heritage with Europeans.

64. James Adair, *Adair's History of the American Indians*, edited by Samuel Cole Williams (Johnson City, Tenn.: Watauga Press, 1930), xxxiii, xxxvi.

65. Ibid., 390.

66. Ibid., 2–3.

67. Ibid., 13.

68. Ibid., 5–6.

69. Ibid., 7.

70. Ibid., 275–76, 303.

71. Ibid., 334.

72. Ibid., 448.

73. Ibid.

74. Ibid., 2–7.

75. Alexander Cameron to John Stuart, 9 February 1774, CO5, vol. 75.

76. Lieut. Colonel Provost to Secretary of War, 7 September 1763, MPAED, 137.

77. George Galphin to James Grant, 26 March 1770, *James Grant Papers*, Reel 20.

78. James Grant to John Stuart, 15 December 1766, *James Grant Papers*, Reel 2.

79. "To the Right Honorable the Lords Commissioners of Trader and Plantations the Humble Representation of the Council and Assembly for the Province of West Florida, 11 November 1766," in *The Minutes, Journals, and Acts of the General Assembly of British West Florida*, edited by Robert R. Rea and Milo B. Howard, Jr. (Tuscaloosa: University of Alabama Press, 1979), 49.

80. "To the Right Honorable the Earl of Hillsborough, His Majesty's Principal Secretary of State for America. The Memorial of the Council and Assembly of His Majesty's Province of West Florida, 24 August 1768," in ibid., 146.

81. James Grant to William Knox, 18 December 1767, *James Grant Papers*, Reel 2.

82. "Council with the Chactaws, by Major Farmar and Mons. Dabbadie, 14 November 1764," MPAED, 86–89.

83. "An Act for the Regulation and Government of Negroes and Slaves" (3 January 1767), in Rea and Howard, *The Minutes, Journals, and Acts of the General Assembly of British West Florida*, 330–36.

84. J. Barton Starr, *Tories, Dons, and Rebels: The American Revolution in British West Florida* (Gainesville: University Press of Florida, 1976), 177–79.

85. Alexander Cameron to Secretary Germain, 31 October 1780, CO5, vol. 82.

86. Peter Chester to John Stuart, 10 September 1771, CO5, vol. 72.

87. Adair, *Adair's History of the American Indians*, 305.

Chapter 7. Conclusion

1. European racialization of natives did not doom intercultural cooperation, however. Throughout the colonial period, the process and its manifestations coexisted with instances of intercommunity harmony, economic exchange, military alliances, and extensive personal and familial relationships. Moreover, racialization did not preclude European hopes of native improvement and possible assimilation into colonial society. Nevertheless, the process provided a basis and historical context for growing doubts among many European Americans that such transformations and long-term accommodation were possible.

2. Entry for 11 May 1781, in Francisco de Saavedra, *Journal of Don Francisco Saavedra de Sangronis During the Commission Which He Had in His Charge from 25 June 1780 Until 20th of the Same Month of 178[?]*, translated by Aileen Moore Topping (Gainesville: University Press of Florida, 1989), 175.

3. Ibid., 183.

4. Ibid., 179.

5. Ibid., 177.

6. Ibid., 176.

Bibliography

Adair, James. *Adair's History of the American Indians*. Edited by Samuel Cole Williams. Johnson City, Tenn.: Watauga Press, 1930.

Adelman, Jeremy, and Stephen Aron. "From Borderlands to Borders: Empires, Nation-States, and the Peoples in Between in North American History." *American Historical Review* 104, no. 3 (October 1999): 814–42.

Adorno, Rolena, and Patrick C. Pautz, eds. *Álvar Núñez Cabeza de Vaca: His Account, His Life, and the Expedition of Pánfilo de Narváez*. 3 vols. Lincoln: University of Nebraska Press, 1999.

Allain, Mathé. *"Not Worth a Straw": French Colonial Policy and the Early Years of Louisiana*. Lafayette: The Center for Louisiana Studies, 1988.

Allen, Theodore. The *Invention of the White Race*. 2 vols. London: Verso, 1994–1997.

The American Gazetteer. Containing a Distinct Account of All the Parts of the New World; Their Situation, Climate, Soil, Produce, Former and Present Condition; Commodities, Manufacturers, and Commerce. Together with an Accurate Account of the Cities, Towns, Ports, Bays, Rivers, Lakes, Mountains, Passes, and Fortifications. 3 vols. London: Printed for A. Millar, 1762.

"Anonymous to M. Faneuil, September 25, 1748." *Louisiana Historical Quarterly* 6 (1923): 547.

Armitage, David. "The New World and British Historical Thought: From Richard Hakluyt to William Robertson." In *America in European Consciousness, 1493–1750*, edited by Karen O. Kupperman, 52–75. Chapel Hill: University of North Carolina Press, 1995.

Arnade, Charles W. *Florida on Trial, 1593–1602*. Coral Gables, Fla.: University of Miami Press, 1959.

———. "Raids, Sieges, and International Wars." In *The New History of Florida*, edited by Michael Gannon, 100–116. Gainesville: University Press of Florida, 1996.

Atkin, Edmund. *Indians of the Southern Colonial Frontier: The Edmund Atkin Report and Plan of 1755*. Introduction and editing by Wilbur R. Jacobs. Columbia: University of South Carolina Press, 1954.

Aubert, Guillaume. "'The Blood of France': Race and Purity of Blood in the French Atlantic World." *William and Mary Quarterly* 61, no. 3 (July 2004): 439–78.

Axtell, James. *The European and the Indian: Essays in the Ethnohistory of Colonial North America.* New York: Oxford University Press, 1981.

Bailyn, Bernard. *Voyagers to the West: A Passage in the Peopling of America on the Eve of the Revolution.* New York: Knopf, 1986.

Bandelier, Fanny, trans. and ed. *The Journey of Alvar Núñez Cabeza de Vaca and His Companions from Florida to the Pacific.* New York: A. S. Barnes, 1905.

Barrientos, Bartolomé. *Pedro Menéndez de Avilés, Founder of Floridas.* Translated by Anthony Kerrigan. Gainesville: University Press of Florida, 1965.

Bartram, William. *Travels of William Bartram.* Edited by Mark Van Doren. New York: Dover, 1955.

Bennett, Charles E. *Laudonnière and Fort Caroline: History and Documents.* Gainesville: University Press of Florida, 1964.

Berkhofer, Robert F., Jr. *The White Man's Indian: Images of the American Indian from Columbus to the Present.* New York: Knopf, 1978; reprint, New York: Vintage Books, 1979.

Bidney, David. "The Idea of the Savage in North American Ethnohistory." *Journal of the History of Ideas* 15 (April 1954): 322–27.

Blackburn, Robin. "The Old World Background to European Colonial Slavery." *William and Mary Quarterly* 54, no. 1 (January 1997): 65–102.

Blome, Richard. *A Geographical Description of the Four Parts of the World, Taken from Notes & Workes of the Famous Monsieur Sanson, Geographer to the French King, and Other Eminent Travellers and Authors Microform.* London: Printed by T. N. for R. Blome, 1670.

Boas, Franz., ed. *Race, Language, and Culture.* New York: The Free Press, 1940.

Bossu, J. B. *Nouveaux Voyages en Louisiane, 1751–1768.* Edited by Philippe Jacquin. Paris: Aubier-Montaigne, 1980.

Bossu, Jean. *Travels in the Interior of North America, 1751–1762.* Translated and edited by Seymour Feiler. Norman: University of Oklahoma Press, 1962.

Boyd, Mark F., Hale G. Smith, and John W. Griffin, eds. *Here They Once Stood: The Tragic End of the Apalachee Missions.* Gainesville: University Press of Florida, 1952.

Braund, Kathryn E. H., and Gregory A. Waselkov, eds. *William Bartram on the Southeastern Indians.* Lincoln: University of Nebraska Press, 1995.

Brasseaux, Carl A., trans. and ed. *A Comparative View of French Louisiana, 1699 and 1762: The Journals of Pierre Le Moyne d'Iberville and Jean-Jacques Blaise d'Abbadie.* Lafayette: University of Southwestern Louisiana, 1981.

Breen, T. H. "Creative Adaptations: Peoples and Cultures." In *Colonial British America: Essays in the New History of the Early Modern Era,* edited by Jack P. Greene and J. R. Pole, 195–232. Baltimore: Johns Hopkins University Press, 1984.

Brooks, Abbie M., ed. *The Unwritten History of St. Augustine,* Copied from the Spanish Archives in Seville, Spain. St. Augustine: The Record Co., 1909.

Brooks, James F. "Confounding the Color Line: Indian-Black Relations in Historical and Anthropological Perspective." *American Indian Quarterly* 22, nos. 1-2 (winter and spring 1998): 125–33.

Brown, Ian. "An Archaeological Study of Culture Contact and Change in the Natchez Bluffs Region." In *La Salle and His Legacy: Frenchmen and Indians in the Lower Mississippi Valley*, edited by Patricia K. Galloway, 176–93. Jackson: University of Mississippi Press, 1982.

Brown, Kathleen M. *Good Wives, Nasty Wenches, and Anxious Patriarchs: Gender, Race, and Power in Colonial Virginia*. Chapel Hill: University of North Carolina Press, 1996.

Bushnell, Amy Turner. *The King's Coffer: Proprietors of the Spanish Florida Treasury, 1565–1702*. Gainesville: University Press of Florida, 1981.

———. *Situado and Sabana: Spain's Support System for the Presidio and Mission Provinces of Florida*. Athens: University of Georgia Press, 1994.

Calderón, Gabriel Díaz Vara. *A 17th Century Letter of Gabriel Díaz Vara Calderón, Bishop of Cuba, Describing the Indians and Indian Missions of Florida*. Washington, D.C.: Smithsonian Institution, 1936.

Calhoun, Robert. "The Taensa Indians: The French Explorers and Catholic Missionaries in the Taensa Country." *Louisiana Historical Quarterly* 17 (1934): 631–41.

Calloway, Colin G. "Neither White nor Red: White Renegades on the American Indian Frontier." *Western Historical Quarterly* 17, no. 1 (January 1986): 43–66.

———. *The American Revolution in Indian Country: Crisis and Diversity in Native American Communities*. New York: Cambridge University Press, 1995.

———. *New Worlds for All: Indians, Europeans, and the Remaking of Early America*. Baltimore: Johns Hopkins University Press, 1997.

Campbell, Thomas. "Thomas Campbell to Lord Deane Gordon, An Account of the Creek Nation, 1764." *Florida Historical Quarterly* 8, no. 3 (January 1930): 156–63.

Canny, Nicholas P. "The Ideology of English Colonization: From Ireland to America." *William and Mary Quarterly* 30, no. 4 (October 1973): 575–98.

Cashin, Edward J. *William Bartram and the American Revolution on the Southern Frontier*. Columbia: University of South Carolina Press, 2000.

Chaplin, Joyce. "Expansion and Exceptionalism in Early American History." *Journal of American History* 89, no. 4 (March 2003): 1431–55.

———. "Natural Philosophy and an Early Racial Idiom in North America: Comparing English and Indian Bodies." *William and Mary Quarterly* 54, no. 1 (January 1997): 229–52.

———. *Subject Matter: Technology, the Body, and Science on the Anglo-American Frontier, 1500–1676*. Cambridge, Mass.: Harvard University Press, 2001.

Charlevoix, Pierre François Xavier de. *Journal of a Voyage to North America*. 2 vols. 1761; reprint, Ann Arbor, Mich.: University Mircroforms, 1966.

Cluny, Alexander. *The American Traveller: Containing Observations on the Present State, Culture and Commerce of the British Colonies in America*. London: E. and C. Dilly, 1769.

Cooke, James J. "France, The New World and Colonial Expansion." In *La Salle and His Legacy: Frenchmen and Indians in the Lower Mississippi Valley*, edited by Patricia K. Galloway, 81–92. Jackson: University of Mississippi Press, 1982.

Connor, Jeannette T., trans. and ed. *Colonial Records of Spanish Florida: Letters and Reports of Governors and Secular Persons*. Deland: Florida State Historical Society, 1925.

Corbett, Theodore G. "Migration to a Spanish Imperial Frontier in the Seventeenth and Eighteenth Centuries: St. Augustine." *Hispanic American Historical Review* 54, no. 3 (August 1974): 414–30.

Covington, James W. *The Seminoles of Florida*. Gainesville: University Press of Florida, 1993.

Covington, James W., and A. F. Falcones, eds. *Pirates, Indians, and Spaniards: Father Escobedo's "La Florida."* St. Petersburg, Fla.: Great Outdoors Publishing, 1963.

Cronon, William. *Changes in the Land: Indians, Colonists, and the Ecology of New England*. New York: Hill and Wang, 1983.

Davis, Frederick T. "History of Juan Ponce de León's Voyages to Florida: Source Records." *Florida Historical Quarterly* 14, no. 1 (July 1935): 5–66.

Deagan, Kathleen. *Spanish St. Augustine: The Archaeology of a Colonial Creole Community*. New York: Academic Press, 1983.

De Brahm, John Gerar William. *Report of the General Survey in the Southern District of North America*. Edited by Louis De Vorsey, Jr. Columbia: University of South Carolina Press, 1971.

Delanglez, Jean. "The Natchez Massacre and Governor Périer." *Louisiana Historical Quarterly* 17 (1934): 631–41.

Deloria, Philip J. *Playing Indian*. New Haven, Conn.: Yale University Press, 1998.

D'Escalante Fontaneda, Hernando. *Memoir of D'Escalante Fontaneda Respecting Florida, Written in Spain about the Year 1775*. Edited by David O. True. Translated by Buckingham Smith. Coral Gables, Fla.: University of Miami Press, 1944.

Diamant, Lincoln. *Bernard Romans: Forgotten Patriot of the American Revolution*. Harrison, N.Y.: Harbor Hill Books, 1985.

Dickason, Olivia P. *The Myth of the Savage and the Beginnings of French Colonialism in the Americas*. Edmonton: University of Alberta Press, 1984.

Dickinson, Jonathan. *Jonathan Dickinson's Journal; or, God's Protecting Providence. Being the Narrative of a Journey from Port Royal in Jamaica to Philadelphia between August 23, 1696 and April 1, 1697*. Edited by Charles Andrews and Evangeline Andrews. New Haven, Conn.: Yale University Press, 1945.

Dowd, Gregory E. "'Insidious Friends': Gift Giving and the Cherokee-British Alliance in the Seven Years' War." In *Contact Points: American Frontiers from the Mohawk Valley to the Mississippi, 1750–1830*, edited by Andrew R. L. Cayton and Fredrika J. Teute, 114–50. Chapel Hill: University of North Carolina Press, 1998.

Dunn, Richard S. *Sugar and Slaves: The Rise of the Planter Class in the English West Indies, 1624–1713*. New York: Norton, 1972.

Du Ru, Paul. *Journal of Paul du Ru.* Translated by Ruth L. Butler. Chicago: Caxton Club, 1934.

Eccles, W. J. *France in America.* East Lansing: Michigan State University Press, 1990.

Elliott, John. "Introduction: Colonial Identity in the Atlantic World." In *Colonial Identity in the Atlantic World, 1500–1800,* edited by Nicholas Canny and Anthony Pagden, 3–13. Princeton, N.J.: Princeton University Press, 1987.

"Excerpt of a Letter Written by Mr. Faucond du Manoir, Director General of the Colony of Ste Catherine, to Those Interested in the Said Colony at the Natchez, July 18th, 1721." *Louisiana Historical Quarterly* 2 (1919): 164–69.

Fabel, Robin F. A. "The Letters of R: The Lower Mississippi in the Early 1770s." *Louisiana History* 24 (1983): 402–27.

———. *The Economy of British West Florida 1763–1783.* Tuscaloosa: University of Alabama Press, 1988.

———. *Colonial Challenges: Britons, Native Americans, and Caribs, 1759–1775.* Gainesville: University Press of Florida, 2000.

Faragher, John M. "'More Motley than Mackinaw': From Ethnic Mixing to Ethnic Cleansing on the Frontier of the Lower Missouri, 1783–1833." In *Contact Points: American Frontiers from the Mohawk Valley to the Mississippi, 1750–1830,* edited by Andrew R. L. Cayton and Fredrika J. Teute, 304–26. Chapel Hill: University of North Carolina Press, 1998.

Forbes, Jack D. *Africans and Native Americans: The Language of Race and the Evolution of Black Peoples.* Chicago: University of Illinois Press, 1993.

French, Benjamin F. *Historical Collections of Louisiana and Florida.* 2 vols. New York: J. Sabin and Sons, 1869; reprint, New York: AMS Press, 1976.

Frye, David. *Indians into Mexicans: History and Identity in a Mexican Town.* Austin: University of Texas Press, 1996.

Gallay, Alan. *The Indian Slave Trade: The Rise of the English Empire in the American South, 1670–1717.* New Haven, Conn.: Yale University Press, 2002.

Galloway, Patricia, ed. *La Salle and His Legacy: Frenchmen and Indians in the Lower Mississippi Valley.* Jackson: University Press of Mississippi, 1982.

———. *Mississippi Provincial Archives: French Dominion.* Vols. 4 and 5. Collected, edited, and translated by Dunbar Rowland and A. G. Sanders. Baton Rouge: Louisiana State University Press, 1984.

Galvão, António. *The Discoveries of the World by Antonie Galvano.* Translated by Richard Hakluyt. London: Impensis G. Bishop, 1601; reprint, New York: Da Capo Press, 1969.

———. *The discoveries of the world from their original unto the year of Our Lord 1555 by Antonio Galvano, governor of Ternate;* corrected, quoted and published in England, by Richard Hakluyt (1601); now reprinted with the original Portuguese text, and ed. by Vice-Admiral Bethune, C.B. Lisbon, 1563; English translation, London, 1601; reprint, London: Hakluyt Society, 1862.

Gannon, Michael. *The Cross in the Sand: The Early Catholic Church in Florida, 1513–1570.* Gainesville: University Press of Florida, 1965.

———. "First European Contacts." In *The New History of Florida*, edited by Michael Gannon, 16–39. Gainesville: University Press of Florida, 1996.

Garcilaso de la Vega. *Obras completas del Inca Garcilaso de la Vega.* 4 vols. Madrid: Ediciones Atlas, 1960–1965.

———. *The Florida of the Inca: A History of the Adelentatdo, Hernando de Soto, Governor and Captain General of the Kingdom of Florida, and of Other Heroic Spanish and Indian Cavaliers, Written by the Inca, Garcilaso de la Vega, An Officer of His Majesty, and a Native of the Great City of Cuzco, Capital of the Realms and Provinces of Peru.* Translated and edited by John G. Varner. Austin: University of Texas Press, 1962.

Geiger, Maynard J. *The Franciscan Conquest of Florida (1573–1618).* Washington, D.C.: Catholic University of America, 1937.

Gentleman of Elvas. *True Relation of the Hardships Suffered by Governor Fernando de Soto & Certain Portuguese Gentlemen During the Discovery of the Province of Florida. Now Newly Set Forth by a Gentleman of Elvas.* Translated and edited by James A. Robertson. 2 vols. Deland: Florida State Historical Society, 1932–1933.

Gilmore, Myron P. "The New World in French and English Histories of the Sixteenth Century." In *First Images of America: The Impact of the New World on the Old*, 2 vols., edited by Fredi Chiappelli, 2:519–28. Berkeley: University of California Press, 1976.

Gold, Robert L. *Borderland Empires in Transition: The Triple Nation Transfer of Florida.* Carbondale: Southern Illinois Press, 1969.

Green, John A. "Governor Périer's Expedition Against the Natchez Indians, December, 1730–January, 1731." *Louisiana Historical Quarterly* 19 (1936): 547–77.

Greenblatt, Stephen. *Marvelous Possessions: The Wonder of the New World.* Chicago: University of Chicago Press, 1991.

Greene, Jack P. *Imperatives, Behaviors, and Identities: Essays in American Cultural History.* Charlottesville: University of Virginia Press, 1995.

Gutiérrez, Ramón A. *When Jesus Came, the Corn Mothers Went Away: Marriage, Sexuality, and Power in New Mexico, 1500–1846.* Stanford, Calif.: Stanford University Press, 1991.

Hand, Wayland D. "The Effect of the Discovery on Ethnological and Folklore Studies in Europe." In *First Images of America: The Impact of the New World on the Old*, 2 vols., edited by Fredi Chiappelli, 1:45–55. Berkeley: University of California Press, 1976.

Hakluyt, Richard. *Divers Voyages Touching the Discoerie of America.* London: Thomas Woodcoke, 1582; Reprint, Ann Arbor, University Microfilms, 1966.

———. *The Principal Navigations, Voyages, Trafiques & Discoveries of the English Nation Made by Sea or Over-Land to the Remote and Farthest Distant Quarters of the Earth at Any Time Within the Compasse of These 1600 Yeeres.* 12 vols. London, 1589; Reprint, Glasgow: J. Maclehose and Sons, 1903–1905.

Hann, John H. *Apalachee: The Land between the Rivers.* Gainesville: University Press of Florida, 1988.

———. *History of the Timucua Indians and Missions.* Gainesville: University Press of Florida, 1996.

———. *Indians of Central and South Florida, 1513–1763.* Gainesville: University Press of Florida, 2003.

———, ed. *Spanish Translation: The History of Florida's Spanish Period.* Tallahassee: Bureau of Archaeological Research, 1986.

———. *Visitations and Revolts in Florida, 1656–1695.* Tallahassee: Bureau of Archaeological Research, 1993.

———, trans. and ed. *Missions to the Calusa.* Gainesville: University Press of Florida, 1991.

Hannaford, Ivan. *Race: The History of an Idea in the West.* Baltimore: Johns Hopkins University Press, 1996.

Harris, Marvin. *Patterns of Race in the Americas.* New York: W. W. Norton, 1964.

Hart, William B. "Black 'Go-Betweens' and the Mutability of 'Race,' Status, and Identity on New York's Pre-Revolutionary Frontier." In *Contact Points: American Frontiers from the Mohawk Valley to the Mississippi, 1750–1830,* edited by Andrew R. L. Cayton and Fredrika J. Teute, 88–113. Chapel Hill: University of North Carolina Press, 1998.

Hernández de Biedma, Luis. *Narratives of the Career of Hernando de Soto in the Conquest of Florida, as Told by a Knight of Elvas and in a Relation by Luys Hernández de Biedma, Factor of the Expedition.* 2 vols. Edited by Edward G. Bourne. Translated by Buckingham Smith. New York: Allerton, 1922.

Herrera, Antonio de. *The General History of the Vast Continent and Islands of America Call'd, the West Indies, From the First Discovery Thereof. . .* 6 vols. Translated by John Stevens. Madrid, 1601–1615; reprint, London: Printed for J. Batley, 1725–1726.

Herrera y Tordesillas, Antonio de. *Historia general de los hechos de los castellanos en las islas I tierra firme del mar oceano.* 8 vols. Madrid: Imprento Real de Nicolas Rodiguez Franco, 1726–28.

Higginbotham, Jay. "Henri de Tonti's Mission to the Chickasaw, 1702." *Louisiana History* 19 (1978): 285–96.

———, trans. and ed. *The Journal of Sauvole.* Mobile, Ala.: Colonial Books, 1969.

Hinderaker, Eric. *Elusive Empires: Constructing Colonialism in the Ohio Valley, 1673–1800.* New York: Cambridge University Press, 1997.

Hoffman, Kathleen. "Cultural Development in La Florida." *Historical Archaeology* 31, no. 1 (spring 1997): 24–35.

Hoffman, Paul E. *A New Andalucia and a Way to the Orient: The American Southeast During the Sixteenth Century.* Baton Rouge: Louisiana State University Press, 1990.

———. *Florida's Frontiers.* Bloomington: Indiana University Press, 2002.

Holt, Thomas C. "Of Blood and Power: An Introduction." *William and Mary Quarterly* 61, no. 3 (July 2004): 435–38.

Horsman, Reginald. *Race and Manifest Destiny: The Origins of American Racial Anglo-Saxonism.* Cambridge, Mass.: Harvard University Press, 1981.

Howard, Clinton N. *The British Development of West Florida, 1763–1769*. Berkeley: University of California Press, 1947.

Hudson, Charles. *The Southeastern Indians*. Knoxville: University of Tennessee Press, 1975.

———. "James Adair as Anthropologist." *Ethnohistory* 24, no. 4 (autumn 1977): 311–28.

———. "The Hernando de Soto Expedition, 1539–1543." In *The Forgotten Centuries: Indians and Europeans in the American South, 1521–1704*, edited by Charles Hudson and Carmen C. Tesser, 74–103. Athens: University of Georgia Press, 1994.

Hudson, Nicholas. "From 'Nation' to 'Race': The Origin of Racial Classification in Eighteenth-Century Thought." *Eighteenth-Century Studies* 29, no. 3 (spring 1996): 247–64.

An Impartial Account of the Late Expedition Against St. Augustine Under General Oglethorpe. Introduction and indexes by Aileen M. Topping. 1742; reprint, Gainesville: University Press of Florida, 1978.

Jackson, Robert H. *Race, Caste, and Status: Indians in Colonial Spanish America*. Albuquerque: University of New Mexico Press, 1999.

Jaenen, Corneilius J. *Friend and Foe: Aspects of French-Amerindian Cultural Contact in the Sixteenth and Seventeenth Centuries*. New York: Columbia University Press, 1976.

Jaimes, Annette M. "American Racism: The Impact on American-Indian Identity and Survival." In *Race*, edited by S. Gregory and R. Sanjek. New Brunswick, N.J.: Rutgers University Press, 1994.

Jefferys, Thomas. *A Description of the Spanish Islands and Settlements on the Coast of the West Indies. Compiled from Authentic Memoirs, Revised by Gentlemen Who Have Resided Many Years in the Spanish Settlements. Illustrated with Thirty-two Maps and Plans, Chiefly from Original Drawings Taken from the Spaniards in the Last War*. London: Printed for T. Jefferys, 1762.

Jennings, Francis. *The Founders of America: From the Earliest Migrations to the Present*. New York: W. W. Norton, 1993.

Johnson, Cecil. *British West Florida, 1763–1783*. New York: Archon Books, 1971.

Jordan, Winthrop. *White Over Black: American Attitudes toward the Negro, 1550–1812*. Chapel Hill: University of North Carolina Press, 1968.

Kamen, Henry. *Empire: How Spain Became a World Power, 1492–1763*. New York: HarperCollins, 2003.

Keen, Benjamin, trans. *The Spanish Character: Attitudes and Mentalities from the Sixteenth to the Nineteenth Century by Bartolomé Bennassar*. Berkeley: University of California Press, 1979.

Kicza, John E., ed. *The Indian in Latin American History: Resistance, Resilience, and Acculturation*. Wilmington, Del.: Scholarly Resources, 1999.

Kimber, Edward. *A Relation or Journal of a Late Expedition to the Gates of St. Augustine, on Florida*. Edited by Samuel Proctor. 1744; Gainesville: University Press of Florida, 1976.

Kip, William I., comp. and trans. *The Early Jesuit Missions in North America; Compiled and Translated from the Letters of the French Jesuits.* 2 vols. New York: Wiley and Putnam, 1847.

Kniffen, Fred B., Hiram F. Gregory, and George A. Stokes, *The Historic Indian Tribes of Louisiana: From 1542 to the Present.* Baton Rouge: Louisiana State University Press, 1987.

Knight, Vernon J., and Sheree L. Adams. "Voyage to the Mobile and Tomeh in 1700 with Notes on the Interior of Alabama." *Ethnohistory* 28, no. 2 (spring 1981): 179–94.

Kolchin, Peter. "Whiteness Studies: The New History of Race in America." *Journal of American History* 89, no. 1 (June 2002): 154–73.

Kornfeld, Eve. "Encountering 'the Other': American Intellectuals and Indians in the 1790s." *William and Mary Quarterly* 52 (1995): 287–314.

Krech, Shepard. *The Ecological Indian: Myth and History.* New York: W. W. Norton, 1999.

Kupperman, Karen O. *Indians & English: Facing Off in Early America.* London: Cornell University Press, 2000.

———. "Presentment of Civility: English Reading of American Self-Presentation in the Early Years of Colonization." *William and Mary Quarterly* 54, no. 1 (January 1997): 193–228.

———. *Settling with the Indians: The Meeting of English and Indian Cultures in America, 1580–1640.* Totowa, N.J.: Rowman & Littlefield, 1980.

La Clue, Jean-François Bertet de. *A Voyage to Dauphin Island to 1720: The Journal of Bertet la Clue.* Edited and translated by Francis Escoffier and Jay Higginbotham. Mobile, Ala.: Museum of the City of Mobile, 1974.

La Harpe, Jean-Baptiste Bénard de. *The Historical Journal of the Establishment of the French in Louisiana.* Translated by Joan Cain and Virginia Koening. Edited by Glenn R. Conrad. Lafayette: Center for Louisiana Studies, 1971.

Landers, Jane, ed. "An Examination of Racial Conflict and Cooperation in Spanish St. Augustine: The Career of Jorge Biassou, Black Caudillo." *El Escribano* 25 (December 1988): 85–100.

———. *The African American Heritage of Florida.* Gainesville: University Press of Florida, 1995.

Laudonnière, René. *Histoire Notable de la Floride. A Foothold in Florida: The Eye-Witness Account of Four Voyages Made by the French to that Region and Their Attempt at Colonization, 1562–1568.* Translated by Sarah Lawson. East Grinstead, England: Antique Atlas Publications, 1992.

Leon-Portilla, Miguel. *Endangered Cultures.* Translated by Julie Goodson-Lawes. Dallas: Southern Methodist University Press, 1990.

Le Page du Pratz, Antoine S. *Histoire de la Louisiane, contenant la decouverte de ce vaste pays; sa description geographique coutumes & religion des naturels, avec leurs origins; deux voyages dans le nord du nouveau Mexique, don't un jusqu'a la mer du Sud.* 3 vols. Paris: De Bure, l'aine, 1758.

————. *History of Louisiana or the Western Parts of Virginia and Carolina.* . . . London: T. Beckett, 1774; reprint, Baton Rouge: Claitor's Publishing, 1972.

Lepore, Jill. *The Name of War: King Philip's War and the Origins of American Identity.* New York: Knopf, 1998.

Lescarbot, Marc. *Histoire de la Nouvelle France.* 3 vols. Edited and translated by H. P. Biggar and W. L. Grant. Paris, 1618; reprint, New York: Greenwood Press, 1968.

Lussagnet, Suzanne, ed., *Le Français en Floride. Textes de Jean Ribault, René De Laudonnière, Nicolas Le Challeux et Dominique de Gourges.* Paris: Presses Universitaires de France, 1958.

Lyon, Eugene. *The Enterprise of Florida: Pedro Menéndez de Avilés and the Spanish Conquest of 1565–1568.* Gainesville: University Press of Florida, 1976.

————. *Pedro Menéndez de Avilés.* New York: Garland, 1995.

————. "Settlement and Survival." In *The New History of Florida*, edited by Michael Gannon, 40–61. Gainesville: University Press of Florida, 1996.

McAlister, Lyle N. *Spain and Portugal in the New World, 1492–1700.* Minneapolis: University of Minnesota Press, 1984.

McEwan, Barbara G., ed. *The Spanish Missions of La Florida.* Gainesville: University Press of Florida, 1993.

McWilliams, Richebourg G., trans. and ed. *Fleur de Lys and Calumet: Being the Pénicaut Narrative of French Adventures in Louisiana.* Baton Rouge: Louisiana State University Press, 1953.

————. *Iberville's Gulf Journals.* Tuscaloosa: University of Alabama Press, 1981.

Mandell, Daniel R. *Behind the Frontier: Indians in Eighteenth Century Eastern Massachusetts.* Lincoln: University of Nebraska Press, 1996.

————. "Shifting Boundaries of Race and Ethnicity: Indian-Black Intermarriage in Southern New England, 1760–1880." *Journal of American History* 85, no. 2 (September 1998): 466–501.

Margry, Pierre. *Découvertes et établissements, des Français dans l'ouest et dans le sud de l'Amérique Septentrionale, 1614–1754.* 6 vols. Paris: D. Jouaust, 1876–1886.

Marichal, Juan. "The New World from Within: The Inca Garcilaso." In *First Images of America: The Impact of the New World on the Old*, 2 vols., edited by Fredi Chiappelli, 1:57–61. Berkeley: University of California Press, 1976.

Matijasic, Thomas D. "Reflected Values: Sixteenth-Century Europeans View the Indians of North America." *American Indian Culture and Research Journal* 11, no. 2 (1987): 31–50.

Merrell, James H. "The Racial Education of the Catawba Indians." *Journal of Southern History* 50, no. 3 (August 1984): 363–84.

————. *Into the American Woods: Negotiators on the Pennsylvania Frontier.* New York: W. W. Norton, 1999.

Merritt, Jane T. "Metaphor, Meaning, and Misunderstanding: Language and Power on the Pennsylvanian Frontier." In *Contact Points: American Frontiers from the Mohawk*

Valley to the Mississippi, 1750–1830, edited by Andrew R. L. Cayton and Fredrika J. Teute, 60–87. Chapel Hill: University of North Carolina Press, 1998.

Milanich, Jerald T. *Florida Indians and the Invasion from Europe*. Gainesville: University Press of Florida, 1995.

———. *Laboring in the Fields of the Lord: Spanish Missions and Southeastern Indians*. Washington, D.C.: Smithsonian Institution Press, 1999.

Milanich, Jerald T., and Charles Hudson. *Hernando de Soto and the Indians of Florida*. Gainesville: University Press of Florida, 1993.

Milfort, Louis LeClerc. *Memoirs, or a Quick Glance at My Various Travels and My Sojourn in the Creek Nation*. Translated by Ben C. McCary. Savannah: Beehive Press, 1972.

Morgan, Edmund S. *American Slavery, American Freedom: The Ordeal of Colonial Virginia*. New York: W. W. Norton, 1975.

Morgan, Philip D. "Encounters between British and "Indigenous' peoples, c. 1500–c. 1800." In *Empire and Others: British Encounters with Indigenous Peoples, 1600–1850*, edited by Martin Daunton and Rick Halpern, 42–78. Philadelphia: University of Pennsylvania Press, 1999.

Morner, Mangus. *Race Mixture in the History of Latin America*. Boston: Little, Brown, 1967.

Mowat, Charles L. "The First Campaign of Publicity for Florida." *Mississippi Valley Historical Review* 30, no. 3 (December 1943): 359–76.

———. *East Florida as a British Province, 1763–1784*. Gainesville: University Press of Florida, 1964.

Mulroy, Kevin. *Freedom on the Border: The Seminole Maroons in Florida, the Indian Territory, Coahuila, and Texas*. Lubbock: Texas Tech University Press, 1993.

Nash, Gary B. "The Image of the Indian in the Southern Colonial Mind." *William and Mary Quarterly* 29, no. 2 (April 1972): 197–230.

Nobles, Gregory H. *American Frontiers: Cultural Encounters and Continental Conquest*. New York: Hill and Wang, 1997.

O'Brien, Greg. "The Conqueror Meets the Unconquered: Negotiating Cultural Boundaries in the Post-Revolutionary Southern Frontier." *Journal of Southern History* 67(2001): 39–72.

O'Daniel, V. F. *Dominicans in Early Florida*. New York: United States Catholic Historical Society, 1930.

O'Donnell, James H. "Armchair Adventurers and Horseback Botanists: Explorations of Florida's Natural History, 1763–1800." *Gulf Coast Historical Review* 8, no. 1 (fall 1992): 85–93.

———. *Southeastern Frontiers: Europeans, Africans, and American Indians, 1513–1840*. Bloomington: Indiana University Press, 1982.

O'Neill, Charles, ed. *Charlevoix's Louisiana: Selections from the History and the Journal*. Baton Rouge: Louisiana State University Press, 1977.

Oberg, Michael L. *Dominion and Civility: English Imperialism and Native America, 1585–1685*. Ithaca, N.Y.: Cornell University Press, 1999.

Oviedo, Gonzalo Fernández de. *Historia general y natural de las Indias*. 5 vols. Madrid: Ediciones Atlas, 1959.

Pagden, Anthony. *Lords of All the World: Ideologies of Empire in Spain, Britain, and France, c. 1500–c. 1800*. New Haven, Conn.: Yale University Press, 1995.

Pearce, Roy H. *Savagism and Civilization: A Study of the Indian and the American Mind*. Berkeley: University of California Press, 1988.

Perdue, Theda. *Slavery and the Evolution of Cherokee Society, 1540–1866*. Knoxville: University of Tennessee Press, 1979.

———. *"Mixed Blood" Indians: Racial Construction in the Early South*. Athens: University of Georgia Press, 2003.

Perkins, Elizabeth. "Distinctions and Partitions amongst Us: Identity and Interaction in the Revolutionary Ohio Valley." In *Contact Points: American Frontiers from the Mohawk Valley to the Mississippi, 1750–1830*, edited by Andrew R. L. Cayton and Fredrika J. Teute, 205–34. Chapel Hill: University of North Carolina Press, 1998.

Phelps, Dawson A. "The Chickasaw, the English, and the French: 1699–1744." *Tennessee Historical Quarterly* 16 (1957): 117–33.

Pittman, Philip. *The Present State of the European Settlements of the Missisipi*. Introduction by Robert R. Rea. 1770; reprint, Gainesville: University Press of Florida, 1973.

Porter, Charlotte M. "William Bartram's Travels in the Indian Nations." *Florida Historical Quarterly* 70, no. 4 (April 1992): 434–50.

Posada, Alonso de. *Alonso de Posada Report, 1686: A Description of the Area of the Present Southern United States in the Late Seventeenth Century*. Translated and edited by Barnaby Thomas. Pensacola, Fla.: Perdido Bay Press, 1982.

The Present State of the Country and Inhabitants, Europeans and Indians, of Louisiana, on the North Continent of America, Containing the Garrisons, Forts, and Forces, Prices of All Manner of Provisions . . . to Which Are Added Letters from the Governor of that Province on the Trade of the French and English with the Natives . . . By an Officer at New Orleans to His Friends at Paris. London: J. Millan, 1744.

Quinn, David B., ed. *New American World: A Documentary History of North America to 1612*. 5 vols. New York: Arno Press, 1979.

"A Ranger's Report of Travels with General Oglethorpe, 1739–1742." In *Travels in the American Colonies*, edited by Newton D. Mereness. New York: Macmillan, 1916.

Rea, Robert R., and Milo B. Howard, Jr., eds. *The Minutes, Journals, and Acts of the General Assembly of British West Florida*. Tuscaloosa: University of Alabama Press, 1979.

Ribault, Jean. *The Whole and True Discovery of Terra Florida*. 1563; reprint, Deland: Florida State Historical Society, 1927.

Richter, Daniel K. *Facing East from Indian Country*. Cambridge, Mass.: Harvard University Press, 2001.

————. "War and Culture: The Iroquois Experience." In *American Encounters: Natives and Newcomers from European Contact to Indian Removal, 1500–1850*, edited by Peter C. Mancall and James H. Merrell. New York: Routledge, 2000.

Riordan, Patrick. "Seminole Genesis: Native Americans, African Americans, and Colonists on the Southern Frontier from Prehistory through the Colonial Era." Ph.D. diss., Florida State University, 1996.

Roberts, William. *An Account of the First Discovery, and Natural History of Florida: With a Particular Detail of the Several Expeditions and Descents Made on That Coast*. 1763; Introduction and index by Robert L. Gold. Gainesville: University Press of Florida, 1976.

Rochefort, César de. *The History of the Caribby-Islands, Viz, Barbados, St Christophers, St Vincents, Martinico, Dominico, Barbouthos, Monserrat, Mevis, Antego, &c.* 2 vols. Translated by John Davies. London: J. M. for Thomas Dring and John Starkey, 1666.

Roediger, David P. "The Pursuit of Whiteness: Property, Terror, and Expansion, 1790–1860." *Journal of the Early Republic* 19, no. 4 (winter 1999): 579–600.

Rogers, George C. "The East Florida Society of London, 1766–1767." *Florida Historical Quarterly* 54, no. 4 (April 1976): 479–96.

Romans, Bernard. *A Concise Natural History of East and West Florida*. 1775; reprint, Gainesville: University Press of Florida, 1962.

Rowland, Dunbar, ed. *Mississippi Provincial Archives, English Dominion, 1763–1766: Letters and Enclosures to the Secretary of State from Major Robert Farmar and Governor George Johnstone*. Vol. 1. Nashville: Brandon Printing, 1911.

Rowland, Dunbar, and A. G. Sanders, eds. and trans. *Mississippi Provincial Archives: French Dominion*. 3 vols. Jackson: Mississippi Department of Archives and History, 1927–1932.

Rowland, Eron O. "Peter Chester, Third Governor of the Province of British West Florida under British Dominion 1770–1781." In *Publications of the Mississippi Historical Society*. Vol. 5. Edited by Dunbar Rowland. Jackson: Mississippi Historical Society, 1925.

Saavedra, Francisco de. *Journal of Don Francisco Saavedra de Sangronis During the Commission Which He Had in His Charge from 25 June 1780 Until 20th of the Same Month of 178[?]*. Translated by Aileen Moore Topping. Gainesville: University Press of Florida, 1989.

Sanders, Ronald. *Lost Tribes and Promised Lands: The Origins of American Racism*. Boston: Little, Brown, 1978.

Saunt, Claudio. *A New Order of Things: Property, Power, and the Transformation of the Creek Indians, 1733–1816*. New York: Cambridge University Press, 1999.

Scarry, John F. "The Late Prehistoric Southeast." In *The Forgotten Centuries: Indians and Europeans in the American South, 1521–1704*, edited by Charles Hudson and Carmen C. Tesser, 17–35. Athens: University of Georgia Press, 1994.

The Scots Magazine. 55 vols. Edinburgh: Sands, Brymer, Murray, and Cochran, 1739–1793.

Searcy, Martha C. *The Georgia-Florida Contest in the American Revolution, 1776–1778.* Tuscaloosa: University of Alabama Press, 1985.

Seed, Patricia. *Ceremonies of Possession in Europe's Conquest of the New World, 1492–1640.* New York: Cambridge University Press, 1995.

Shannon, Timothy J. "Dressing for Success on the Mohawk Frontier: Hendrick, William Johnson, and the Indian Fashion." In *American Encounters: Natives and Newcomers from European Contact to Indian Removal, 1500–1850,* edited by Peter C. Mancall and James H. Merrell, 351–76. New York: Routledge, 2000.

Shea, John G. *Discovery and Exploration of the Mississippi Valley.* New York: J. S. Redfield, 1852.

Sheehan, Bernard W. *Savagism and Civility: Indians and Englishmen in Colonial Virginia.* Cambridge, Mass.: Harvard University Press, 1980.

Shoemaker, Nancy. "How Indians Got to Be Red." *American Historical Review* 102, no. 3 (June 1997): 625–44.

———. *A Strange Likeness: Becoming Red and White in Eighteenth-Century North America.* New York: Oxford University Press, 2004.

Silver, Timothy. *A New Face on the Countryside: Indians, Colonists, and Slaves in South Atlantic Forests, 1500–1800.* New York: Cambridge University Press, 1990.

Slotkin, Richard. *Regeneration through Violence: The Mythology of the American Frontier, 1600–1860.* Middletown, Conn.: Wesleyan University Press, 1973.

Smedley, Audrey. "'Race' and the Construction of Human Identity." *American Anthropologist* 100, no. 3 (September 1998): 690–702.

———. *Race in North America: Origin and Evolution of a Worldview.* 2nd. ed. Boulder, Colo.: Westview Press, 1999.

Smith, Buckingham. *Coleccion de varios documentos para la historia de la Florida y tierras adyacentes.* Londres, Argentina: Trübner, 1857.

Sobel, Mechal. "The Revolution in Selves: Black and White Inner Aliens." In *Through A Glass Darkly: Reflections on Personal Identity in Early America,* edited by Ronald Hoffman, Mechal Sobel, and Fredrika Teute, 163–205. Chapel Hill: University of North Carolina Press, 1997.

Starr, J. Barton. *Tories, Dons, and Rebels: The American Revolution in British West Florida.* Gainesville: University Press of Florida, 1976.

Steele, Ian K. *Warpaths: Invasions of North America.* New York: Oxford University Press, 1994.

Stine, Linda F. "Mercantilism and Piedmont Peltry: Colonial Perceptions of the Southern Fur Trade, Circa 1640–1740." In *Volumes in Historical Archaeology XIV,* edited by Stanley South, 1–49. Columbia: University of South Carolina, 1990.

Stork, William. *An Account of East Florida; with a Journal Kept by John Bartram of Philadelphia, Botanist of His Majesty for the Floridas; Upon a Journey from St. Augustine up the River St. Johns*. London: Sold by Nicol, 1765; reprint, Fernandina: The Florida Mirror, 1881.

Sturtz, Linda L. "Spanish Moss and Aprons: European Responses to Gender Ambiguity in the Exploration and Colonization of South-Eastern North America." *Seventeenth Century* 11 (1996): 125–40.

Swanton, John R. *Indian Tribes of the Lower Mississippi Valley and the Adjacent Coast of the Gulf of Mexico*. Bureau of American Ethnology Bulletin 43. Washington, D.C.: Government Printing Office, 1911.

———. *The Indians of the Southeastern United States*. 1946; reprint, Washington, D.C.: Smithsonian Institution Press, 1979.

Sweet, James H. "The Iberian Roots of American Racist Thought." *William and Mary Quarterly* 54, no. 1 (January 1997): 143–66.

Takaki, Ronald. "The Tempest in the Wilderness: The Racialization of Savagery." *Journal of American History* 79, no. 3 (December 1992): 892–912.

TePaske, John J. *The Governorship of Spanish Florida, 1700–1763*. Durham, N.C.: Duke University Press, 1964.

Thelen, David. "The Nation and Beyond: Transnational Perspectives on United States History." *Journal of American History* 86. no. 3 (December 1999): 965–76.

Thomas, David H., ed. *Spanish Borderlands Sourcebooks: The Missions of Spanish Florida*. New York: Garland, 1991.

Thomas, G. E. "Puritans, Indians and the Concept of Race." The *New England Quarterly* 48, no. 1 (March 1975): 3–27.

Transcriptions of the British Colonial Office Records. Copied from the Library of Congress Collections of the Files of the Florida Writers' Project, Works Project Administration. 2 vols. N.p.: 1939.

Usner, Daniel H., Jr. *American Indians in the Lower Mississippi Valley*. Lincoln: University of Nebraska Press, 1998.

———. *Indians, Settlers, & Slaves in a Frontier Exchange Economy: The Lower Mississippi Valley before 1783*. Chapel Hill: University of North Carolina Press, 1992.

Vaughan, Alden T. *Roots of American Racism: Essays on the Colonial Experience*. New York: Oxford University Press, 1995.

Wade, Peter. *Race and Ethnicity in Latin America*. London: Pluto Press, 1997.

Weber, David J. "Blood of Martyrs, Blood of Indians: Toward a More Balanced View of Spanish Missions in Seventeenth Century North America." In *Columbian Consequences*, 3 vols., edited by David H. Thomas, 429–48. Washington, D.C.: Smithsonian Institution Press, 1990.

———. *The Spanish Frontier in North America*. New Haven, Conn.: Yale University Press, 1992.

Weddle, Robert S., ed. *La Salle, the Mississippi, and the Gulf: Three Primary Documents*. Translated by Linda Bell and Robert S. Weddle. College Station: Texas A&M University Press, 1987.

White, Richard. *The Roots of Dependency: Subsistence, Environment, and Social Change among Choctaws, Pawnees, and Navajos*. Lincoln: University of Nebraska Press, 1983.

———. "Race Relations in the American West." *American Quarterly* 38, no. 3 (1986): 396–416.

———. *The Middle Ground: Indians, Empires, and Republics in the Great Lakes Region, 1650–1815*. New York: Cambridge University Press, 1991.

Williams, Glyndwr. "'Savages Noble and Ignoble': European Attitudes towards the Wider World before 1800." *Journal of Imperial and Commonwealth History* 6, no. 3 (1978): 303–13.

Willis, William S. "Divide and Rule: Red, White, and Black in the Southeast." *Journal of Negro History* 48, no. 3 (July 1963): 157–76.

Wood, Peter H. "The Changing Population of the Colonial South: An Overview by Race and Region, 1685–1790." In *Powhatan's Mantle: Indians in the Colonial Southeast*, edited by Peter H. Wood, Gregory A. Waselkov, and M. Thomas Hatley, 35–103. Lincoln: University of Nebraska Press, 1989.

Woods, Patricia D. *French-Indian Relations on the Southern Frontier, 1699–1762*. Ann Arbor, Mich.: University Microfilms International Research Press, 1980.

Wright, J. Leitch, Jr. *Creeks and Seminoles: The Destruction and Regeneration of the Muscogulge People*. Lincoln: University of Nebraska Press, 1986.

———. *The Only Land They Knew: The Tragic Story of the American Indians in the Old South*. New York: The Free Press, 1981.

Index

Daniel S. Murphree is assistant professor of history at the University of Texas at Tyler. He is the author of "Race and Religion on the Periphery: Disappointment and Missionization in the Spanish Floridas, 1566–1763," in *Race, Nation, and Religion in the Americas*, edited by Henry Goldschmidt and Elizabeth McAlister (2004) and "Constructing Indians in the Colonial Floridas: Origins of European Floridian Identity, 1513–1573," in the *Florida Historical Quarterly* 81 (Fall 2002), winner of the Arthur W. Thompson Award for the best article published in the journal that year.